Windows® 7
Digital
Classroom™

Windows® 7
Digital
Classroom™

Kate Shoup & the AGI Training Team

Wiley Publishing, Inc.

Windows® 7 Digital Classroom™

Published by
Wiley Publishing, Inc.
10475 Crosspoint Boulevard
Indianapolis, IN 46256

Copyright © 2009 by Wiley Publishing, Inc., Indianapolis, Indiana
Published by Wiley Publishing, Inc., Indianapolis, Indiana
Published simultaneously in Canada
ISBN: 978-0-4705-6802-6
Manufactured in the United States of America
10 9 8 7 6 5 4 3 2 1

For general information on our other products and services or to obtain technical support, please contact our Customer Care Department within the U.S. at (800) 762-2974, outside the U.S. at (317) 572-3993 or fax (317) 572-4002.

Please report any errors by sending a message to errata@agitraining.com

Library of Congress Control Number: 2009935832

About the Authors

Kate Shoup has authored more than 20 books, including Windows Vista Visual Encyclopedia, Internet Visual Quick Tips, The Agassi Story, Rubbish: Reuse Your Refuse, and Webster's New World English Grammar Handbook, and has edited scores more. She has also co-written a feature-length screenplay and starred in the ensuing film, and worked as the Sports Editor for NUVO Newsweekly. When not writing, Kate loves to ski (she was once nationally ranked), read, and ride her motorcycle—and she plays a mean game of 9-ball. Kate lives in Indianapolis with her daughter and their dog.

The AGI Training team develops training content and delivers training classes and programs. They are available to deliver private and customized training programs. More information at *agitraining.com* and *digitalclassroombooks.com*.

Credits

President, American Graphics Institute and Digital Classroom Series Publisher
Christopher Smith

Executive Editor
Jody Lefevere

Technical Editors
Greg Heald, Cynthia Greene-Share, Michael Lattari

Editor
Marylouise Wiack

Editorial Director
Robyn Siesky

Editorial Manager
Cricket Krengel

Business Manager
Amy Knies

Senior Marketing Manager
Sandy Smith

Vice President and Executive Group Publisher
Richard Swadley

Vice President and Executive Publisher
Barry Pruett

Senior Project Coordinator
Lynsey Stanford

Graphics and Production Specialist
Lauren Mickol

Media Development
Chris Leavey, Jeremy Osborn

Proofreading
Barn Owl Publishing

Indexing
Potomac Indexing, LLC

Contents

Starting Up

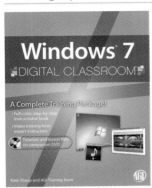

Lesson 1: Getting Started with Windows 7

Lesson 2: Working with Windows 7 Programs

Lesson 3: Working with Files and Folders

Lesson 4: Customizing Windows 7

Lesson 5: Surfing the Web with Internet Explorer 8

Lesson 6: Enjoying Audio and Video with Windows 7

Lesson 7: Maintaining Windows 7

Lesson 8: Setting Up User Accounts

Lesson 9: Networking Your Computer

Lesson 10: Securing Your Computer

Lesson 11: Getting Organized with Windows 7

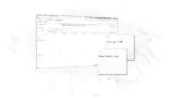

Lesson 12: Communicating via E-mail and IM

Lesson 13: Working with images

Lesson 14: Using Windows 7 on a Laptop or Netbook Computer

Appendix

Starting up

About Windows 7 Digital Classroom

Windows 7 is the foundation for everything you do on your computer. You can use it to run software applications faster than ever, organize your documents and files, and quickly connect your computers to others or the Internet. Because Windows 7 does so many things for all types of users, you need a guide—and that where the Digital Classroom helps you. The *Windows 7 Digital Classroom* is like having your own personal tutor. You can jump to any lesson in the book at any time—they are completely self-contained. Each lesson has detailed step-by-step instructions They're called lessons, not chapters, because each one is written by an expert instructor and you complete each lesson understanding what you need to know so you are up-and-running quickly, in plain, simple language.

Maybe you're new to Windows. If so, start at the absolute basics in the first three chapters and discover the essential things you can do with Windows 7, including how to work with applications, windows, and folders. If you're interested in customizing Windows 7 and getting connected to the Internet, jump right into Lesson 4, "Customizing Windows 7" and Lesson 5, "Surfing the Web with Internet Explorer 8."

Maybe you want to get productive immediately, using word processing, instant messaging, e-mail, and organizing and sharing photos. If so, skip ahead to Lessons 11 through 13. If you're interested in getting under-the-hood, setting up accounts, creating a network, and securing your system you can move right to Lessons 7 through 10. There's even a lesson devoted to getting the most from Windows 7 on a laptop or netbook computer—it's Lesson 14.

So go ahead, flip through the book and you'll find that the Digital Classroom is the fastest, easiest way to understanding Windows 7. Filled with hundreds of images, illustrations, and plain-language step-by-step instructions, It is like having your own personal tutor.

Is this book for you?

This book is for anyone who wants to gain a better understanding of how to use and configure Windows 7. If you're using Windows 7 at home or managing a small network at your office, the *Windows 7 Digital Classroom* is for you. It is filled with useful, easy-to-understand advice and instructions. The *Windows 7 Digital Classroom* is written for anyone who wants clear, plain explanations for how to get Windows 7 computers to work efficiently, organize their files, and keep their computer safe. Simply put, this book helps you get the most from all that Windows 7 offers. If you're already an IT professional managing a large computer network, this book is probably not the type of resource you need. But if you've been given the role of managing Windows 7 computers in your office or need to do it at home, and you want a companion to help you, the *Windows 7 Digital Classroom* is a good choice for you.

About operating systems

An operating system is the software that provides the user interface that you use to interact with your computer. It is the direct link between your computer's hardware—the memory, hard drive, mouse, keyboard, webcam, speakers—and the software such as Microsoft Word, PowerPoint, Photoshop, Internet Explorer, and the thousands of other programs that are available to run on your computer. Some common operating systems in use today include Windows, Linux, UNIX, Solaris, and, Mac OS. The most widely used operating system is Windows, and the latest version of the windows software is Windows 7. The Windows 7 operating system is what gives your computer its personality so that things look and act consistently from one program to the next. The operating system also makes it so each software program can interact with the other in harmony—so you can browse the Internet, edit photographs, and write an e-mail at the same time. Understanding your operating system is the first step to being able to work effectively with any program on your computer.

Prerequisites

Before starting the *Windows 7 Digital Classroom*, you should have Windows 7 installed. This book does not include the Windows 7 operating system, which you must purchase separately.

The lessons in the book will help you connect to a network, the Internet, and to a printer—so these can wait if you haven't yet set up those elements.

If you have purchased a computer that includes Windows 7, start with the first lesson. If you are upgrading to Windows 7, and have not yet installed the software, you should continue with the Starting Up section which includes installation and upgrade instructions.

Windows 7 versions

There are three separate versions of Windows 7. There is Windows 7 Home, Windows 7 Professional, and Windows 7 Ultimate. This book covers most features found across all three versions, so it is a good companion for you gaining an understanding of Windows 7, regardless of which version you are using. You can learn about the different versions of Windows 7 in Appendix A.

System requirements

Before starting the lessons in the *Windows 7 Digital Classroom*, make sure that your computer is set up and running Windows 7. If you're planning to upgrade to Windows 7, make sure your computer is equipped for running the Windows 7 operating system. Note that you must purchase Windows 7 separately from this book. The minimum system requirements for your computer to effectively use Windows 7 are listed below:

- 1 GHz or faster 32-bit (x86) or 64-bit (x64) processor
- 1 GB RAM (32-bit) or 2 GB RAM (64-bit)
- 16 GB available hard disk space (32-bit) or 20 GB (64-bit)
- DirectX 9 graphics device with WDDM 1.0 or higher driver
- CD or DVD drive

Additional requirements to use certain features:
- Internet access
- Depending on resolution, video playback may require additional memory and advanced graphics hardware
- Music and sound require audio output

Installing Windows 7

If you purchased Windows 7 separately and need to install it on your computer. You'll want to get Windows 7 installed on your computer before going ahead with the lessons in this book. We cover three common scenarios:

- **Upgrading to Windows 7 from Windows XP**. Use the steps in this section to upgrade from Windows XP and keep your files, settings, and programs.

- **Upgrading to Windows 7 from Windows Vista**. Go to this section to see how you can easily upgrade from Windows Vista and keep your files, settings, and programs.

- **Installing Windows using custom settings**. Follow these instructions to completely replace your current operating system or if you are installing an operating system for the first time.

Starting up

To get started with the Windows 7 installation or upgrade process you will need:

- **The Windows 7 disc.** You'll need the software to get started or if you purchased and downloaded Windows 7 online you'll need the Windows installation file.

- **Your Windows 7 product key.** You can find your product key on the installation disc holder inside the Windows 7 software or in a confirmation e-mail if you purchased and downloaded Windows 7 online. A product key uses this format where the X's represent the numbers in the key: XXXXX-XXXXX-XXXXX-XXXXX-XXXXX

- **The Windows 7 Upgrade Advisor.** You can download this free utility from *Microsoft.com*. It helps locate any potential problems before you upgrade. You can find the upgrade advisor here: *http://www.microsoft.com/windows/windows-7/get/upgrade-advisor.aspx*. Be sure to download and run this before performing an upgrade or installation of Windows 7.

The Windows 7 Upgrade Advisor.

- **A place to back up your files.** You'll be going through a major change in your computer, and you want to make sure you have a second copy of any important files before you start this process. You can back up your files to an external hard disk, a DVD or CD. If you have a network, you can back them up to another folder or use Windows Live Mesh. It doesn't really matter where you put your files—just make sure you have a second copy of them before you start this process.

- **An Internet connection.** Before you start the upgrade, confirm that your Internet connection is working. You'll likely have certain drivers and updates that Windows 7 will want to access as part of the installation process. You can still install Windows without an Internet connection, but a connection is helpful.

- **An antivirus program.** You will want to make sure it is updated, and then run it. This helps to make sure that you're starting the Windows 7 installation without any vulnerabilities. Turn it off after you have updated and run it. After you install Windows 7, be sure to turn your antivirus program on again, or install new antivirus software that works with Windows 7.

Deciding which version of Windows 7 to install: 32 bit or 64 bit

If you're running a 32-bit version of Windows Vista, you can only upgrade to a 32-bit version of Windows 7, and if you are current using a 64-bit version of Windows Vista, you can only upgrade to a 64-bit version of Windows 7. To switch from a 32-bit version of Vista to a 64-bit version of Windows 7, use the Custom installation option.

A 64-bit operating systems can handle large amounts of memory—typically 4 gigabytes (GB) of random access memory. This is useful if you work with CAD files, image editing programs with really large images, or do extensive professional video editing. 64-bit software and computers are relatively new, so if you don't work with the software mentioned above or your computer is more than a few years old, you are likely better off sticking with your 32-bit operating system.

To find out whether your computer is capable of using the 64-bit version of Windows, do the following on your computer:

1   Open Performance Information and Tools by pressing the Start button, clicking Control Panel, clicking System and Maintenance, and then clicking Performance Information and Tools.

2   Click View and print details.

3   Under System, you can see what type of operating system you're currently running next to System type, and, next to 64-bit capable, whether you can run a 64-bit version of Windows. If your computer is already running a 64-bit version of Windows, the 64-bit capable listing is not displayed.

If the Upgrade option is not available

Some versions of Windows don't work with all installation discs you're utilizing. You might not see the option if you've inserted the 64-bit installation disc and you are using a 32-bit version of Windows Vista, or if you are trying to upgrade to Windows Vista Ultimate from a lower edition, like Home Premium. To make this type of change, you will need to use the Custom option during installation.

Remember that the upgrade options does not preserve your files, settings, or programs so it is important that you back up your files and settings before installing Windows 7. You'll also need to reinstall your programs using the original installation discs or files.

Perform an Upgrade installation of Windows 7

Most users of Windows Vista can select the Upgrade option to install Windows 7. This is the most convenient way to install Windows 7 on your computer. It keeps your files, settings, and programs from Windows Vista. If you are upgrading from Windows XP, you will select the Custom option, which is described later in this section.

Choose the Upgrade option to upgrade your Vista system to Windows 7.

1   Insert the Windows 7 installation disc into your computer or double-click the installation file if you downloaded Windows 7. Setup should start automatically. If it doesn't, press the Start button, click Computer, double-click your DVD drive to open the Windows 7 installation disc, and then double-click setup.exe.

2   On the Install Windows page, press Install now.

3   The Get important updates for installation page appears. Choose to get the latest updates to protect your computer against security threats. You computer will need to be connected to the Internet during Windows 7 installation to get these updates.

4   On the Please read the license terms page click I accept the license terms, then press Next.

5   On the Which type of installation do you want? page, select Upgrade.

6   Continue to follow the on-screen instructions to finish installing Windows 7.

Upgrading from Windows XP to Windows 7

Upgrading your computer from Windows XP to Windows 7 requires a custom installation, which doesn't preserve your programs, files, or settings so you'll want to follow the steps here to help transfer your files and user accounts.

Starting up

To transfer your files and settings, you'll need the following:

- **External hard drive**. You'll need to move your files off your computer before you install Windows 7 so they do not get destroyed. To make this easier, we recommend a free download called Windows Easy Transfer, which will require an external hard disk. They're readily available at electronics and office supply stores, and they provide an easy way to add additional storage space to your computer.

- **The original installation discs for your software programs**. You'll need to reinstall your programs after installing Windows 7.

Moving files and settings

Windows Easy Transfer is a free software utility from Microsoft that helps you move files and settings to your new version of Windows 7.

Windows Easy Transfer creates a single, large file containing your files and settings and it's best to have it placed on an external hard drive. Windows Easy Transfer moves only your files and settings—not your programs. You'll need to reinstall your programs once the Windows 7 installation is finished.

1   Download Windows Easy Transfer. Go to *http://www.microsoft.com/windows* and type **Windows Easy Transfer** in the search terms.

2   Navigate to the download site and click Download, then press Open.

Run Windows Easy Transfer to save your files and settings

1   Make sure your external hard disk or other storage device is connected to your computer.

2   Click Start > Programs > Windows Easy Transfer. The Windows Easy Transfer dialog box appears. Press Next.

The Windows Easy Transfer process moves your user accounts and program settings from your Windows XP computer to Windows 7.

3   Select an external hard disk or USB flash drive to indicate the destination where you will back-up the files.

4   Click This is my old computer.

5   Deselect any user accounts that you do not want to transfer, then press Next.

6   If you want to password protect the backup file, do so, otherwise leave the boxes blank, then press Save.

7   Browse to the external hard disk or other storage device where you want to save your Easy Transfer file, then press Save. Be certain to save the Easy Transfer file to your external hard disk, otherwise it will be deleted during the installation of Windows 7.

8   Windows Easy Transfer will back-up your files and settings. When completed, the location of the files will be confirmed along with the file name. Press Next, then press Close.

9   Disconnect the external drive, you will need it later in this process.

Gather your program discs and setup files

It's important to remember that the Custom installation option doesn't keep any of your programs, so you'll need to reinstall the programs that you want to use in Windows 7.

1   Make sure you have the installation discs for the programs you want to keep using in Windows 7.

2   You might have downloaded some programs from the Internet. If you still have the installation files on your computer (often called setup.exe, install.exe, or similar), copy those setup files to your external hard disk as well. If you don't have the installation files, you'll need to download them again after Windows 7 installation is complete.

Performing a Custom installation of Windows 7

If you are upgrading from Windows XP, you will use the Custom installation option.

1   Insert the Windows 7 installation disc into your computer or double-click the installation file if you downloaded Windows 7. Setup should start automatically. If it doesn't, press the Start button, click Computer, double-click your DVD drive to open the Windows 7 installation disc, then double-click setup.exe.

2   On the Install Windows page, press Install now.

3   The Get important updates for installation page appears. Choose to get the latest updates to protect your computer against security threats. You computer will need to be connected to the Internet during Windows 7 installation to get these updates.

4   On the Please read the license terms page click I accept the license terms, then press Next.

5   On the Which type of installation do you want? page, select Custom.

Choose Custom (advanced) to perform a custom installation.

6   Choose the partition containing Windows XP (this is often the computer's C: drive), and then click Next. Be certain to not select an external hard drive that connects via USB.

7   In the Windows.old dialog box, press OK to continue.

8   Continue to follow the instructions to finish installing Windows 7. You will need to name your computer and set-up user accounts, as these are not carried-over as part of the installation process. You can use the same names that you used in Windows XP, which is a good idea if you have devices such as a network scanner that need to connect to your computer.

Dealing with installation problems

If an error message appears indicating that Windows can't be installed to the partition you chose, click Show details. If the details indicate that Windows must be installed to a partition formatted as NTFS, then you will want to convert your hard disk to the NTFS format.

1   Cancel the Windows 7 installation, and remove the installation disc.

2   Click Start > All Programs > Accessories and right-click Command Prompt and select Run as....

3   Select The following user, choose a user with administrator permissions, type the password for this user, then press OK. The command prompt appears.

4   At the command prompt, type **convert** <drive letter>: **/fs:ntfs** and press Enter to convert the drive. For example, typing **convert c: /fs:ntfs**. Note that there is a space immediately before /fs.

```
Command Prompt
Microsoft Windows XP [Version 5.1.2600]
(C) Copyright 1985-2001 Microsoft Corp.

C:\Documents and Settings\Andy>convert c: /fs:ntfs
```

Convert your hard drive to the NTFS format.

5   If asked if you would you like to force a dismount on this volume, type **Y**, then press Enter.

6   If asked if you want to schedule the drive to be converted the next time the system restarts, type **Y**, press Enter, then click to close the Command Prompt window.

7   Turn off your computer, then start your computer. Use this process instead of using the Restart command. Windows will convert the disk to NTFS and then restart your computer. When Windows XP starts again, return to section Performing a custom installation of Windows 7.

Transferring your files to Windows 7

After you've installed Windows 7, you can transfer you files by running Windows Easy Transfer a second time. You will want to run Windows Easy Transfer before reinstalling any programs because Windows Easy Transfer moves your files back to where your software programs need them to be located, and the program will expect to find them

1   Connect the external hard drive or storage device to your computer that contains your Windows Easy Transfer migration file.

2   Click the Start > Computer, and under Hard Disk Drives, double-click the storage device that contains the migration files. The default name of the file should be Windows Easy Transfer – Items from old computer. Double-click the file.

3   A window titled Choose what to transfer to this computer appears; select which user accounts from Windows XP are transferred to in Windows 7, then press Transfer. If you transfer more than one account, you may be asked to change the password the first time you log on. If so, enter a new password and then press Enter. If you don't want to have a user account password, leave the boxes empty, and then press Enter.

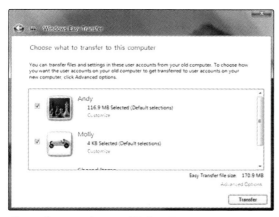

Choose what to transfer to your Windows 7 computer.

4   When the transfer is finished, a window appears with the title Your transfer is complete. You can click to see what was transferred to view the user accounts and files that were transferred.

5 Click See a list of programs you might want to install on your new computer to view what was previously installed on Windows XP, then press Close. You may be asked to restart your computer.

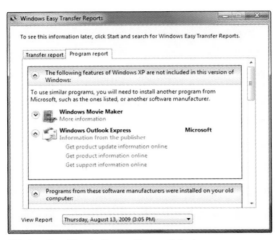

Windows Easy Transfer Program Reports dialog box.

Reinstalling your programs and updating drivers

After using Windows Easy Transfer, it is time to reinstall your programs and update any drivers that help your computer to run better with Windows 7. Some programs such as Windows Mail are not included in Windows 7. Many of these have improved versions that are available at no additional cost from the Microsoft Live web site. See Lessons 12 and 13 for an overview of these Windows Live services.

Other programs, such as Microsoft Office or other software, will require you to use the original discs and to go through the process of installing the software, as the custom installation process removed these applications.

Updating drivers

Software drivers allows your computer to communicate with hardware such as your computer speakers, monitor, and keyboard—so they are pretty important! Many drivers come with Windows, or you can find them by using Windows Update and checking for updates. Press the Start button and choose All Programs > Windows Update. If you can't locate a driver using Windows Update, you'll want to locate the disc that came with the hardware or visit the web site of the device manufacturer. For example, if you have a printer from Epson, you would go to the Epson web site to find the latest drivers.

Cleaning up

The Windows 7 installation keeps many of the files were used under Windows XP. It places them in a folder named Windows.old. If you're confident that you won't need these again, you can delete them. You may want to do this if you're trying to transfer files and you receive an error message that you don't have enough free disk space to transfer your files and settings. To clean-up your old files:

1   Press the Start button. In the Search text field, type Disk Cleanup. In the list of results, double-click Disk Cleanup. Select the drive where you installed Windows 7, then press OK.

2   Click Clean up system files.

3   Select Previous Windows installation(s) then click OK, and then click Delete Files.

Note that this cleanup process does not have an option to undo, and all files deleted will be permanently deleted.

Working with the video tutorials

The DVD that is included with this *Windows 7 Digital Classroom* contains video tutorials developed by the authors to help you understand the concepts explored in each lesson. Each tutorial demonstrates and explains the key concepts and features covered in the lesson. The tutorials vary in length from five to ten minutes per lesson.

The videos are designed to supplement your understanding of the material in the chapter. We have selected exercises and examples that we feel will be most useful to you. You may want to view the entire video for each lesson before you begin that lesson.

DVD video icon.

Setting up for viewing the video tutorials

The DVD included with this book includes video tutorials for each lesson. Although you can view the lessons on your computer directly from the DVD, we recommend copying the folder labeled Videos from the *Windows 7 Digital Classroom* DVD to your hard drive.

Copying the video tutorials to your hard drive:

1　Insert the *Windows 7 Digital Classroom* DVD supplied with this book.

2　On your computer desktop, navigate to the DVD and locate the folder named Videos.

3　Drag the Videos folder to a location onto your hard drive.

Viewing the video tutorials

The videos on the *Windows 7 Digital Classroom* DVD are saved in a projector format. A projector file wraps the Digital Classroom video player into a program file known as an .exe executable file. While the .exe extension may not always be visible to you, the projector file allows the video content to be played on your system without the need for a browser or other player.

Playing the video tutorials:

1　On your computer, navigate to the Videos folder you copied to your hard drive from the DVD. Playing the videos directly from the DVD is possible, but if you encounter problems playing from the DVD, copy the video files to your hard drive.

2　Open the Videos folder and double-click the Win7videos projector file to view the video tutorial.

3　Press the Play button to view the videos.

   The player has a simple user interface that allows you to control the viewing experience, including stopping, pausing, playing, and restarting the video. You can also rewind or fast-forward, and adjust the playback volume.

A. Go to beginning. *B*. Play/Pause. *C*. Fast-forward/rewind. *D*. Stop. *E*. Volume Off/On. *F*. Volume control.

Playback volume is also affected by the settings in your operating system. Be certain to adjust the sound volume for your computer, in addition to the sound controls in the Player window.

Loading lesson files

The Windows 7 Digital Classroom DVD includes files that can be used for many of the lessons. You may also use your own files with these lessons, or work with the sample files found in the lessons folder on the supplied DVD. Copying the lesson files to your hard drive:

1   Insert the Windows 7 Digital Classroom DVD supplied with this book.

2   On your computer desktop, navigate to the DVD and locate the folder named lessons.

3   You can install all the files, or just specific lesson files. Do one of the following:

- Install all lesson files by dragging the lessons folder to your hard drive.
- Install only some of the files by creating a new folder on your hard drive named lessons. Open the lessons folder on the supplied DVD, select the lesson you wish to copy and drag the folder(s) to the folder you created on your hard drive.

Additional resources

The Digital Classroom series goes beyond the training books. You can continue your learning online, with training videos, at seminars and conferences, and in-person training events.

DigitalClassroomBooks.com

The *DigitalClassroomBooks.com* site includes updates, notes, and makes it easy for you to contact the authors. You can also learn more about the other books in the series, including many books on popular creative software.

Learn from the authors

The authors of the Digital Classroom seminar series frequently conduct in-person seminars and speak at conferences. Learn more about their regularly scheduled classes at *agitraining.com*. The authors also provide private classes for groups and organizations, including speaking engagements. Contact AGI training at *info@agitraining.com*.

Follow the authors on Twitter

Follow the Digital Classroom authors on Twitter at *Twitter.com/agitraining*.

Resources for educators

Contact your Wiley publishing education representative to access resources for educators including guides for adoptions Digital Classroom books into your curriculum. Get more information at *Wiley.com*.

What you'll learn in this lesson:

- What you can do with Windows 7
- Activating your copy of Windows 7
- Starting Windows 7
- The Windows 7 desktop
- Getting help

Getting Started with Windows 7

The public spoke, and Microsoft listened. Windows 7 boasts hundreds of improvements based on feedback from users of previous versions of the Windows operating system. The result: a faster, more intuitive, more reliable, and more streamlined operating system.

Starting up

Before you start, be sure you have Windows 7 installed on your computer. If you haven't installed Windows 7 yet, refer to the section "Installing Windows 7" on page 3 of this book.

See Lesson 1 in action!

Use the accompanying video to gain a better understanding of how to use some of the features shown in this lesson. The video tutorial for this lesson can be found on the included DVD.

What you can do with Windows 7

The Windows 7 operating system has been designed with productivity in mind. In addition to being streamlined for speed, Windows 7 contains and supports a collection of tools, programs, and other resources to help you:

- **Get work done.** Windows 7 contains a word-processing program, WordPad, for generating documents; a calculator, which supports four modes—Standard, Scientific, Programmer, and Statistics—as well as several templates for calculating such real-world numbers as mortgages, salaries, etc. Windows 7 offer many productivity applications to help you be more efficient.

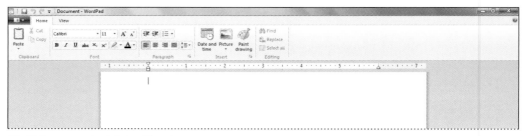

WordPad serves as a simple but useful word processor.

Calculator's four modes: Standard (top left), Scientific (top right), Programmer (bottom left), and Statistics (bottom right).

- **Create and edit pictures**. Use Windows 7 to import images from a digital camera, scan images with a scanner, or download images from the Internet. Then view them individually or in slide show format using Windows Photo Viewer. You can also use the Paint program to create images of your own. For even more photo features, use the Windows Live Photo Gallery, which is covered in more detail in Lesson 13, "Working with Images." When your images look the way you want them to, you can print them, e-mail them, burn them to a CD or DVD, or create a video DVD.

View your images in Windows Photo Viewer.

Windows Live Photo Gallery lets you edit and organize your images.

- **Play music and other media**. The Windows Media Player makes it easy to listen to audio CDs (and burn your own), play digital audio and video clips. You can also watch movies on DVD and tune into Internet radio. Using the Windows Media Center, you can locate and stream your favorite Internet TV shows, record regular TV, if your computer has a TV tuner, and view movies.

Use Windows Media Player to enjoy your favorite music and videos.

- **Get online**. With Windows 7, getting online is a breeze. Once you're connected, you have all the tools you need to get the most out of the Web, including the Internet Explorer 8 web browser, which makes surfing a snap.

Surf the Web with Internet Explorer 8.

What is an operating system?

A computer's operating system is a set of programs that enable the computer to perform such basic tasks as recognizing user input from a keyboard or mouse, sending output to the computer screen, keeping track of files on the hard disk, and controlling peripheral devices, such as external hard drives and printers. It also acts as an interface between the computer and the user, and serves as the host for any other programs, or applications, running on the computer, such as word-processing programs, games, web browsers, etc.

If you're not sure which version of Windows 7 you have, you can easily find out.

1   Press the Start button (⊙) to display the Start menu.

2   Click Control Panel in the Start menu.

Click the Start button and choose Control Panel.

3   In the Control Panel window that appears, click the System and Security link.

Click the System and Security link.

4   In the System and Security window, click the System link. The System window opens, displaying the version of Windows 7 installed on your computer, among other things.

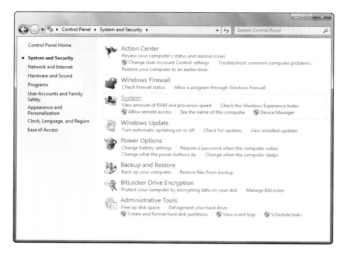

Click the System link to find out which edition of Windows 7 is running on your computer.

You can learn about the different versions of Windows 7 in Appendix A.

Activating your copy of Windows 7

When you install Windows 7, you have the option of activating your copy of the software. If you prefer to wait, you can activate it later—you have 30 days to do so. Activating your copy of Windows 7, which is mandatory, enables Microsoft to verify that your copy of the software is authentic, and ensures that you'll be able to use every feature of the software. It also makes you eligible to receive updates to the software as well as product support from Microsoft.

In this exercise, you will learn how to activate your copy of Windows 7. If you opted to activate Windows 7 when prompted during the installation rather than waiting until later, skip to the next section. Note that you must be connected to the Internet to complete this exercise.

1 Press the Start button (⊕) to display the Start menu.

2 Click Control Panel in the Start menu.

3 In the Control Panel window that appears, click the System and Security link.

4 In the System and Security window, click the System link. The System window opens.

5 The Windows activation section of the System window indicates how many days you have left to activate your copy of Windows 7. You may have to scroll down to see this section of the window. Click the Activate Windows now link.

Activate your copy of Windows 7 from the System window.

6 The first screen of the Windows Activation Wizard appears. Click Activate Windows online now.

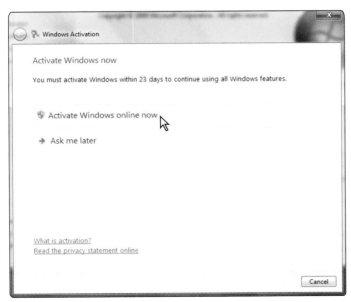

Windows 7 launches the Windows Activation Wizard.

7 Microsoft verifies the product key, then activates the software. When activation is complete, press the Close button (■) in the upper right corner.

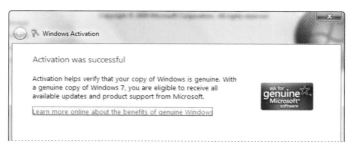

Windows 7 verifies the product key, then notifies you when activation is successful.

 If you don't have an Internet connection, you can activate your copy of Windows 7 via phone. To find out what number to call, click Show Me Other Ways to Activate in the first screen of the Windows Activation Wizard (this option is visible only if you are not connected to the Internet) and follow the onscreen prompts.

What's new with Windows 7

Windows 7 incorporates hundreds of improvements based on feedback provided by users of previous versions of the operating system—most notably Windows 7's immediate predecessor, Windows Vista.

The Windows 7 Taskbar buttons are larger and easier to see. In Windows 7, you can pin a button for any program on the Taskbar, so it's always a click away. You can also change the order in which Taskbar buttons appear. Finally, the Windows 7 Taskbar supports thumbnail and full-screen previews of open windows. Hover your mouse over a Taskbar button to preview the associated window in thumbnail mode. Click the thumbnail to preview the window in full-screen mode.

Preview the associated window in thumbnail mode.

Jump lists offer a handy way to quickly access your most recent files—right from the Taskbar. If you frequently access a particular file, you can pin it to the Taskbar. Right-click a Taskbar button to view a jump list of recent documents.

To view a jump list of recent documents right-click a Taskbar button.

Windows 7 makes window management a snap—literally. For example, in previous operating systems, to compare the contents of two open windows, you were required to manually resize and position each one. In contrast, with Windows 7's new Snaps feature, you can drag one window to the right edge of the screen and the other to the left; Snaps automatically resizes them as needed and snaps them into place.

Revealing your desktop when windows are open is also simple: Just hover your mouse over the Show Desktop button on the right-most edge of the Taskbar, and the open windows hide from view. To hide all open windows but one, click and *shake* the title bar of the window you want to remain; all other open windows are minimized. Shake the open window again; the minimized windows reappear.

Windows 7 adds a new feature called libraries. A library displays all content of a particular type, for example, image files, in one easy-to-find location, no matter where on your computer those files are located.

Windows 7 also has improved device-management features that enable you to easily connect, manage, and use any devices, such as printers, scanners, cameras, that are connected to your computer.

Manage devices connected to your computer from one convenient location.

If you have a home network, the HomeGroup feature makes it painless to connect any computers running Windows 7 to that network, and to share files, folders, and even devices such as printers with other Windows 7 computers on the network. Accessing these files and devices is as easy as if they were on your hard drive.

If you use a laptop computer, you'll appreciate Windows 7's improved power-management features. One feature, adaptive display brightness, dims the display if your system has been idle for a time; another ensures that less power is used to play DVDs—especially handy on long trips where AC power is unavailable.

If you were one of the countless Windows Vista users frustrated by the seemingly endless stream of pop-up alerts, you'll appreciate Windows 7's new notification system. Rather than launching a pop-up, Windows 7 displays a special icon (🏳) in the Taskbar's Notification area. Click the icon whenever you want to open the new Windows 7 Action Center. This special window offers one-stop access to alerts and tasks related to keeping your computer in good form.

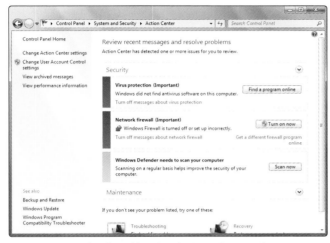

Review messages and resolve problems from the Action Center window.

If you have a touch-screen monitor, you can use your fingers to scroll, resize windows, play media, pan, and zoom. The Start menu, Taskbar, and Windows Explorer window also support touch input.

Live from Redmond

In the interest of streamlining, Microsoft also omitted some features from Windows 7 that existed in earlier versions of Windows. These include the following:

- The sidebar
- Windows Calendar
- Windows Mail
- Windows Photo Gallery
- Windows Movie Maker

Some of these features, such as Windows Mail, Windows Photo Gallery, and Windows Movie Maker, are now available free from Windows Live, a collection of web services and downloadable applications from Microsoft. You'll explore the programs that are available on Windows Live later in this book in Lesson 13, "Working with Images.".

Starting Windows 7

The first time you start Windows 7, you may be prompted to complete a series of configuration steps. Simply follow the onscreen prompts. After completion, whenever you turn on your computer, Windows 7 starts automatically, displaying the Welcome screen. From there, you must specify which account you want to use by clicking it. If you've set a password for the selected account, enter it when prompted. Note that the characters you type appear as dots to prevent others from seeing your password as you type, and the Windows 7 desktop appears.

Be sure to remember your password, or write it down and store it somewhere safe. If you forget your password, press the Go button to the right of the password field; Windows 7 displays the password hint you set when you created your password. For more about creating passwords and other user account details, see Lesson 8, "Setting Up User Accounts."

The Windows 7 desktop

The Windows 7 desktop serves as the jumping-off point for any task you want to perform using your computer. Take a moment to familiarize yourself with the various components of the desktop.

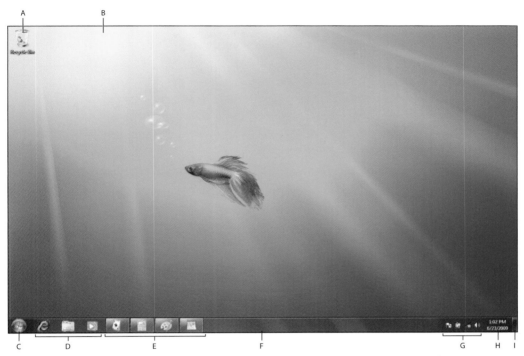

*A. Shortcut Icon. **B.** Work area. **C.** Start Button. **D.** Quick Launch Program Icons. **E.** Programs that are currently running. **F.** Taskbar. **G.** Notification area. **H.** Time & Date. **I.** Show Desktop Button.*

- **The Start button**. Clicking this button reveals the Start menu, from which you can launch any Windows 7 application.

- **The Windows Taskbar**. Buttons representing any programs you have open appear on the Taskbar. Also, by default, the Taskbar features icons for launching Internet Explorer 8, Windows Explorer, and Windows Media Player. You can *pin* additional program icons—or even icons for frequently accessed documents or folders—to the Taskbar if you like. You'll learn more about customizing the Taskbar in Lesson 4, "Customizing Windows 7." Note that open programs appear highlighted; buttons for launching programs do not.

- **The Notification area.** This area displays important information about your computer, such as whether you are connected to a wireless network, whether your laptop is plugged in, and the system volume level. It also displays special alert icons if your system is in need of attention. You can click the icons displayed in this area to view additional information or to make necessary adjustments.

- **Time and date.** Your computer displays the time and date to the right of the Notification area. For more a more detailed calendar and clock, you can click the Time and Date. From there you can click the Change date and time settings link to make any changes to the Time, Date, and Time zone.

- **Show Desktop button.** If you need to access the desktop, but have several programs running at once, press the Show Desktop button to minimize all open windows and reveal the desktop. If you just need to glance at the desktop, but don't want to minimize the open program windows, hover your mouse over the Show Desktop button to take a quick peek at the desktop underneath.

- **Work area.** Any programs, folders, and files that you open display in the work area.

- **Shortcut icon.** You double-click icons on the Windows 7 desktop to launch a program or Windows 7 feature. Often, when you install new programs, these shortcut icons are added by default; if not, you can create them yourself. You'll learn how to create or *pin* shortcut icons in Lesson 4, "Customizing Windows 7."

Getting help

If you run into a problem with Windows 7, or you aren't sure how to accomplish a task, for example, you may want to find out how to set a password for your user account, the Windows Help and Support Center is your first stop for expert assistance. Here, you can search for help by typing a keyword or phrase, such as **password** or **user account password**, to view a list of links to related help articles. Another approach is to browse help articles.

 If your computer is connected to the Internet, help includes online resources.

1   Press the Start button (●). The Start menu appears.

2   Click Help and Support.

Choose Help and Support from the Start menu.

3   The Windows Help and Support window appears. Type a keyword or phrase, for example **user account password**, in the Search text field and press Enter.

Type a keyword or phrase in the Search box and press Enter.

4 Windows 7 displays a list of links to articles that relate to the word or phrase you typed. Click a link that looks relevant, and Windows 7 displays the article.

Click a relevant link, and then read the help article.

You can also browse the help articles in the Help and Support Center. Here's an example of how you might browse for an article. Keep in mind that locating other articles may involve more or fewer screens of subcategories or topics.

5 Press the Back button (⊙) twice to return to the Windows Help and Support window.

6 Click the Browse Help topics link.

Click the Browse Help topics link.

7   A screen containing a table of contents appears. Click a link in the table of contents that relates to what you need help with. In this example, Security and privacy was chosen.

Click a link in the table of contents.

8   Windows 7 lists a series of topics and categories to help you refine your search. Click the option that best matches your needs.

9   A list of subcategories appears. Click the one that is most relevant to your inquiry.

10 A list of topics in the selected subcategory appears. Click the link for the topic that looks most promising. Windows 7 displays the article you selected.

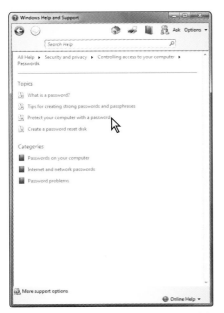

Click the most promising topic, and then read the help article.

Finding program-specific help

Although the Help and Support Center is a great way to get help with Windows 7, it can't help you with a program that's not included with the Windows 7 operating system, such as Microsoft Excel or Adobe Photoshop. To access the Help function in these programs, click the Help menu in the specific program window and choose View Help, Help Topics, or something similar (the precise terminology varies). Alternatively, press the F1 key on your keyboard. You can also access program-specific Help information from within certain dialog boxes and screens, indicated by a question mark icon or a text link.

Shutting down Windows 7

When you are not using your computer, you should power it down to conserve energy. While your instinct may be to press the machine's power button, you should not do so, as unsaved changes in open documents could be lost. In addition, Windows system files could be damaged, which could make your system less stable. Instead, you should power down Windows 7. When you do, you have three options:

- **Sleep**. Sleep is essentially a stand-by mode. Power is withheld from non-essential components and operations in order to conserve energy. When a *sleeping* system is *awakened*, it resumes operation quickly.

- **Hibernate**. When in Hibernate mode, your Windows 7 system saves your data to your hard disk, then completely powers down your computer. When you are ready to use the computer again, press the machine's power button; the system restarts, reverting to the state it was in before it entered hibernation with all the same programs, folders, and files displayed on the desktop. The advantage of using Hibernate mode over Sleep mode is that no power is consumed. Although it does take the system a bit longer to resume operation after hibernating. When the system restarts, it remembers any open programs or documents on which you were working.

If your Hibernate option is missing, you might have Hybrid sleep turned off. The Hybrid sleep option can be found by opening the Control panel and clicking the Hardware and Sound link. Click the Power Options link and click the Change plan settings link of your current power plan. In the Edit Plan Settings window, click the change advanced power settings link. In the Power Options Advanced settings dialog box that appears, look for the Allow hybrid sleep option under the Sleep category. If the setting is On, then the Hibernate option is missing due to a setting in your computer's BIOS, which are changed outside of Windows 7,

- **Shut Down**. Like Hibernate, Shut Down completely powers down your computer. The difference is that the next time you start it back up, you begin with a fresh desktop.

1   To shut down Windows 7, press the Start button (⬤). The Start menu appears.

2   Press the Shut Down button. Windows 7 shuts down your computer. Click the arrow to the right of the Shut Down button to view additional options.

Choose Shut Down from the Start menu or click the arrow to the right for additional options.

3   Choose Sleep or Hibernate. Windows 7 puts your computer in Sleep mode or Hibernate mode, depending on which option you choose.

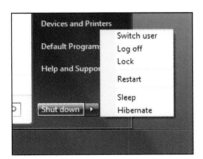

Choose Sleep or Hibernate.

Note that in addition to providing Sleep and Hibernate options, the Shut Down menu also includes the following choices:

- **Switch User**. Choose this to switch to a different user account without closing the programs you have open in the current session. You'll learn more about user accounts in Lesson 9, "Networking Your Computer."

- **Log Off**. Choose this to close all open programs and log out of your account. This returns Windows 7 to the Welcome screen that appears immediately after startup, where users indicate which account they want to use.

- **Lock**. Choose this to lock the computer. To unlock the computer, you will need to enter the password you have specified for the current user account, assuming one has been set.

- **Restart**. Choose this option to close all open programs, shut down Windows 7, then start Windows 7 back up again. You might choose this option if, for example, you've installed new software, and the new software requires that Windows 7 be restarted before it can be used.

Self study

1 Click and right-click the various icons currently on display in the Notification area on the right side of the Taskbar, and explore the options and windows that appear.

2 Press the Ask button in the Windows Help and Support window to learn about additional ways to obtain help and support.

Review

Questions

1 What is an operating system?

2 How many versions of the Windows 7 operating system are there?

3 How do you obtain Windows Mail, Windows Photo Gallery, and Windows Movie Maker?

4 On what part of the Windows 7 desktop do you find important information about your computer, such as whether you are connected to a wireless network, or whether your system is in need of attention?

5 What are the two main ways to find help using the Windows Help and Support Center?

Answers

1 An operating system is a set of programs that enable the computer to perform basic tasks, such as recognizing user input from a keyboard or mouse, sending output to the computer screen, keeping track of files on the hard disk, and controlling peripheral devices such as external hard drives and printers. It also acts as an interface between the computer and the user, and serves as the host for any other programs, or applications, running on the computer, such as word-processing programs, games, web browsers, etc.

2 In all, there are three versions of the Windows 7 operating system:

- Windows 7 Home
- Windows 7 Professional
- Windows 7 Ultimate

3 Windows Mail, Windows Photo Gallery, and Windows Movie Maker—as well as other free software for Windows 7 users—are available from Windows Live, a Microsoft-run Web site offering various web services and downloadable applications.

4 You find this information in the Taskbar's Notification area. You can click the icon's display in this area to view additional information or to make necessary adjustments.

5 You can obtain help from the Windows Help and Support Center by searching using a keyword or phrase, or by browsing Help topics.

What you'll learn in this lesson:

* Starting and exploring programs in Windows 7

* Using dialog boxes

* Working with files in a program

* Working with multiple program windows

Working with Windows 7 Programs

Windows 7 includes several programs and there are countless other Windows 7-compatible programs available. While not all programs operate in exactly the same way, they share many common attributes.

Starting up

Before you start, be sure to download all the files for this lesson from the accompanying DVD to your hard drive.

See Lesson 2 in action!

Use the accompanying video to gain a better understanding of how to use some of the features shown in this lesson. The video tutorial for this lesson can be found on the included DVD.

Exploring programs in Windows 7

Windows 7 includes several programs, also referred to as applications. These include the following:

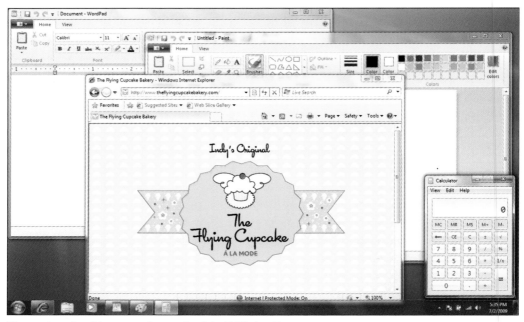

These are just a few of the programs that come bundled with Windows 7.

- **Internet Explorer 8.** This most recent version of the Microsoft web browser is faster, easier, and safer than ever, and is loaded with new features to improve your online experience.

- **WordPad.** A full-featured word-processing program, WordPad enables you to create and edit documents that include rich formatting and graphics, as well as linked or embedded objects, such as pictures or other documents.

- **Paint.** Windows 7 includes an improved version of Microsoft Paint, used to create drawings and otherwise edit digital images.

- **Calculator.** Windows 7's Calculator utility benefits from an upgrade, offering several modes: Standard, Scientific, Programmer, and Statistics.

- **Games.** Windows 7 features numerous games: Chess Titans, FreeCell, Hearts, Internet Backgammon, Internet Checkers, Internet Spades, Mahjong Titans, Minesweeper, Purble Place, Solitaire, and Spider Solitaire.

- **Windows Media Player 12.** This digital media player is ideal for playing audio and video, and viewing images on your computer. You can also use Windows Media Player to rip music from and burn music to CDs, and to purchase or rent music from various online music stores.

- **Windows Media Center.** Along with the appropriate hardware, for example, a TV tuner and an FM tuner, Windows Media Center enables you to turn your Windows 7 computer into an entertainment center. With it, you can watch and record TV shows, listen to digital music, view digital pictures and videos, play games, listen to and burn CDs, watch and burn DVDs, listen to FM and Internet radio stations, and access content from online services.

In addition to these pre-installed, or bundled, programs, countless others Windows 7-compatible programs are available, some are free, and others are available for purchase. You'll learn how to install additional programs on your Windows 7 system in Lesson 8, "Setting Up User Accounts."

Starting a program

In order to work with a program in Windows 7, you must first instruct Windows 7 to launch it. When you do, Windows 7 starts the program and displays it on your desktop.

1　Press the Start button (⊙). The Start menu appears.

2　If the program you want to start appears in the first pane of the Start menu, click it to launch it. Otherwise, click All Programs.

Click All Programs if the program you want to run is not listed here.

3 The All Programs menu appears. Click the program you want to start. You may need to open a submenu to locate the program. For example, the WordPad program is located under the Accessories submenu. To locate the WordPad program, you must click the Accessories submenu to open it. Windows 7 starts the program, displaying the program's window on the desktop. Note that a button for the program also appears in the Taskbar.

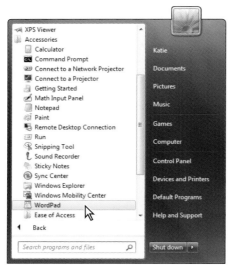

Click the program you want to start; Windows 7 starts the program.

Another way to start a program is by launching a file associated with that program from Windows Explorer. For example, you can start WordPad by opening a Rich Text format document file in Windows Explorer. For more information, refer to Lesson 3, "Working with Files and Folders."

To open a second program window for the same program, for example, if you want to work on two similar documents at the same time, shift-click the program's button in the Taskbar after launching the program initially. Windows 7 launches an additional program window.

Navigating program windows

When you start a program, its program window appears on the Windows 7 desktop. While not all program windows are the same, many have certain navigation elements in common:

A. Window Menu. ***B.*** *System Menu Icon.* ***C.*** *Quick Access Toobar.* ***D.*** *Ribbon.* ***E.*** *Title Bar.* ***F.*** *Work Area.*
G. *Minimize Button.* ***H.*** *Maximize Button.* ***I.*** *Close Button.* ***J.*** *Scroll Bar.* ***K.*** *Zoom Settings.*

- **Window Menu button.** Pressing this button reveals commands for restoring, moving, resizing, minimizing, maximizing, and closing the program window. Note that the appearance of this button changes, depending on the program that is running.

- **System Menu button.** Press the System Menu button to access options for creating a new document, opening an existing document, saving a document, printing a document, and more.

- **Quick Access toolbar.** Use the buttons in this toolbar to quickly launch save, undo, and redo commands. You can customize it to change which buttons it contains. For more information on customizing the Quick Access toolbar, see the section, "Working with files in a program" in this lesson.

- **Title bar.** The title bar displays the name of the program as well as the name of any documents that are open in the program window.

- **Work area.** This is where any files you have opened in the program appear.

- **Ribbon**. In lieu of the traditional drop-down menu and toolbars that appear in many Windows programs, some now offer the Ribbon, which displays groups of related buttons and options in tabs. To view a different tab, click it. Press a button or option in the tab to activate its associated command or feature. Note that some groups of options feature a special diagonal arrow icon (▾) in the bottom-right corner; click this icon to reveal a dialog box with additional related options. You can see the ribbon listed as item D in the figure on the previous page.

Although the Ribbon has become popular in certain Windows 7 programs, traditional drop-down menus and toolbars do still exist in others.

- **Minimize button**. Press the Minimize button (▭) to minimize the program window—that is, clear it from the desktop without closing the program. A button for the program window remains on the Taskbar. Press this button on the Taskbar to re-display the window.

- **Maximize button**. Pressing the Maximize button (▢) enlarges the program window to cover the entire desktop. Note that when you press the Maximize button, it's replaced with a Restore Down button (▣). Press this Restore Down button to return the window to its original size.

- **Close button**. Press the Close button (▬✕▬) to clear the program window from the desktop and shut down the program.

- **Scroll bars**. If your file is too large to be viewed in its entirety in the work area, vertical and/or horizontal scroll bars appear to enable you to see the rest of the file. To scroll up or down in a window, click the scroll box that appears along the right side of the program window and drag up or down. To scroll left or right in a window, click the scroll box that appears along the bottom of the program window and drag left or right.

An even easier way to scroll up and down in a file is to use the wheel on your mouse. Move the wheel backward, away from your wrist, to scroll up; move the wheel forward, toward your wrist, to scroll down.

- **Zoom**. Use the Zoom In and Zoom Out buttons or the Zoom slider to zoom in or out of the file displayed in the work area.

Using dialog boxes

When a program needs you to supply information, it displays a dialog box. For example, when you save a document for the first time, Windows 7 displays the Save As dialog box. Here you can indicate the folder in which you want to save the file, the name you want to give the file, and so on. Similarly, when you print a file, Windows 7 displays a Print dialog box, where you enter such information as how many copies you want to print, which portion of the file you want to print, which printer you want to use, and so on.

Dialog boxes feature various types of input controls to enable you to supply information to the program, including the following:

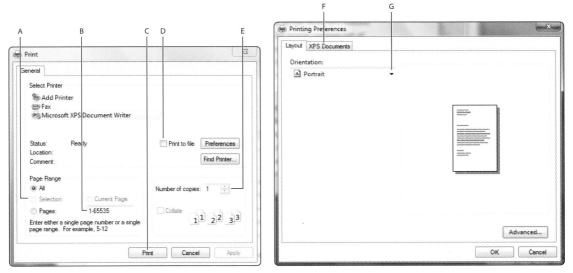

A. Option button. B. Text field. C. Command button. D. Checkbox. E. Spin box. F. Tab. G. Drop-down menu.

- **Option button**. Click an option button to enable or disable the feature associated with it. Note that only one option button in a group can be enabled at once. When an option button is selected, it appears colored in; deselected option buttons appear empty.

- **Text field**. You type text in a text field. To do so, you click inside the text field and when the blinking vertical bar, called a cursor or insertion point, appears inside the text field, you press the Backspace or Delete key to delete any existing characters and then type your text.

- **Command button**. You click a command button to execute the command that appears on the button. For example, you can press the OK command button to implement the settings you choose in a dialog box. Alternatively, you can press the Cancel command button to close the dialog box without changing the settings.

- **Checkbox**. As with an option button, clicking a checkbox enables or disables the feature associated with it. Unlike an option button, however, multiple checkboxes in a group can be enabled at once. When a checkbox is selected, it contains a checkmark; deselected checkboxes are empty.

- **Tab**. Some dialog boxes have multiple tabs along the top, each displaying a different set of input controls. To switch to a different tab in a dialog box, click the desired tab.

- **Drop-down menu**. A drop-down menu looks like a text field, but with a down-arrow button on the right side. To change the setting that appears in the menu, click the down-arrow button to display a list of available settings, then select the desired setting in the list.

- **Spin box**. You use a spin box to set a numeric value. Click the top arrow on the spin box to increase the value that appears in the text field alongside the spin box, and the bottom arrow to decrease it. You can also type a value in the text field.

Keyboard Shortcuts

To speed up your input, you can use certain keyboard shortcuts to navigate dialog boxes in Windows 7. For example:

- **Enter**. Press Enter to select the default command button (indicated by a highlight).

- **Esc**. Press Esc to close the dialog box without implementing your changes. (Pressing Esc is the same as pressing the Cancel command button.)

- **Tab**. Press Tab to move forward through the controls in the dialog box.

- **Shift+Tab**. While pressing the Shift key, press Tab (an action called Shift-tabbing) to move backward through the dialog box controls.

- **Up arrow/Down arrow**. Press these keys to move up or down within a group of option buttons.

- **Alt+Down arrow**. While pressing the Alt key, press the Down-arrow key to reveal the available options in the selected drop-down menu.

Working with files in a program

In many cases, the entire purpose of a program is to create, edit, and/or print files, whether they are documents, image files, spreadsheets, or database entries. Windows 7 makes it easy to perform all these tasks, placing the necessary commands in the System menu.

Creating a new file

1   Press the System Menu button in the program window. The System menu appears.

2   Click New. A new, empty file (in this case, a document file) appears in the work area.

 Depending on the program you are using, you may be required to provide additional information when creating a new file. For example, if you are creating a new document in Microsoft Word, which is available as a part of the Microsoft Office suite of products, you are prompted to indicate what type of document you want to create.

Click New in the System menu and a new file appears in the work area.

 An even faster way to create a new file is to press the Ctrl+N keyboard shortcut.

Saving a file

If you make changes to a file, it's critical that you save them and do so early and often. The first time you save a document, Windows 7 prompts you to specify the folder in which the file should be saved and to provide a name for the file. Subsequent saves require no additional input, as the original file is updated.

1   Press the System Menu button in the program window. The System menu appears.

2   Click Save. If you have saved this file before, Windows 7 saves the changes made to the file since the last time you saved it. No additional input is required from you.

Click Save in the System menu.

3   If this is the first time you have saved this file, Windows 7 displays the Save As dialog box. In the Save As dialog box's Navigation pane, click the library in which you want to save the file, in this example, the Documents library. To save the file in a subfolder, double-click the subfolder in the file list.

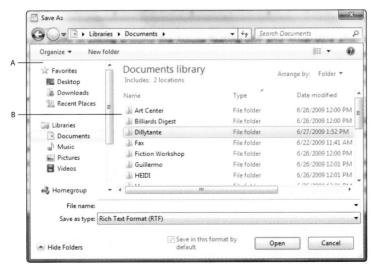

A. Navigation pane. B. File list.

4   Type a name for the file in the File name text field.

5   To change the file type, click the Save as type drop-down menu to reveal additional options and select the desired type from the list.

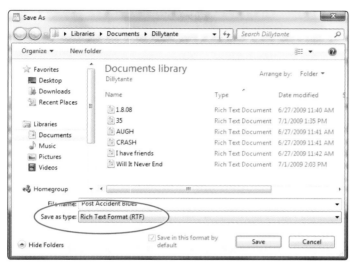

Change the file type, if necessary.

6   Press the Save button. Windows 7 saves the file in the folder you chose, giving it the name you indicated. Notice that this name now appears in the program window's title bar.

 An even faster way to save a file is to press the Ctrl+S keyboard shortcut.

If you want to make changes to a file but leave the original version intact, for example, if you are making changes to a form letter that you send out to clients, but you want to keep a copy of the previous version for your records, you can easily do so.

7   Press the System Menu button in the program window. The System menu appears.

8   Click Save As.

9   As before, Windows 7 displays the Save As dialog box. In the Navigation pane, click the library in which you want to save the file, in this example, the Documents library. To save the file in a subfolder, double-click the subfolder in the file list.

10 If you are saving the updated file in the same folder as the original, type a unique name for the updated file in the File name text field. That way, you won't overwrite the original file by accident.

11 Press Save. Windows 7 saves the file in the folder you chose, giving it the name you indicated.

Opening an existing file

You can open files you've created or received from others to edit them or add more data. Windows 7 lists files you've accessed most recently in the System menu as well as in jump lists, which are accessible from the program's button on the Windows 7 Taskbar, assuming the program is already running in Windows 7. If the file you need to open does not appear in either of these lists, you can find it in the Open dialog box.

1 Right-click the program's button in the Windows 7 Taskbar.

2 A list of recently opened files appears. Click the file you want to open. Windows 7 opens the file in the program window. Alternatively, click the System Menu button in the program window to open a file. The System menu appears.

Right-clicking the program's button in the Windows 7 Taskbar displays a jump list of recently used files.

3 If the file you want to open appears in the Recent Documents list, click it to open it. Otherwise, press Open. Windows 7 displays the Open dialog box.

Click Open in the System menu.

4   In the Open dialog box's Navigation pane, click the library in which the file is stored, in this example, the Documents library. If the file is in a subfolder, double–click the subfolder in the file list to open it.

An even faster way to launch the Open dialog box is to press the Ctrl+O keyboard shortcut.

If you're not sure where a file is located, you can search for it using the Search text field in the upper-right corner of the Open dialog box. Simply type a keyword or phrase that relates to the file and press Enter to see a list of files matching the criteria you typed. You'll learn more about searching in Lesson 3, "Working with Files and Folders."

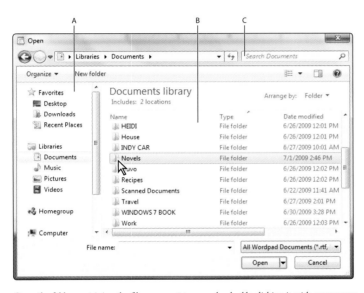

Open the folder containing the file you want to access by double-clicking it with your mouse.

5   Click the file you want to open.

6   Press Open. Windows 7 opens the file in the program window.

Printing a file

Assuming you have a printer connected to your computer, you can create printed copies of your files. This is handy if, for example, you need to print handouts for a meeting.

1   Press the System Menu button in the program window. The System menu appears.

2 Click Print.

Click Print in the System menu.

3 Windows 7 displays the Print dialog box. Under Select Printer, click the printer you want to use for the job.

An even faster way to launch the Print dialog box is to use the keyboard shortcut, Ctrl+P.

4 Under Page Range, indicate whether Windows 7 should print the whole document, a selection of pages, the current page, or a specific page range.

5 Use the Number of Copies spin box to specify how many copies to print. If you are printing multiple copies, use the *Collate* checkbox to specify whether they should be collated. You can also type the number of copies you would like to print in the text field to the left of the spin box.

6 Press Print. Windows 7 prints the file from the selected printer.

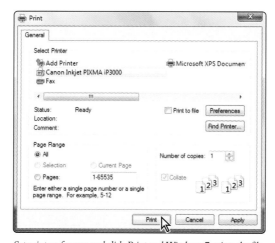

Set print preferences and click Print and Windows 7 prints the file.

Managing program windows

As noted previously in the section, "Navigating program windows," you can click the Minimize (⊟) button to minimize the program window which clears it from the desktop without closing the program.

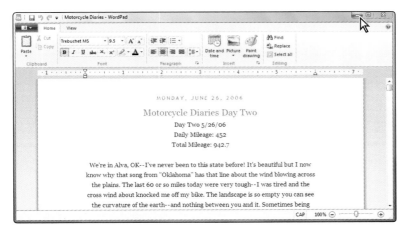

Press the Minimize button and the program window disappears, but its Taskbar button remains in place. To restore the window to its original location, click its Taskbar button.

The Maximize (⊡) button enlarges the program window to cover the entire desktop.

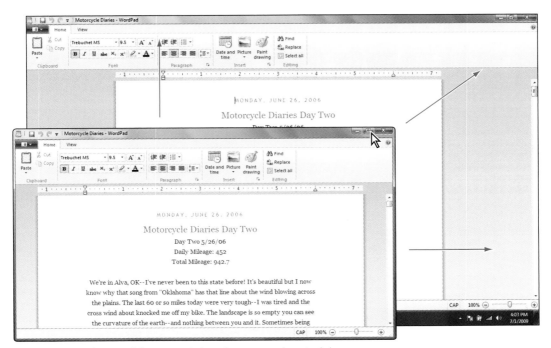

Press the Maximize button and the program window enlarges to cover the entire desktop.

The Restore Down (🗗) button returns a maximized window to its original size.

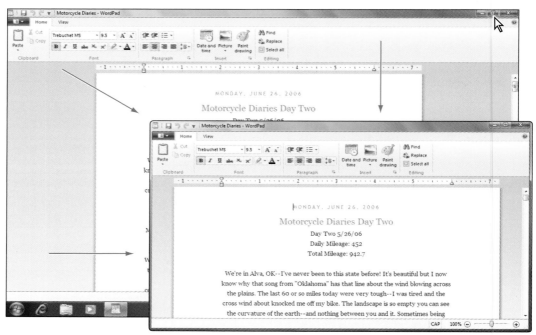

Press the Restore Down button to shrink the window to its original size.

The Close (❌) button to close the program window. The program window and its Taskbar button disappear. Note that if the program window contains a file with unsaved changes, you are prompted to save them before the program window closes.

Press the Close button.

Manually resizing a window

In addition to resizing a window using the Maximize/Restore Down buttons, you can also resize it manually, enabling you to fine-tune its dimensions.

1 Position your mouse pointer over the edge of the window border you want to move. The pointer changes to a two-headed arrow.

2 Click and drag the two-headed arrow to resize the window. Drag inward (toward the center of the window) to make the window smaller. Drag outward (away from the center of the window) to enlarge it.

3 Release the mouse button. Windows 7 resizes the window.

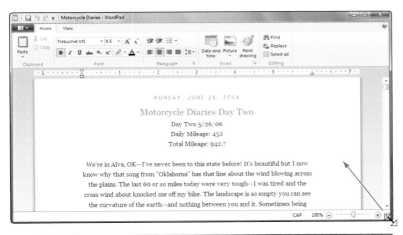

Position your mouse pointer over the window border and drag (top). Windows 7 resizes the window (bottom).

To resize the window's vertical and horizontal dimensions at the same time, position your mouse pointer over a corner of the window. When it changes to a two-headed arrow, click and drag inward or outward to make the window smaller or larger.

Moving a window

There may be times that you need to move a window to a different area of your desktop, for example, to access a shortcut icon on your desktop or to make room for an additional program window.

1 Click an empty section of the program window's title bar. Drag the window in the direction you want it to move.

2 When the window is in the desired location, release the mouse button.

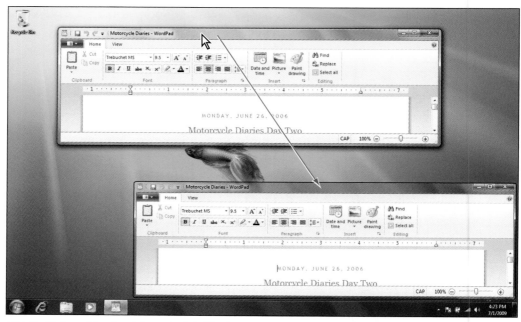

Click the title bar and drag the window to the desired location.

Working with multiple program windows

Many Windows users multitask, for example, run multiple programs at once or launch multiple files in a single program. While multitasking can certainly be an efficient way to work, it can make navigating your Windows 7 system difficult. Fortunately, Windows 7 includes several tools for navigating the various open windows, viewing open windows side by side or minimizing windows not currently in use.

Switching between open windows

Windows 7 supports several methods for switching between your open windows. Some of these methods involve using your keyboard; others involve using the Taskbar.

- **Alt+Tab**. While holding down the Alt key, press the Tab key. Windows 7 displays thumbnail images of each window currently open in the system; with the Alt key still pressed, press the Tab key as many times as needed until the thumbnail for the window you want to switch to is highlighted. Alternatively, you can click the desired thumbnail using the mouse.

Press Alt+Tab to switch to a different window.

- **Alt+Esc**. While holding down the Alt key, press the Esc key. Windows 7 displays the next window in the cycle.

- **Windows logo+Tab**. While holding down the Windows logo key on your keyboard, press Tab. Windows 7 displays all open windows in a 3D stack, bringing the next window in the cycle to the top of the stack each time you press Tab.

Press Windows logo+Tab to view all open windows in a 3D stack.

To switch between open windows using the Taskbar, press the Taskbar button that represents the window you want to view.

1 Place your mouse pointer over the button for the window you want to preview. A thumbnail image of the window appears.

Placing your mouse pointer over a Taskbar button displays a thumbnail image of the associated program window.

2 To see a full-size preview, place your mouse pointer over the thumbnail image. Windows 7 displays a full-size preview of the program window.

Place your mouse pointer over the thumbnail for a full-size preview.

3 To switch to the previewed window, click the thumbnail icon. Otherwise, move your mouse pointer away from the thumbnail icon, and the full-screen preview disappears.

Minimizing windows by shaking

If the window you want to view is already visible on the desktop, but you're distracted by the open windows underneath it, you can quickly minimize the extra windows.

Click the title bar of the window you want to leave open and, holding down the mouse button, *shake* it—quickly move your mouse pointer back and forth. Windows 7 minimizes all the open windows except the one you shook. To re-display the other windows, *shake* the visible window a second time.

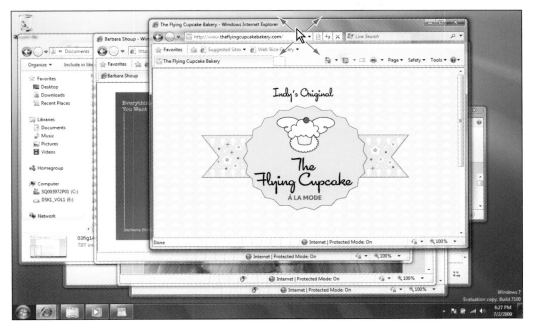

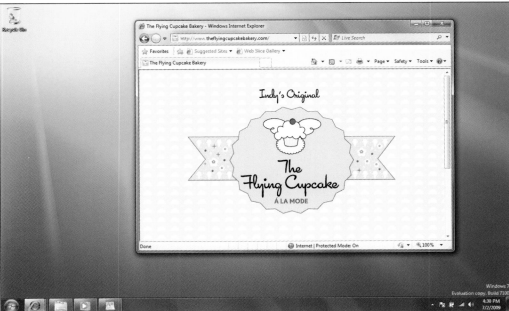

Click the title bar of the window you want to leave open and shake it. Windows 7 minimizes all the other windows.

If you're running multiple windows in the same program, you can easily switch to the one you need by doing one of the following:

1   Place your mouse pointer over the program's button in the Taskbar. Thumbnail images of each program appear. Click the thumbnail for the desired program window to switch to it.

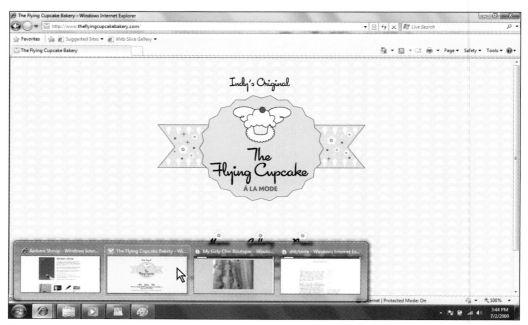

Hover your mouse pointer over the program icon and select the desired window from the thumbnails that appear.

2   While holding down the Ctrl key, click the program's button to cycle through the open windows.

Displaying windows side-by-side

In previous versions of Windows, displaying windows side-by-side was a cumbersome process that involved manually resizing the windows you wanted to view and dragging them to the desired position. Windows 7 simplifies this process with a new feature called Snaps. With Snaps, you can drag a window to either edge of the screen and Windows 7 *snaps* it into place, resizing it to fill half the screen.

1 Click the title bar of one window and drag that window to the left edge of the screen.

2 When the mouse pointer reaches the edge of the screen, release the mouse button. The window snaps into place, filling the left half of the work area.

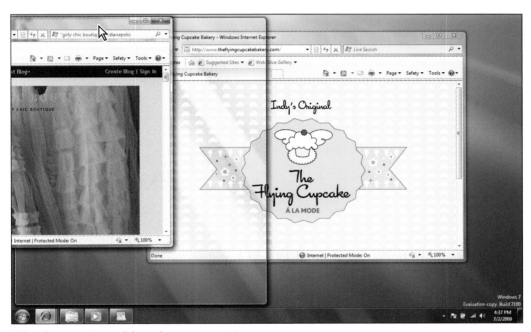

Release the mouse pointer and the window snaps into position.

3 Repeat steps 1 and 2, this time dragging the other window's title bar to the right edge of the screen. The window snaps into place, enabling you to view the two windows side-by-side.

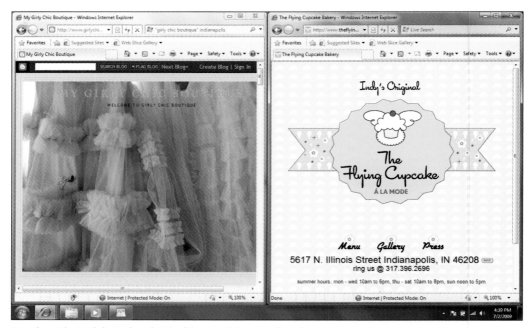

Drag the window's title bar to the right side of the screen. When you release the mouse pointer, the window snaps into position, enabling you to view the two windows side-by-side.

You can also view windows top-to-bottom. To do so, drag one window's title bar to the top edge of the screen to snap it into place and drag the other window's title bar to the bottom edge of the screen.

Showing the desktop

As you work, you may find it necessary to take a quick look at your desktop—perhaps to open a file you've saved there. You can minimize all open windows to view your desktop using a few different techniques:

- Using your Keyboard press the Alt+Tab, Alt+Esc, or Windows logo+Tab keys. Use this shortcut to cycle through your open windows, stopping when the desktop is revealed.

Cycle through your open windows until the desktop is revealed.

- Click the Show Desktop button (▮) on the far-right side of the Taskbar a second time to restore the windows to their original locations. Alternatively, hover your mouse pointer over this button; this enables you to take a quick look at the desktop without minimizing your open windows.

• Right-click an empty area of the Taskbar and choose Show the Desktop from the menu that appears.

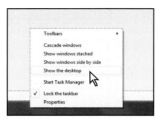

Right-click an empty area of the Taskbar and choose Show the Desktop.

Self study

1 Practice using the various keyboard shortcuts: Ctrl+N to open a new file, Ctrl+S to save a file, Ctrl+O to launch the Open dialog box, Ctrl+P to launch the Print dialog box, and the various keyboard shortcuts for navigating dialog boxes. To find more shortcuts, launch Windows Help and Support and type **keyboard shortcuts** in the Search text field.

2 Compare the various techniques for switching between open windows to decide which one works best for you. Press Alt+Tab, Alt+Esc, or Windows logo+Tab; press a window's Taskbar button; preview windows using the Taskbar button,

Review

Questions

1 What are three programs that come pre-installed with Windows 7.

2 What feature replaces traditional drop-down menus and toolbars in some Windows 7 programs?

3 Name three types of input controls in dialog boxes.

4 Which menu do you use to create new files, save files, open existing files, print files, etc?

5 Where are the buttons for minimizing, maximizing/restoring down, and closing program windows located?

Answers

1   Programs that come pre-installed with Windows 7 include, but are not limited to, are Internet Explorer 8, WordPad, Paint, Calculator, Windows Media Player 12, Windows Media Center, and several games.

2   In lieu of the traditional drop-down menus and toolbars, some programs offer the Ribbon, which displays groups of related buttons and options in clickable tabs. Pressing a button or option in the tab activates its associated command or feature.

3   Dialog boxes gather input from users by way of option buttons, checkboxes, text fields, drop-down menus, spin boxes, and command buttons. Some dialog boxes also contain tabs. Clicking a tab reveals an additional set of input controls.

4   You use the System menu to create new files, save files, open existing files, print files. To view this menu, press the System Menu button in the program window's upper left corner.

5   Buttons for minimizing, maximizing, restoring, and closing are found in the window's upper right corner. In addition, you can access a menu with equivalent commands in the Window menu, which you access by pressing the Window Menu button in the upper left corner of the program window.

What you'll learn in this lesson:

- Viewing files and folders
- Creating new files and folders
- Managing files and folders
- Searching for files
- Opening files

Working with Files and Folders

As you work in Windows 7, you will create many files and folders. Keeping them organized is critical to your productivity. In this lesson, you'll learn how to view, create, manage, organize, and find your files and folders using Windows 7.

Starting up

Before you start, be sure to download all the files for this lesson from the accompanying DVD to your hard drive.

See Lesson 3 in action!

Use the accompanying video to gain a better understanding of how to use some of the features shown in this lesson. The video tutorial for this lesson can be found on the included DVD.

Viewing files and folders

Like previous versions of Windows, Windows 7 includes a program called Windows Explorer. Windows Explorer acts like a sort of digital filing cabinet, with folders, or libraries, to store and organize your files, for example, your documents, digital pictures, music, etc., and programs. Each folder contains tools for searching, navigating, and organizing the files and subfolders within it.

Windows Explorer contains three main folders for storing files:

• **Documents**. This is where word-processing files, spreadsheets, and web pages are stored by default.

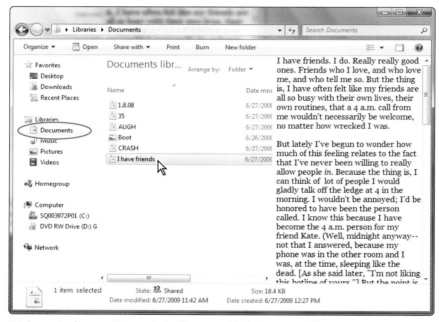

Word-processing files, spreadsheets, and other files are stored in the Documents folder

- **Pictures**. This folder acts as a central repository for digital image files that are imported from a digital camera or scanned using a scanner. It contains special toolbar buttons for viewing your pictures in a slide show, printing your pictures, sharing them with others, and burning them to a CD or DVD.

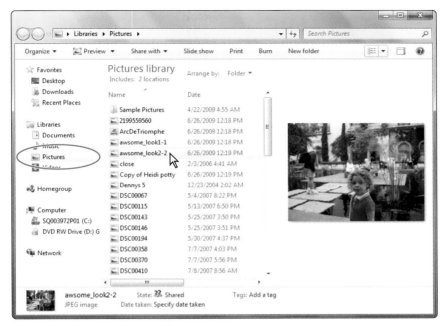

Digital images are stored in the Pictures folder.

- **Music.** This is where audio files, MP3 files, WMA files, WAV files, etc., that you've downloaded or ripped are saved.

Windows 7 places music files that you've downloaded or ripped in the Music folder.

1   Press the Start button (⬤). The Start menu appears.

2   Select either Documents, Pictures, or Music. The folder you've chosen opens. To open a subfolder within any of these folders, double-click it.

Another way to access these three main folders, and several others, is to launch your User folder.

3   Press the Start button again. Click your username, located in the top-right of the Start menu.

4   The User folder opens. From here, you can access several folders by double-clicking them. Note that the Download folder is where items you've download from the Internet are stored by default, and the My Videos folder is where videos are stored by default.

Use the User folder to access downloaded content.

Yet another way to view files in Windows Explorer is to launch it from the Taskbar.

5   Close any open windows, then press the Windows Explorer button ( ) on the Taskbar.

6   The Libraries folder opens, providing quick access to the Documents, Music, Pictures, and Video folders. Again, you open these folders by double-clicking them.

The Libraries folder offers quick access to the Documents, Music, Pictures, and Videos folders.

Viewing files on external media

If the file you need to view is not on your computer's hard drive, but is instead on a CD, DVD, memory card, or an external hard drive, you can access it from Windows Explorer's Computer option:

1   Insert the media into the appropriate drive.

2   The AutoPlay dialog box opens. Select Open folder to view files. A window containing the files on the removable media appears.

Select Open folder to view files in the AutoPlay dialog box.

If the auto play dialog box doesn't appear, or if you need to access the disk at a later time use the Computer option:

3   Press the Start button (⬤). The Start menu appears.

4   Select Computer. The Computer folder opens, listing all the drives on your computer— your internal hard drive and any external media such as DVDs, and memory cards. Double-click a drive to view its contents.

The Computer folder displays an icon for your computer's hard drive and for any external media. Double-clicking a drive displays its contents.

Navigating folder windows

Windows Explorer contain four panes to make it easier to find the files you need:

A. Toolbar. B. Navigation pane. C. Details pane. D. Preview pane. E. Library pane. F. File list.

- **Navigation pane.** This pane contains clickable links to other folders on your computer.
- **File list.** This is where the files in the selected folder are listed.
- **Library pane.** Here you can specify how files in the file list should be arranged—by folder, date, rating, or tag.
- **Preview pane.** When you select a file in the file list, a preview of that file appears in the Preview pane.
- **Details pane.** This pane includes details about the selected file in the file list. These details vary by the type of file selected.

If any of the panes listed are not visible in your folder window, you can display them by clicking the Organize button in the upper left corner of the window, choosing Layout, and selecting the missing pane from the list that appears.

Each folder also window contains a toolbar with various buttons for organizing, sharing, burning discs, creating new folders, changing how files in the folder window are displayed, and getting help. You'll also find a search text field. Type a keyword or phrase in this text field to locate a file in the selected folder.

Changing file views

Windows 7 offers several options for displaying files in the Windows Explorer file list. These include Extra Large Icons, Large Icons, Medium Icons, and Small Icons.

Extra Large Icons view (top left), Large Icons view (top right),
Medium Icons view (bottom left), and Small Icons view (bottom right).

The Extra Large option, in which the icons that represent files in the file list are quite large, is handy if you are viewing pictures, as the icons are identical to the pictures they represent.

Other options include:

- **List.** This view displays more files at one time in the file list.
- **Details.** This view is similar to List, but includes additional information about each file (such as the date last modified, size, type, etc.) and clickable columns for sorting.

- **Tiles**. This view is similar to Medium Icons but, like the Details view, shows information about each file displayed.

- **Content**. Places greater emphasis on the name of each file.

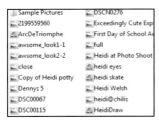
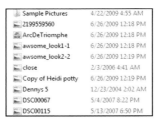

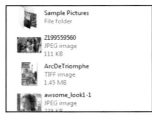

List view (top left), Details view (top right), Tiles view (bottom left), and Content view (bottom right).

1   Click the down arrow to the right of the Change your view button (■). The appearance of this button differs, depending on whether you are in the Documents library, the Pictures library, or the Music library. A list of the available views appears, with a slider pointing to the current view.

2   Click the desired view; in this example, Details. Alternatively, click and drag the slider to select a view. Note that using the slider enables you to fine-tune the available views to make the icons smaller or larger than the default.

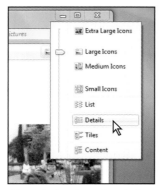

Choose the desired view from the list.

Another way to quickly change views is to press the Change your view button (⊟). Pressing this button cycles through the available views.

Creating new files and folders

As you learned in Lesson 2, "Working with Windows 7 Programs," you can create new files from within various Windows programs. You can also create new files from within Explorer windows. This method may be more convenient if the program associated with the file you want to create is not currently running.

Creating a new file

1 Open the folder in which you want to create the new file. The Documents folder is used in this example.

2 Right-click a blank area of the File list.

3 From the menu that appears, choose New.

4 From the types of documents listed, choose Rich Text Document.

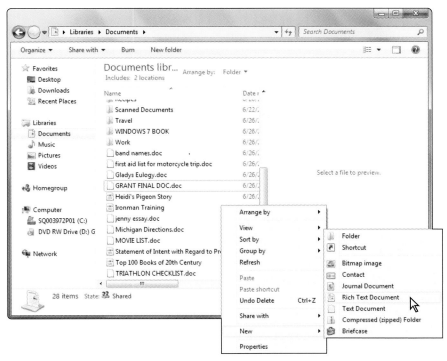

Create a new file from inside Windows Explorer.

5 A new file is created, with the default name, New Rich Text Document, selected. Type a descriptive name for the file and press Enter.

Type a descriptive name for the file.

Creating a new folder

In addition to creating new files, you can also create new folders. This is handy as you start to collect many documents and need folders to keep them organized. You can create subfolders within folders as well. For example, in your Documents folder, you might create a subfolder to contain any correspondence or other files that pertain to a particular client. Alternatively, you might create folders for each project you're working on, for storing all the files associated with them. You can move and copy files into folders you create.

1 Open the folder in which you want to create the new folder.

2 Press the New Folder button.

3 A new folder is created, with the default name, New Folder, selected. Type a name for the folder, for example, the name of your client or the title of your project, so that later, you'll be able to quickly identify what it contains, and press Enter.

Type a descriptive name for the folder.

Two subfolders within the same folder cannot have the same name. If you try to use the same name for a second folder, Windows 7 asks whether you want to merge the contents of the two folders into a single folder.

Managing files and folders

Windows Explorer enables you to manage your files and folders or allows you to copy and move files and folders, rename them as needed, and delete them when you're finished using them. Additionally, Windows Explorer also enables you to assign certain properties to your files, such as ratings and tags to make it easier to sort and locate them.

Selecting files and folders

Before you can copy, move, rename, delete, rate, or tag a file, you must first select it. That way, Windows 7 knows exactly the file with which you want work. You can select files one at a time or select multiple files at once if you want to move several files into a new folder. Note that although the following exercises cover selecting files, the technique for selecting folders is exactly the same.

Selecting a single file

1 Open the folder that contains the file with which you want to work. For this example, the Pictures library is used.

2 Click a file. Notice that a preview of the selected file appears in the Preview pane, and the name of the file is highlighted in the File list.

Click to select a single file.

Selecting multiple files

1   Open the folder that contains the files with which you want to work.

2   Click the first file you want to select.

3   While pressing the Ctrl key, click each additional file you want to select. This action is known as *Ctrl-clicking*. Each of the files you Ctrl-clicked is now selected allowing you to perform actions on multiple files at the same time.

Ctrl-click to select multiple files.

Selecting consecutive files

1   Open the folder that contains the files you want to work with.

2   Select a file, then while pressing the Shift key, click the last file you want to select in the list. This action is known as *Shift-clicking*. The first file, the last file, and all the files in between are selected.

Shift-click to select consecutive files.

Selecting by dragging

Alternatively, you can drag a selection rectangle around the files you want to select:

1   Open the folder that contains the files you want to work with.

2   Click a blank area in the file list above and to the left of the first file you want to select.

3   Holding your mouse button down, drag down and to the right until your mouse pointer is below and to the right of the last file you want to select.

Drag a selection rectangle around the files you want to select.

Selecting all the files in a folder

1   Open the folder that contains the files you want to work with.

2   Press the Organize button.

3   Press Select All. Windows 7 selects all the files in the folder.

Choose Select All from the Organize menu.

An even easier way to select all the files in a folder is to open the folder, then press the keyboard shortcut, Ctrl+A.

Deselecting files

Deselecting files is as easy as selecting them:

- If you've selected multiple files but need to deselect one, hold down the Ctrl key and click the file you want to deselect.

- To deselect all files, click an empty area in the file list.

Moving files and folders

After you create files, you'll often need to move them to the correct folder. Note that although the steps here cover moving files, the technique for moving folders is exactly the same.

1 Open the folder that contains the file or files you want to move.

2 Select the file or files you want to move.

3 Right-click the selected file or files. If multiple files are selected, right-click any of the selected files.

4 Select Cut in the menu that appears.

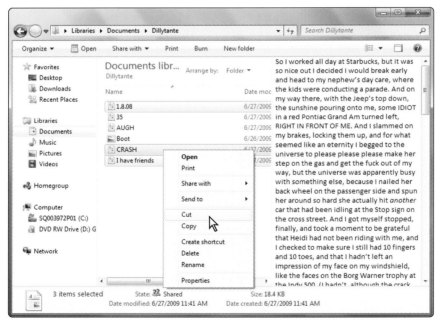

Right-click the selected files and choose Cut from the menu that appears.

5   Open the folder into which you want to move the selected file or files. Right-click a blank area of the File list.

6   Select Paste in the menu that appears. Each selected file is moved from the old location to the new one.

Copying files and folders

In addition to moving files and folders, you can also copy them. When you move a file or folder, you remove it from the original location and place it in a new location. When you copy a file or a folder, you make a duplicate of it, so that there are two versions of it—one in the original location and one in the new location. You might copy a file if, for example, you send the same document to multiple clients, and you want a copy of that document to appear in each client's folder. Note that although the steps here cover copying files, the technique for copying folders is exactly the same.

1   Open the folder that contains the file or files you want to copy.

2   Select the file or files you want to copy.

3   Right-click the selected file or files. If multiple files are selected, right-click any of the selected files. Select Copy in the menu that appears.

5   Open the folder into which you want to copy the selected file or files. Right-click a blank area of the file list.

6   Select Paste in the menu that appears. A copy of each selected file is placed in the new location.

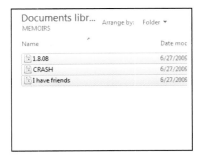

The files are copied to the new location.

You can also copy files to an external storage device such as a memory stick or external hard drive. This is handy if you need to transport your data or you want to create a backup copy for safekeeping. To do so, repeat the preceding steps, but in step 5, open your Computer folder, by pressing the Start button and choosing Computer, then double-click the icon for the external drive to open its folder window.

Copying files and folders to CD or DVD

If your computer has a recordable CD or DVD drive, you can copy files and folders to a recordable disc. Here's how:

1   Insert a recordable CD or DVD into your drive.

2   Press the Close button (⬛) in the upper-right corner of the AutoPlay dialog box that appears.

3   Open the folder containing the files you want to copy to the disc.

4   Select the files you want to copy.

5   Press the Burn button in the folder window.

6   If this is the first time you are burning files to this disc, Windows 7 displays the Burn a Disc dialog box. Type a title for your disc.

7   Choose Like a USB Flash Drive. Choosing With a CD/DVD player results in a disc that you can play using a CD or DVD player rather than a disc containing data files. You'll learn about creating these types of discs later in the book.

8   Press Next. Windows 7 formats the disc, and then copies the files.

9   When the copying is complete, a folder window for the disc appears, containing the files you burned to the disc.

Renaming files and folders

Giving your files and folders descriptive names makes it much easier to keep things organized. If the current name of a file or folder is not as descriptive as you'd like, you can rename it. File and folder names can be as long as 255 characters, although the following characters cannot be used: < > , ? : \ *

Note that you should only rename files and folders that you have created yourself or that have been given to you by others. Never rename Windows 7 system files or folders, or files or folders associated with programs you have installed on your computer. Otherwise, your computer could behave erratically or even crash. Note that although the following exercise cover renaming files, the technique for renaming folders is exactly the same:

1   Open the folder that contains the file you want to rename.

2   Click the file you want to rename to select it.

3   Right-click the selected file.

4 Choose Rename from the menu that appears.

Right-click the selected file and choose Rename from the menu that appears.

5 Windows 7 selects the current filename. Type the new name you want to use for the file and press Enter. Windows 7 renames the file.

Type the new filename and press Enter.

Deleting files and folders

If you no longer need a file or folder, you can delete it to avoid cluttering up your Windows 7 system. As with renaming files and folders, you should only delete files and folders that you create yourself or that have been given to you by others. Note that although the following exercise cover deleting files, the technique for deleting folders is exactly the same.

Warning! Deleting a folder also deletes any files stored in that folder:

1 Open the folder that contains the file or files you want to delete.

2 Select the file or files you want to delete.

3 Right-click the selected file or files. If multiple files are selected, right-click any of the selected files.

4   Select Delete in the menu that appears.

5   Windows 7 prompts you to confirm the deletion. Press Yes, and the file or files are deleted.

Confirm the deletion; the file or files no longer appear in the folder window.

Restoring a deleted file or folder

When you delete a file or folder, it is moved to the Recycle Bin, where it remains until the Recycle Bin is emptied. As long as the Recycle Bin has not been emptied, you can restore deleted files to their original folder location. Although the following exercise covers restoring deleted files, the technique for restoring deleted folders is exactly the same:

1   Right-click the Recycle Bin shortcut icon on the Desktop. If you can't see the Desktop because you have program or folder windows open, press the Show Desktop button (▮) on the right edge of the Taskbar.

2   Choose Open from the menu that appears.

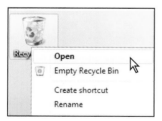

Choose Open from the menu that appears.

3   The Recycle Bin window appears. Click the file you want to restore to select it.

4   Press the Restore this item button in the window's toolbar. Windows 7 removes the file from the Recycle Bin, placing it back in its original folder.

Emptying the Recycle Bin

To permanently remove files you have deleted from your system, you must empty the Recycle Bin. This frees-up space on your hard drive, allowing you to store new items.

1   Right-click the Recycle Bin icon on your Desktop. If you can't see the Desktop because you have program or folder windows open, press the Show Desktop button on the right edge of the Taskbar.

2   Choose Empty Recycle Bin from the menu that appears.

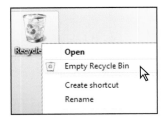

Right-click the Recycle Bin shortcut icon
and choose Empty Recycle Bin.

3   Windows 7 prompts you to confirm that you want to permanently delete the files in the Recycle Bin. Press Yes, and Windows 7 empties the Recycle Bin.

Confirm that you want to permanently delete the files, and Windows 7 empties the Recycle Bin. Notice that
the Recycle Bin shortcut icon now depicts an empty, rather than full, recycling bin.

Tagging files

Windows 7 applies certain properties to files, such as Name, Date Modified, Author, File Type, etc. You can use these properties as criteria when searching for files. In addition, Windows 7 enables you to apply tags, or brief descriptions that are embedded in the files' metadata, to certain types of files, which you can also use as sort, filter, and search criteria. You'll learn more about searching for files later in this lesson. These tags can be anything you choose, such as, the name of the person featured in a digital photo, or the project with which a document is associated.

1   Open the folder that contains the file you want to tag.

2   Select the file you want to tag.

3   In the Details pane, select Add a tag.

Click Add a tag in the Details pane.

4   A blinking cursor appears. Type a tag name. You can apply multiple tags to a file. To add multiple tags, separate each one by a semicolon.

Type a tag.

5   If the tag you type has already been applied to other files, a menu appears with the tag listed alongside a checkbox. Click the checkbox to select it.

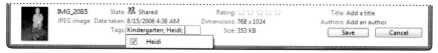

If the tag you type has been applied to other files, a check box for that tag appears.

6. Press the Save button in the Details pane. Windows 7 saves your tag or tags.

 You can also tag a file from the file's Properties dialog box. You'll learn how to open this dialog box later in this lesson.

Rating files

In addition to tagging certain types of files, you can also rate them. Windows 7's rating feature uses a star system, with five stars as the highest rating. After you rate a file, you can locate it by sorting, filtering, or searching by file rating.

1   Open the folder that contains the file you want to rate.

2   Select the file you want to rate.

3   In the Details pane, next to the Rating entry, click the star that represents the rating you want to apply. For example, to apply a five-star rating, click the fifth star.

Click a star in the Details pane.

4   Press the Save button in the Details pane. Windows 7 saves your rating.

You can also rate a file from the file's Properties dialog box. You'll learn how to open this dialog box in the next section.

Viewing file and folder properties

As mentioned, each file and folder in Windows 7 contains various properties. These include the file or folder's name, size, date modified, permissions, such as, whether it is read-only, meaning it can be read but not modified, and any tags or ratings. Sometimes it's necessary to view or modify these properties—for example, to turn off a file's read-only permission if you need to modify the file. You can view and change a file or folder's properties in its Properties dialog box.

1   Right-click the file or folder whose properties you want to view or change.

2   Choose Properties from the menu that appears. The file or folder's Properties dialog box opens.

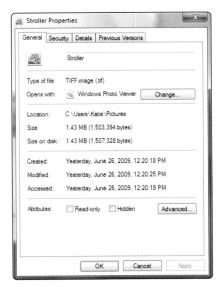
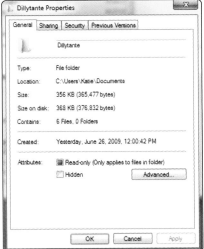

The file or folder's Properties dialog box appears.

3   Click the Details tab in the file or folder's Properties dialog box to see and set additional properties, such as tags, ratings, and more.

Click the Details tab to see and set tags, ratings, and other properties.

4   Once you are finished making any necessary changes to the file or folder's properties, press OK to close the dialog box.

Before sharing a file with others, it's wise to remove its tags, especially if they contain personal information.

1   To remove a file's tag (or any other property you've applied), open the file's Properties dialog box.

2   Click the Details tab, and click the Remove Properties and Personal Information link. The Remove Properties dialog box appears.

3   Click the Create a Copy with All Possible Properties Removed option button and press OK.

4   In Windows Explorer, alongside the original file, you see a copy of the file. The copy is stripped of any properties you set, which you can now share with others.

Sorting files

If you have many files in a folder, you can sort them in the folder window based on their properties. This can make it easier to find the file you need. By default, files are sorted by name, but you can sort by any other property, such as, Date Modified, Author, Type, Rating, and Tags.

The easiest way to sort your files is to click the column header that contains the property you want to sort by. Note that these column headers are visible only in Details view. For example, to sort the files in a folder window by file type, click the Type column header.

To switch the sort order from ascending to descending or vice versa, click the column header.

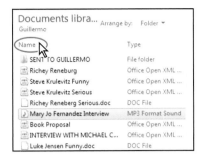

Click a column header to sort files in a folder.

If there is no column header for the property you want to use to sort your files, you can add one.

1 Open the folder that contains the files you want to sort. Make sure the folder window is in Details view by pressing the Change your view button (⊟) in the upper right corner of the window and selecting Details from the menu that appears.

2 Right-click one of the existing column headings.

3 Choose the property you want to sort by from the list that appears. Alternatively, click More.

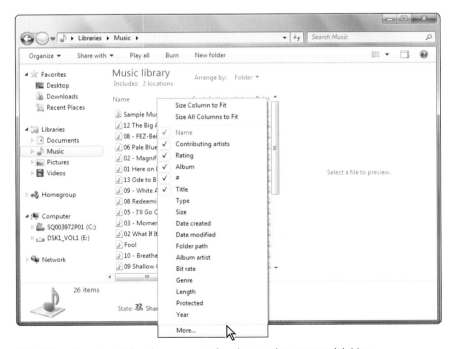

Right-click a column header. Then choose a property from the menu that appears or click More.

4　Clicking More opens the Choose Details dialog box. Click the checkbox next to a property to select it.

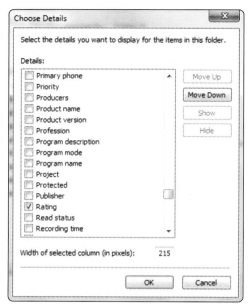

Select the check box next to the property you want to sort by.

5　Press OK.

6　Windows 7 adds a column for the property you chose. Click the column header to sort by that property.

To change the order of the columns in the folder window, click the header for a column you want to move, drag the column to the desired position, then release the mouse button.

Filtering files

You can also filter the files in a folder window so that only the files with a particular property attribute are shown. For example, you can filter all the files in the folder with a five-star rating, all the files in the folder that are of the TIFF file type, all the files in the folder created on a certain date.

1   Open the folder that contains the files you want to filter, such as, the sample images folder. Make sure the folder window is in Details view.

2   Place your mouse pointer over the Rating column header. A down arrow appears on the right side of the column header.

3   Click the down arrow to see a list of values associated with the column's property. In this example, 1 Star, 2 Stars, 3 Stars, etc.

4   To display only files with a particular property value, for example, a Rating property value of five stars, click the appropriate checkbox. Only the files with the property value you chose are displayed.

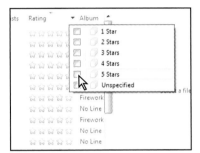
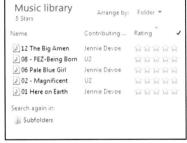

Choose the desired property value and Windows 7 displays only the files with that value.

Compressing files and folders

Windows 7 can reduce the number of bytes in a file or folder on your hard drive in order to save space. This is especially useful if, for example, you need to send a large file or folder via e-mail. Uploading and downloading very large files is time-consuming. So reducing the size of a file lets you send it more quickly. A compressed file or folder needs to be uncompressed by the recipient. When a compressed file or folder is uncompressed, it is identical to the original, uncompressed file or folder.

1   Open the folder that contains the files and folders you want to compress, such as the sampled images folder.

2   Select the files and folders you want to compress.

3 Right-click a selected file or folder.

4 In the menu that appears, select the Send to command.

5. Select Compress (zipped) folder.

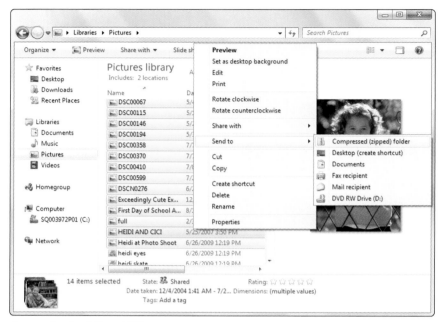

Compress the selected files and folders.

6 Windows 7 copies the selected files and folders, compresses the copies, and places them in a special compression folder, also called a ZIP folder—hence the *zipper* icon (🗜). Type a descriptive name for the compression folder and press Enter.

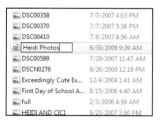

Type a descriptive name for the compression folder.

Uncompressing files and folders

To uncompress a file or folder, you must *extract* it from the compression folder. The uncompressed file or folder is identical to the original version, before it was compressed.

1   Open the folder that contains the compressed folder you want to decompress.

2   Right-click the compressed folder. Choose Extract All from the menu that appears.

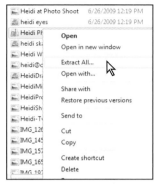

Right-click the compression folder and choose Extract All.

3   The Extract Compressed (Zipped) Folders window appears. To extract the files to a location other than the default, press the Browse button.

4   The Select a destination dialog box opens. Locate and select the folder to which you want to extract the compressed files.

Specify where you want the extracted files and folders to be saved.

5   Press OK to close the Select a Destination dialog box.

6   Press Extract. Windows 7 extracts the files and folders into the folder you specified.

Searching for files

As you work with more files and folders on your computer, finding the ones you need can become difficult. Fortunately, Windows 7 offers a robust search function which you can use in a number of different ways. For example, if you have a general idea where the file you're looking for is located, for example, somewhere in your Documents folder, you can search from within that folder's window in Windows Explorer. Alternatively, if you're not sure where the file you need is located, you can search for files located anywhere on your hard drive or attached computers by searching from the Start menu.

Searching in a folder window

Use the Search text field found in the upper right corner of each Explorer window to locate files or folders within a folder. Type the name of the file or folder, a broad description of what the file contains (such as *music*), the file type (DOC, JPG, MP3, etc.), tags you've added to your file, the author, the date the file was last modified, even words or phrases that appear within the file in the Search text field. As you type, Windows 7 sifts through the files and folders in the folder window, displaying only those that match your criteria.

1   Open the folder that contains the file or folder you need to find.

2   Type part or all of the file's name, type, author, or other criteria in the Search text field. As you type, Windows 7 displays the files and folders within the folder that match your criteria.

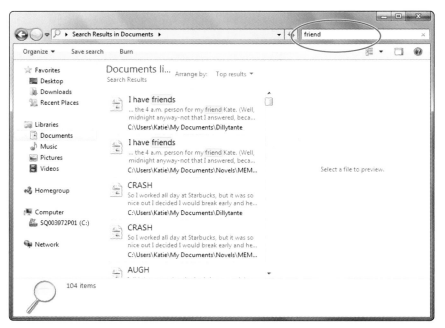

As you type, Windows 7 displays the files and folders that match your criteria.

Searching from the Start menu

You can also run searches from the Windows 7 Start menu. When you do, Windows 7 scours your entire system for files, folders, and programs that match your search criteria.

1 Press the Start button (). The Start menu appears.

2 In the Search text field at the bottom of the Start menu, type part or all of the file's name, type, author, or other criteria. As you type, Windows 7 displays the files, folders, and programs that match your criteria.

The Start menu displays the files, folders, and programs that match your criteria.

Opening files

Once you've located the file you want to work with, you can open it. When you open a file, Windows 7 automatically launches the application associated with that file, then opens the file in that application's window. For example, if the file you want to open is a Rich Text file, Windows 7 launches the WordPad application and then displays the contents of the file in the WordPad window.

1 Open the folder that contains the file you want to open.

2 Right-click the file you want to open.

3. Choose Open in the menu that appears. Windows 7 opens the file in the program associated with it.

Choose Open if the file you are opening is a text, spreadsheet, or image file. Other types of files may display different options. For example, music files display a Play option rather than an Open option.

An even faster way to open a file is to double-click it in the folder window.

Opening a file with a different program

When you open a file, Windows 7 launches the application associated with that file. You can also open a document or file in a program other than the default choice. You might do this if because a different program enables you to edit or view the file in a way that the default program does not.

1 Open the folder that contains the file you want to open.

2 Right-click the file you want to open.

3 Choose Open With from the menu that appears.

4 Choose the program you want to use to view or edit the file. Windows 7 opens the file in the program you chose.

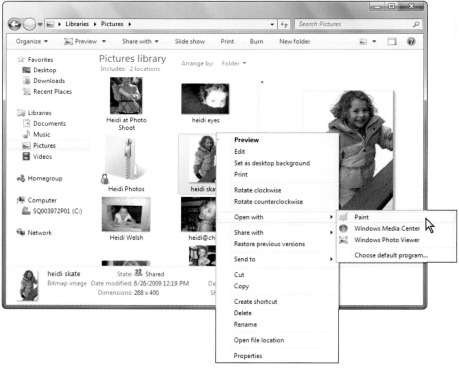

Right-click the file, choose Open With, and choose the program you want to use to view or edit the file. Windows 7 opens the file in the selected program.

Setting a new default program

If the program that Windows 7 uses to open a certain type of file by default doesn't suit your purposes, you can set a new default program that windows will use to open all the files of this type. For example, if you always want image files to open using a certain photo editor, or music files to always open with a certain music player.

1   Open the folder that contains a file whose default program you want to change, such as, the sample images folder.

2   Right-click the file.

3   Choose Open With from the menu that appears.

4   Select Choose default program from the submenu that appears.

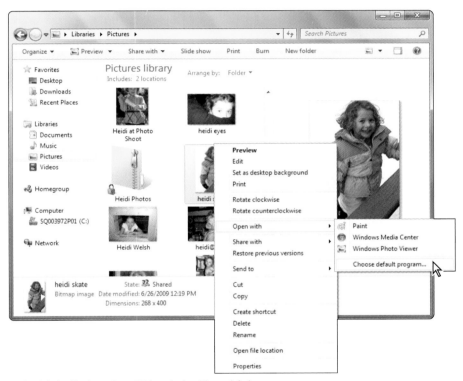

Right-click the file, choose Open With, and select Choose default program.

5   The Open With dialog box appears. Select the program you want to use as the default program.

6   Make sure the *Always use the selected program to open this kind of file* checkbox is checked.

7 Press OK. Windows 7 opens the file in the new default program.

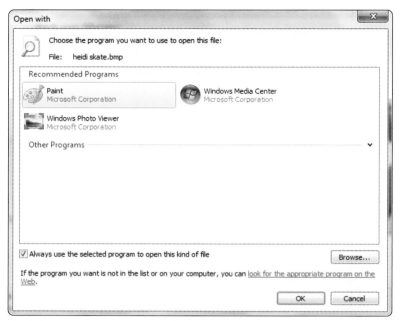

Specify the program you want to set as the default.

Self study

1 Experiment with the various ways of opening folder windows, by clicking the Windows Explorer button in the Taskbar, launching them from the Start menu, opening the user folder, and determine which way works best for you.

2 Determine which program you want to use as the default program for various file types. If the program you want to use does not appear in the Recommended Programs list in the Open With dialog box, click the Look for the Appropriate Program on the Web link to find other options.

Review

Questions

1. Where is the default location where Windows 7 stores documents? What about music files? Digital images?

2 What is the difference between moving files and folders and copying them?

3 What is a tag?

4 Name three types of criteria you can use when searching.

5 What are two ways to search for files?

Answers

1 Windows 7 stores documents in the Documents folder. Music files are stored in the Music folder, and digital images are stored in the Pictures folder.

2 When you move a file or folder, you remove it from the original location and place it in a new location. When you copy a file or folder, you make a duplicate of it, so that there are two versions of it—one in the original location and one in the new location.

3 A tag is a brief description of a file that is embedded in the file's metadata. You can use tags to sort, filter, and search.

4 Types of search criteria include the name of the file or folder, a broad description of what the file contains (such as *music*), the file type (DOC, JPG, MP3, etc.), tags you've added to the file, the author, the date the file was last modified, and even words or phrases that appear within the file, assuming you're looking for a text document as opposed to a digital image or music file.

5 You can find Search text boxes in the Windows 7 Start menu and in folder windows in Windows Explorer.

What you'll learn in this lesson:

- Changing the display and sound settings

- Setting language options

- Customizing the Start menu and Taskbar

- Creating and managing shortcuts

Customizing Windows 7

Even an operating system as sophisticated as Windows 7 is not one-size-fits-all—which is why Windows 7 offers so many customization options.

Starting up

Before you start, be sure to download all the files for this lesson from the accompanying DVD to your hard drive.

See Lesson 4 in action!

Use the accompanying video to gain a better understanding of how to use some of the features shown in this lesson. The video tutorial for this lesson can be found on the included DVD.

Changing Windows 7 display and sound settings

One of the most popular way to personalize Windows is to change its display and sound settings, which you access right from the Windows 7 work area on the Desktop.

Changing the screen resolution

You can change your computer's screen resolution. A lighter screen resolution lets more information fit in the same area on your computer monitor while this can be good for editing images, it may be bothersome if you prefer to see larger size text and windows on your Desktop. This is because the higher the screen resolution, the smaller windows appear when they are open on the Desktop. For example, the windows in a screen with a resolution of 800x600 appear much larger than in a screen with a resolution of 1280x800 or higher. How you set your screen resolution is largely a matter of personal taste, but larger monitors often require a higher screen resolution. At a higher resolution, most items appear to be more clear.

1   Right-click a blank area of the Desktop.

2   Click Screen Resolution in the shortcut menu that appears.

Right-click an empty area of the Desktop and choose Screen Resolution.

3   The Screen Resolution window appears. Click the Resolution drop-down menu to display its options.

4   Drag the Resolution slider to the desired resolution. Press OK. Each monitor has unique display capabilities and recommended resolutions. If you have the documentation that came with your monitor, you can check this to determine the best setting. Windows 7 will also list a recommended setting.

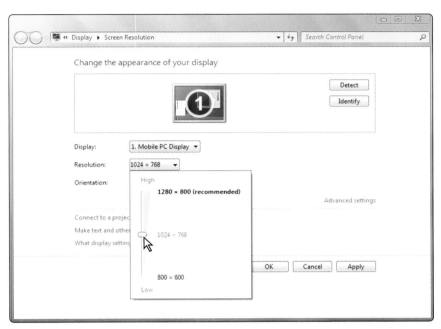

Set the screen resolution.

5   Windows 7 prompts you to confirm the change. Press Keep changes or to revert to the original settings, press Revert. Windows 7 changes the screen resolution.

Press Keep changes when prompted.

Adding gadgets to the Desktop

Windows 7 lets you access mini-programs called gadgets. Some of these gadgets display news headlines, weather conditions, exchange rates, and stock quotes, others offer quick access to frequently used tools such as a clock, a Slide Show gadget which cycles through the images in your Pictures folder.

Some gadgets, such as those that display weather or stock information, require that your computer be connected to the Internet to work.

1 Right-click a blank area of the Desktop.

2 Click Gadgets in the shortcut menu that appears.

Right-click an empty area of the Desktop and choose Gadgets.

3   The Desktop Gadgets window appears. To add a gadget to the Windows 7 Desktop, click the gadget you want in the Desktop Gadgets window and drag it to the spot on the Desktop where you want the gadget to appear.

Add a gadget to your Windows 7 Desktop by dragging it to you Desktop.

In addition to adding the gadgets that come bundled with Windows 7, you can access additional gadgets online. To do so, click the Get More Gadgets Online link in the bottom-right corner of the Desktop Gadgets window.

4   Some gadgets might require a bit of customization. For example, by default, the Weather gadget needs you to input the city for which you want weather information. To configure a gadget, hover your mouse pointer over the gadget until a toolbar appears.

Hover your mouse pointer over the gadget to display a toolbar.

5   Press the Options button (⚲) in the toolbar.

Some gadgets can be enlarged to display even more information. To enlarge your gadget, press the Larger Size button (◪) in the toolbar.

6 In the dialog box that appears, indicate your preferences for the gadget. For example, in the dialog box displayed for the Weather gadget, indicate your current location and if the temperature should be shown in Fahrenheit or Celsius.

7 Press OK. Windows 7 updates the gadget per your specifications.

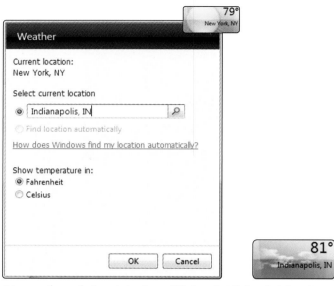

Set your preferences for the gadget and press OK; the gadget displays the information you specified.

 In some cases, you can click a gadget to see more information. For example, clicking the city name in the Weather gadget launches an MSN Weather page that contains an extended forecast, a radar map, and more for that area.

8 Press the Close button (▭) of the Desktop Gadgets window to close it.

If, after you add a gadget, you decide you'd like to place it somewhere else on your Desktop, you can easily move it. To do so, hover your mouse pointer over the gadget to reveal the gadget's toolbar; then press the Drag Gadget button (⠿) and drag the gadget to the desired location on the Desktop. To remove a gadget from the Desktop altogether, hover your mouse pointer over the gadget to reveal the toolbar, and press the Close button (✕). Windows 7 removes the gadget from the Desktop.

Changing the Desktop background

You can change the Desktop background that Windows 7 displays by default. You can choose a single or set of images that rotate their display, like a slide show. You can select from Windows 7's pre-designed backgrounds or choose from your own photos.

1   Right-click a blank area of the Desktop.

2   Click Personalize in the shortcut menu that appears.

3   The Personalization window appears. Click the Desktop Background link along the bottom of the window.

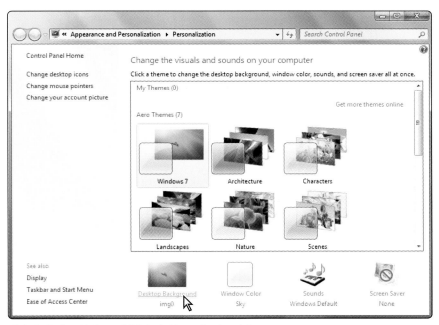

Click the Desktop Background link in the Personalization window.

4 The Desktop Background window opens. Place your mouse pointer over the image you want to use as the Desktop background. A checkbox appears; click it to select it. If you want to select all the images in a category, for example, in the Landscapes category, click the category name.

5 By default, the entire screen is covered by the Desktop background image. To fit the image to the screen, stretch it, tile it, or center it, choose the desired option from the Picture position drop-down menu in the lower left portion of the screen.

6 If you've selected multiple images, Windows 7 changes the picture every 30 minutes by default. To change this setting, choose the desired setting from the Change picture every drop-down menu.

7 If you'd like Windows 7 to shuffle the images, that is, display them in a random order, click the *Shuffle* checkbox to select it.

Save your changes.

8 Press the Save changes button. Windows 7 changes the Desktop background.

The new Desktop background.

9 To use your own image as a background image, click the Desktop Background link in the Personalization window.

10 Press the Browse button next to the Windows Desktop Backgrounds drop-down menu. The Browse for Folder dialog box appears.

11 Locate and click the folder that contains the image or images you want to use as the Desktop background, then press OK.

Browse to your own images folder in the Browse for Folder dialog box to specify your own Desktop picture.

12 Windows 7 creates a new category in the Desktop Background window for the folder you chose, with all images in that folder selected by default.

The images in the folder you chose appear in the Desktop Background window.

13 To fit the image to the screen, stretch it, tile it, or center it, choose the desired option from the Picture position drop-down menu.

14 If you've selected multiple images, specify how often Windows 7 changes the picture by choosing the desired setting from the Change picture every { } drop-down menu.

16 If you'd like Windows 7 to shuffle the images—that is, display them in a random order— click the *Shuffle* checkbox to select it.

17 Press the Save changes button. Windows 7 changes the Desktop background. The background is updated with your image.

Changing the window color

In addition to changing your Desktop background, you can change the color of the Taskbar and of windows displayed on your screen.

1   If necessary, right–click the Desktop and select Personalize from the menu that appears.

2   Click the Window Color link in the Personalization window.

3   The Window Color and Appearance window opens. Click a color to select it.

4   To heighten or diminish the selected color's intensity, drag the Color intensity slider to the right or left, respectively.

5   To ensure that what's underneath a window's title bar remains visible, click the *Enable transparency* checkbox to select it.

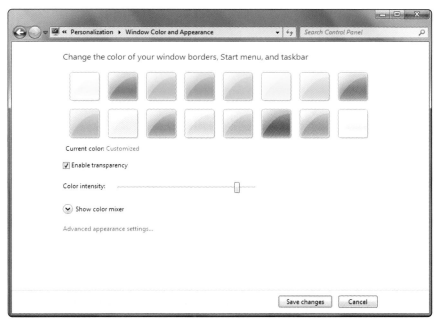

Change the window color.

6   Press the Save changes button.

Changing the sound scheme

By default, Windows 7 plays certain sounds when events occur. For example, when you log on to Windows 7, it plays the Windows Logon sound; when you log off, it plays the Windows Logoff sound; when you connect a device to your Windows computer, it plays a sound called Device Connect. You can change individual sounds or all sounds. You can even use sounds you've recorded or downloaded from the Internet for playback when certain events occur. You can also configure Windows 7 to play no sounds for system events.

1   If necessary, right-click the Desktop and select Personalize from the menu that appears.

2   Click the Sounds link in the Personalization window.

3   The Sound dialog box opens with the Sounds tab displayed. From the Sound Scheme drop-down menu, choose a different scheme. To disable the playback of sounds when system events occur, for example, the Windows Logon, choose No Sounds.

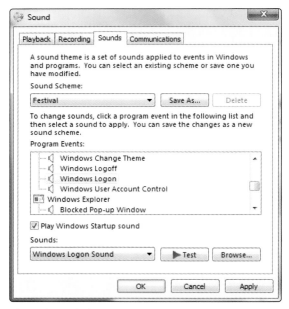

Change the sound scheme.

4   Press OK. Windows 7 applies the scheme you chose.

Changing an individual system sound

You can also change an individual system sound using the sound dialog box. To do so, click the Sounds link in the Personalization window.

1   Click the Sounds link in the Personalization window.

2   In the Program Events window, select the sound you want to change.

3   Choose the sound you want to associate with the selected program event from the Sounds drop-down menu.

4   To test the selected sound, press the Test button.

To use a sound of your own—one you've recorded or downloaded from the Internet—press the Browse button. Windows 7 displays a Browse dialog box; locate and select the sound you want to use, then press the Open button.

5   If you like the sound you've chosen, press the Save As button. This enables you to save this modified version of the selected sound scheme as a separate scheme.

6   The Save Scheme As dialog box opens. Type a name for this new, modified scheme and press OK.

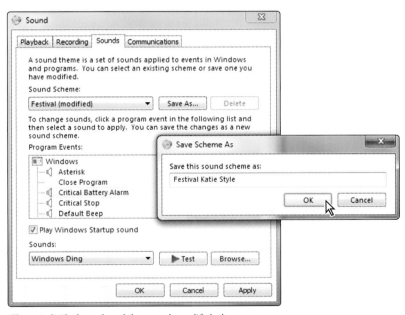

Change individual sounds, and then save the modified scheme.

7   Press OK to close the Sound dialog box.

Setting the screen saver

Setting a screen saver, still or animated pictures that appear on your screen when the mouse and keyboard have been inactive for a period of time, prevents others from seeing the contents of your Desktop when you are away from your computer. When you return to your computer, move your mouse or press a key on your keyboard to turn off the screen saver and display your Windows 7 Desktop.

Windows 7 comes with several screen savers pre-installed. You can also create your own personalized slide show screen saver featuring images in your Pictures folder. When you set a screen saver, you control options, such as how long your computer should be inactive before the screen saver appears and whether Windows 7 should require a password to redisplay the Desktop. This ensures that unauthorized users cannot click your mouse to deactivate the screen saver and work at your computer.

1   Click the Screen Saver link in the Personalization window.

2   The Screen Saver Settings dialog box opens. Choose the screen saver you want to use from the Screen saver drop-down menu. Windows 7 displays a preview of the screen saver in the dialog box.

Some screen savers have settings you can change. For example, the 3D Text screen saver enables you to specify what text should be displayed, the font, how the text rotates, and more. To access these settings, select the desired screen saver in the drop-down list and press the Settings button.

3   Use the Wait text field to specify how long your system should be idle before the screen saver starts.

4   If you want Windows 7 to require a password to redisplay the Desktop, click the *On resume, display logon screen* checkbox to select it.

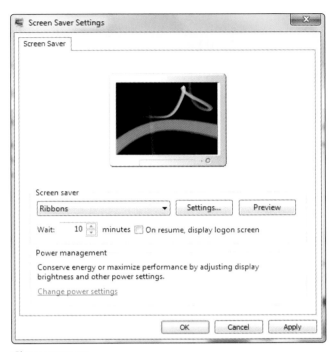

Choose a screen saver.

5   Press the Preview button. Windows 7 displays a preview of the screen saver.

6   Press OK to close the Screen Saver Settings dialog box. The next time your system is idle for the specified duration, Windows 7 will launch the screen saver. To return to the Desktop, move your mouse or press any key on the keyboard.

7   You can also create a custom screen saver that cycles through the photos in your Pictures folder. To do so, click the Screen Saver link.

8   In the Screen Saver Settings dialog box, choose Photos from the Screen Saver drop-down menu.

9   The Photos Screen Saver Settings dialog box opens. To change how quickly Windows 7 cycles through your photos, choose a different speed from the Slide show speed drop-down menu.

10 If you want Windows 7 to shuffle the photos in the slide show, click the *Shuffle Pictures* checkbox to select it.

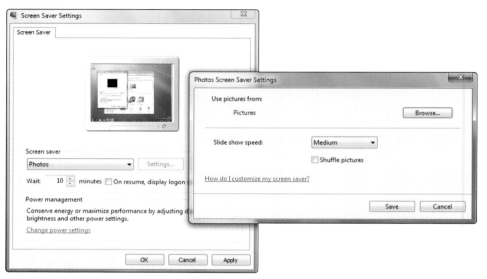

Adjust the settings for the Photos screen saver.

By default, Windows 7 cycles through the photos in your Pictures folder. To use photos in a different folder, press Browse in the Photos Screen Saver Settings dialog box. Then, in the Browse for Folder dialog box that appears, locate and select the folder that contains the images you want to use, then press OK.

11 Press Save to close the Photos Screen Saver Settings dialog box.

12 Press OK to close the Screen Saver Settings dialog box. The next time your system is idle for the specified duration, Windows 7 will launch the screen saver.

Applying a theme

If you want to customize your Windows 7 Desktop, but don't feel like spending a lot of time setting the various individual options—the Desktop background, window color, sound scheme, and so on, you can apply a Windows 7 theme to change the overall appearance. When you apply a theme, Windows 7 displays the Desktop background or backgrounds, window color, sound scheme, and screen saver associated with that theme.

1   Select a theme from any of the Theme categories in the Personalization window; Windows 7 applies it to the Desktop.

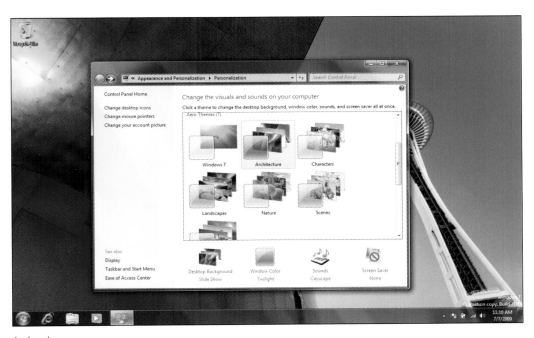

Apply a theme.

You can customize a theme by changing the Desktop Background, Window Color, Sounds, or Screen Saver. Simply follow the steps outlined in the preceding sections to do so. If you modify an existing theme, Windows 7 creates a new theme with your changes. To save this theme, right-click it in the Personalization window, choose Save Theme, type a descriptive name for the theme in the Save Theme As dialog box, and press Save.

4   You can also download additional themes from the Microsoft web site. In the Personalization window, click the Get more themes online link.

5   Windows 7 launches Internet Explorer 8, directing you to a page on the Microsoft site with additional themes. When you find a theme you like, press its Download button.

Download a theme from the Microsoft web site.

6   Windows 7 asks whether you want to open or save the file; press Open. Windows 7 flashes a security notification; click Allow.

7   Windows 7 downloads the theme and applies it to your Desktop.

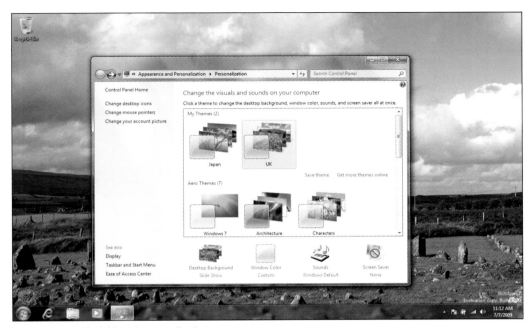

The theme is downloaded from the Microsoft web site.

8   Press the Close button (▬) in the Personalization window to close it.

Setting language options

Windows 7 includes support for several languages, including English, French, German, Japanese, Portuguese, Chinese, Arabic, and more. If you plan to use the keyboard setup associated with a language other than the English-language QWERTY keyboard, or you want Windows 7 to use a different language in dialog boxes, and menus, you must add support for that language to Windows 7.

If you plan to use Windows 7 only in English, you should skip this section of the book and move on ahead to "Changing accessibility settings."

Downloading and installing language-support software

Before you can add support for a language to your Windows 7 system, you must first download the necessary software from Microsoft and install it on your computer.

1   Press the Start button (⊙).

2   Click Control Panel.

3   Click the Clock, Language, and Region link.

Click the Clock, Language, and Region link in the Control Panel window.

4   The Clock, Language, and Region window opens. Click the Install or uninstall display languages link.

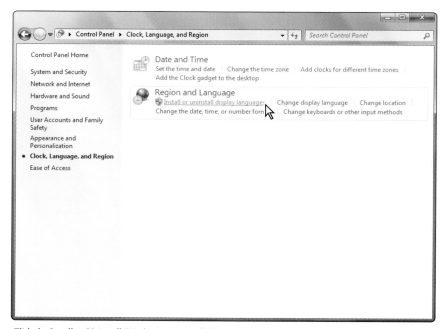

Click the Install or Uninstall Display Languages link.

5 The Install or uninstall display languages Wizard starts. Click Install display languages.

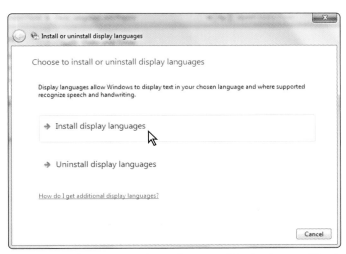

Click Install Display Languages in the Install or Uninstall Display Languages Wizard screen.

6. The next screen of the wizard appears. Click Launch Windows Update.

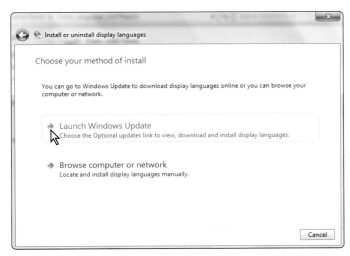

Click Launch Windows Update.

7. Windows 7 displays the Windows Update screen. Click the Optional Updates Are Available link.

An even faster way to access the Windows Update window is to open the Start menu, choose Control Panel, click the System and Security link in the Control Panel window, then click the Windows Update link in the System and Security screen.

8   Windows 7 displays the Windows Update screen. Click the optional updates are
     available link.

Click the Optional Updates Are Available link.

9   Click the checkbox next to the language you want to install to select it.

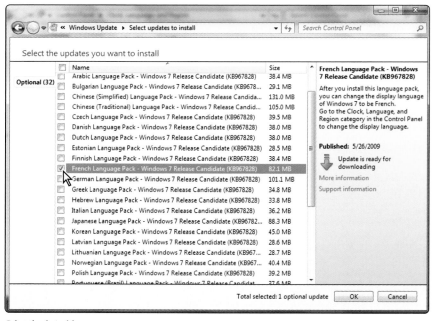

Select the desired language.

10   Press the OK button.

11 In the Windows Update screen, click Install Updates.

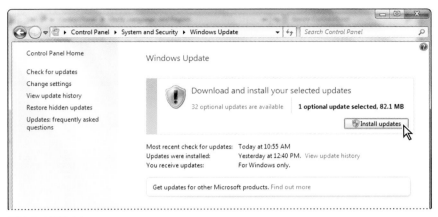

Click Install Updates.

12 Windows 7 downloads and installs the software, notifying you when the update is complete. Press the Close button (▬) of the Windows Update screen to close it.

Changing the display and input language

Only perform these steps if you wish to change the language Windows uses to display menus and warnings, otherwise move on to the next exercise, "Changing accessibility settings."

Once you've downloaded the necessary software, you're ready to change the display and input language or the language Windows 7 displays in wizards, dialog boxes, menus, and the like, and the language you use to enter information into your computer, respectively.

1 Click the Change display language link in the Control Panel window.

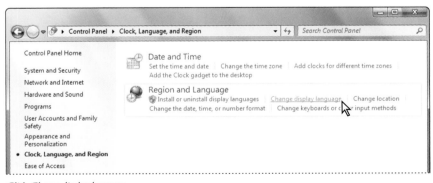

Click Change display language.

2   The Region and Language dialog box opens with the Keyboards and Languages tab
    displayed. Choose the desired language from the Choose a display language drop-down
    menu (in this example, français).

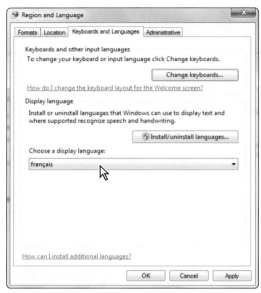

*Choose the language you want to use from the Choose a display
language drop-down menu.*

3   Press OK.

4   Windows 7 informs you that you must log off for the settings to take effect. Press the
    Log off now button.

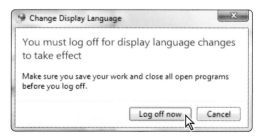

Log off.

5 The next time you log on, the language settings you chose will be in effect.

The next time you log on, your changes will be in effect.

You can also use the Region and Language dialog box to specify that Windows 7 display such information as dates, times, currency, and measurements in a format that's in keeping with a particular region in the world. To do so, click the dialog box's Formats tab and select the desired locale from the Format drop-down list; Windows 7 changes how the date, time, and other information is displayed. To access even more settings, press the Additional Settings button.

Changing the keyboard configuration

Suppose you want Windows 7 to display information in wizards, dialog boxes, menus, etc. in English, but you want to be able to type using the keyboard configuration associated with a different language; this changes which characters appear onscreen when you press certain keys on your keyboard. In that case, you can add support for a second (or third, or fourth…) keyboard configuration. When you add support for an additional keyboard configuration, Windows 7 displays the Language bar, which you can use to quickly switch from one keyboard to another.

1 Open the Control Panel window.

2 In the Control Panel window, click the Clock, Language, and Region link.

3 The Clock, Language, and Region window appears; click the Change Display Language link.

4 The Region and Language dialog box opens with the Keyboards and Languages tab displayed. Press the Change keyboards button.

5 The Text Services and Input Languages dialog box appears. Choose the desired language from the Default input language drop-down menu.

Add support for a second keyboard.

6 Press OK to close the Text Services and Input Languages dialog box.

7 Press OK to close the Region and Language dialog box.

8 Press the Close button (▣) in the Control Panel window to close it.

9   The Language bar appears in the Taskbar. To switch to the other keyboard configuration, click the Language bar icon and choose the desired configuration from the menu that appears.

Click the Language bar and select the keyboard configuration you want to use.

Changing accessibility settings

Windows 7 includes several features designed to help users that may have difficulty seeing the screen or using the mouse and keyboard use their computer more easily and more effectively.

•   **Magnifier.** This feature magnifies the Desktop to make it easier to read.

Accessing the Magnifier from the Ease of Access Control Panel.

- **On-Screen Keyboard**. This accessibility option displays a virtual Desktop keyboard through which you can type in one of three ways: by clicking an onscreen key, by hovering over a key with your mouse, or by using alternative input devices such as a toggle switch to select a key.

The On-screen Keyboard.

- **Narrator**. This accessibility option, designed to help those people who are visually impaired work on a Windows computer, reads aloud onscreen items, such as dialog box options, aloud. You can personalize various aspects of Narrator, such as the text-reading speed, the voice pitch, and the overall volume.

The Navigator.

You access these and other accessibility tools from Windows 7's Ease of Access Center; it serves as a centralized repository for Windows 7's sensory and dexterity settings. The Ease of Access Center also serves as a launching point for Windows 7's Speech Recognition program, which lets you dictate text and verbally issue commands to your computer.

1   Open the Control Panel window.

2   Click the Ease of Access link.

3   The Ease of Access window opens. Click the Ease of Access Center link; the Ease of Access Center opens.

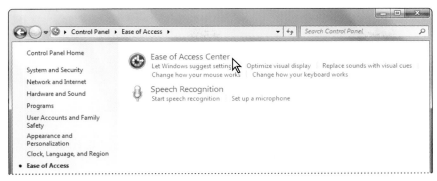

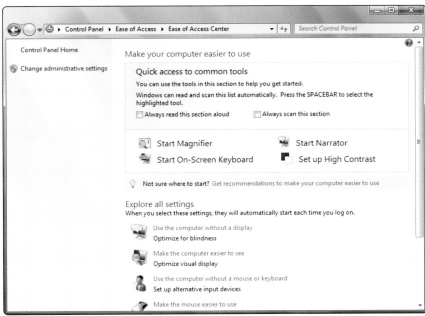

Click the Ease of Access Center link to open the Ease of Access Center.

To determine which (if any) of the Windows 7 accessibility tools may be helpful to you, click the Get Recommendations to Make Your Computer Easier to Use link in the Ease of Access Center window. Windows 7 asks a series of questions related to eyesight, hearing, dexterity, speech, and so on; answer them, pressing Next to move through the screens. When you finish, Windows 7 lists technologies that may prove useful and provides a link to additional information about assistive technologies online.

Customizing the Start menu

When you press the Start button, Windows 7 displays the Start menu; the menu's main pane features a list of shortcuts to programs that you've opened recently. You access additional programs by clicking the All Programs option. You can *pin* shortcuts to the programs you use most often to this main pane. When you pin a program shortcut to the main pane, it remains there indefinitely until you *unpin* it.

Pin a program to the Start menu

1 Click the Start button ( ). The Start menu appears.

2 Click All Programs. Right-click the program you want to pin to the Start menu. In this example, the Paint application.

3 Choose Pin to Start Menu.

Pin a program shortcut to the Start menu.

4   Windows 7 adds a shortcut for the program to the main pane of the Start menu.

The programs shows in the Start menu.

If you pin multiple program shortcuts to the Start menu, you can arrange them in any order you like. To move a pinned shortcut in the list, click it and drag it to the desired position. To remove a pinned program shortcut from the Start menu, right-click it and choose Unpin from Start menu.

More Start menu customizations

To further customize the Start menu, you use the Windows 7 Taskbar and Start Menu Properties dialog box.

1   Right-click a blank area of the Windows 7 Taskbar.

2   Choose Properties from the menu that appears.

3   The Taskbar and Start Menu Properties dialog box opens. Click the Start Menu tab.

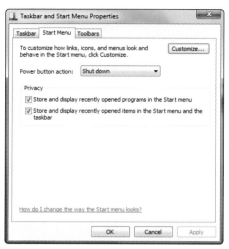

The Start Menu tab.

From the Taskbar and Start Menu Properties dialog box, you can specify Start menu settings including:

- **The default power button action**. By default, Windows 7 displays a Shut Down option in the Start menu. If you more frequently use Hibernate, or Sleep, you can configure Windows 7 to display that option rather than the Shut Down option. To do so, choose the desired option from the Power Button Action drop-down menu.

- **Whether shortcuts to recently opened programs should be displayed in the Start menu and/or Taskbar**. To do so, select the appropriate checkbox under Privacy.

4 For more personalization options, press the Customize button. This launches the Customize Start Menu dialog box, where you can do the following:

- Add, customize, or remove certain shortcuts from the right side of the Start menu.

- Adjust the number of shortcuts to recently used programs in the main pane of the Start menu. You can also display how many recently opened items should appear in jump lists on the Taskbar.

- Revert to the default settings.

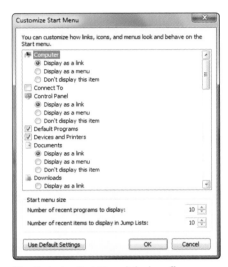

The Customize Start Menu dialog box offers more personalization settings for the Start menu.

Customizing the Taskbar

You can modify the Windows 7 Taskbar to match the way you work. Here are just a few ways to modify your Taskbar:

- You can reposition the Taskbar on your Desktop, moving it to the top, left, or right side of the screen.

- You can maximize your Desktop space by auto-hiding the Taskbar. This is helpful if you have a small monitor or work on a laptop with limited display space. When you auto-hide the Taskbar, it disappears. To view it, move your mouse pointer to the bottom of the screen.

- You can resize the Taskbar. For example, you might make it larger to better see the buttons, or smaller to create a little extra room in the Desktop's work area.

- You can change what icons appear in the Taskbar's notification area, hiding icons you don't use and showing those you want to monitor.

- You can pin shortcut icons to the programs you use most often to the Taskbar for fast access.

- You can change the system date and time, which is displayed in the Taskbar, to reflect your current location.

Repositioning the Taskbar

1   Open the Taskbar and Start Menu Properties dialog box.

2   If necessary, click the Taskbar tab.

3   Choose the desired location from the Taskbar Location on Screen drop-down menu (in this example, Top).

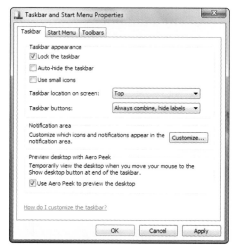

Select a location for the Taskbar.

4   Press OK to close the Taskbar and Start Menu Properties dialog box. Windows 7
     repositions the Taskbar.

The repositioned Taskbar.

Auto-hiding the Taskbar

1   Open the Taskbar and Start Menu Properties dialog box.

2   If necessary, click the Taskbar tab.

3 Click the *Auto-Hide the Taskbar* checkbox to select it.

Auto-hide the Taskbar.

4 Press OK to close the Taskbar and Start Menu Properties dialog box. Windows 7 hides the Taskbar, displaying it only when you move your mouse pointer to the bottom of the screen.

Resizing the Taskbar

You can make the Taskbar larger or smaller, depending on your preference.

1 To make the Taskbar smaller, open the Taskbar and Start Menu Properties dialog box.

2 If necessary, click the Taskbar tab.

3 Click the *Use Small Icons* checkbox to select it.

4 Press OK to close the Taskbar and Start Menu Properties dialog box. Windows 7 shrinks the Taskbar buttons, thereby making the Taskbar smaller as well.

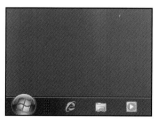

Resize the Taskbar.

5 To enlarge the Taskbar, you must unlock it. Right-click a blank area of the Windows 7 Taskbar.

6   Choose Lock the Taskbar from the menu that appears. Notice that Windows 7 removes the check mark that initially appeared alongside this menu entry.

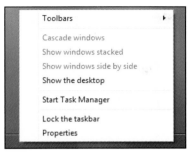

Unlock the Taskbar.

7   Once you've unlocked the Taskbar, you're ready to resize it. Place your mouse pointer over the top edge of the Taskbar. The mouse cursor changes to a two-headed arrow.

8   Click and drag upward.

9   When the Taskbar is the size you want, release the mouse button; Windows 7 resizes the Taskbar.

Resize the Taskbar.

Customizing the notification area

1 Open the Taskbar and Start Menu Properties dialog box.

2 If necessary, click the Taskbar tab.

3 Press the Customize button in the Notification Area section of the dialog box.

4 Windows 7 launches the Notification Area Icons screen. Choose the desired setting from the drop-down menu next to the icon you want to change; Show Icon and Notifications, Hide Icon and Notifications, or Only Show Notifications.

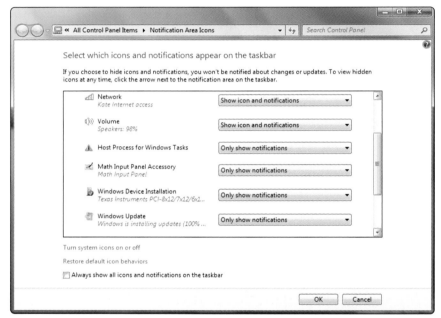

Customize the notification area.

5 Press OK to close the Notification Area Icons screen.

6 Press OK to close the Taskbar and Start Menu Properties dialog box. Windows 7 puts your changes into effect.

Pinning a program button to the Taskbar

Windows 7 enables you to pin program, folder, and file buttons to the Taskbar allowing for one-click access. You can also unpin any buttons you don't need.

1   Open the program, folder, or file you want to pin to the Taskbar. A Taskbar button for the opened program appears—by default this is at the bottom of your display.

2   Right-click the Taskbar button for the program, folder, or file.

3   A shortcut menu appears. If the item you want to pin to the Taskbar is a program, click Pin This Program to the Taskbar. If it's a folder or file, place your mouse pointer over it in the Recent list and click the pushpin icon that appears. Windows 7 pins a button for the program, folder, or file to the Taskbar.

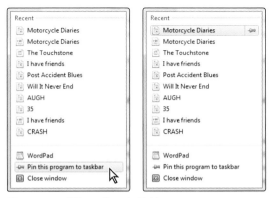

Pin a program, folder, or file to the Taskbar.

4   To unpin a program, folder, or file you no longer want from the Taskbar, right-click its button on the Taskbar and choose Unpin This Program from Taskbar. Windows 7 removes the program's button.

Unpin a program, folder, or file from the Taskbar.

5 In addition to pinning buttons to the Taskbar (and unpinning those buttons you don't use), you can also change the order in which the buttons appear on the Taskbar. To do so, click a button you want to move, and drag it to the desired position. When you release the mouse button, Windows 7 drops the button in the position you chose.

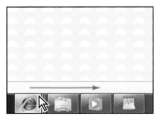 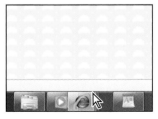

Change the order of your Taskbar buttons.

Changing the system date and time

You may need to adjust your Windows 7 date and time settings if you travel to other time zones. When you create and modify files on your computer, the time and date information is automatically recorded so you want to keep your clock accurate.

1 Click the date and time display to the right of the notification area on the Taskbar.

2 Windows 7 displays a clock and calendar. Click the Change Date and Time Settings link.

3 The Date and Time dialog box opens. Press the Change Date and Time button.

Press the Change Date and Time button in the Date and Time dialog box.

4 The Date and Time Settings dialog box opens. Select today's date in the calendar.

5   To change the time, click in the Hour field in the digital clock text field, and click the up or down arrow to increase or decrease the value. Repeat this in the Minutes, Seconds, and AM/PM fields.

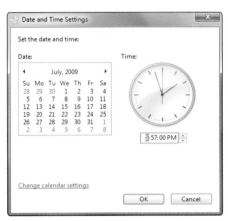

Make your changes in the Date and Time Settings dialog box.

6   Press OK to close the Date and Time Settings dialog box.

7   In the Date and Time dialog box, press the Change Time Zone button.

8   The Time Zone Settings dialog box opens. Choose your time zone from the Time Zone drop-down menu.

9   If you are in an area that observes daylight saving time, click the *Automatically Adjust Clock for Daylight Saving Time* checkbox to select it.

Make your changes in the Time Zone Settings dialog box.

10   Press OK to close the Time Zone Settings dialog box.

11   Press OK to close the Date and Time dialog box.

Displaying multiple clocks

If you like, you can configure Windows 7 to display as many as two additional clocks when you click the date and time display on the Taskbar. This is handy if you frequently communicate with colleagues, friends, or family members who work or live outside your time zone.

1   Open the Date and Time dialog box by clicking the date and time in the Taskbar's notification area, then clicking the Change date and time settings link.

2   Click the Additional Clocks tab.

3   Click the *Show This Clock* checkbox to select it.

4   Choose the desired time zone from the Select Time Zone drop-down menu.

5   Type a name for this second clock—for example, the name of the region it reflects or the name of someone who lives there.

Make your changes in the Date and Time dialog box.

6   Press OK to close the Date and Time dialog box.

7 Hover your mouse pointer over the date and time display on the Taskbar; Windows 7 displays the local time and date as well as the time and date in the second location. Alternatively, click the date and time display to view both clocks side by side.

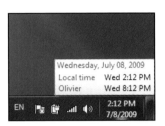

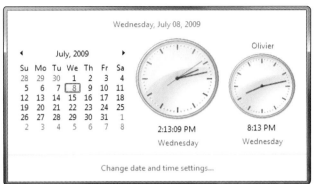

Display the date and time.

Adding an address bar to your Windows 7 Taskbar

When you want to visit a web site, you typically launch your web browser, then type the web address for the page you want to visit in your browser window's address bar. You can save yourself a step, however, by adding an address bar to your Windows 7 Taskbar. Then, anytime you wish to visit a web site, you can type its address in the address bar on the Taskbar; Windows 7 automatically launches the Internet Explorer 8 web browser and opens the page you specified.

You'll learn more about browsing the Web using Internet Explorer 8 in Lesson 5, "Surfing the Web with Internet Explorer 8."

1 Right-click a blank area of the Windows Taskbar.

2 Click Toolbars in the menu that appears.

3   Click Address in the sub-menu that appears.

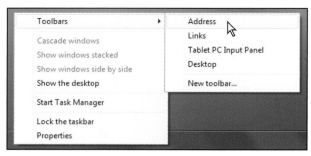

Add an address bar to your Windows 7 Taskbar.

4   Windows 7 adds an address bar to your Taskbar.

Add an address bar to your Windows 7 Taskbar.

Creating and managing shortcuts

Just as you can pin programs to the Taskbar and Start menu, so, too, can you place shortcuts to programs—as well as to files, folders, drives, and even network resources—on your Windows 7 Desktop. A shortcut is special icon that you can double-click to launch the associated program, file, folder, drive, or what have you on your system. Often, when you install a new program on your Windows computer, Windows 7 prompts you to add a shortcut to that program on the Desktop during the installation process; in addition, you can create your own shortcuts.

Creating a shortcut

1   In Windows Explorer, locate the program, file, folder, drive, or other system resource for which you want to create a shortcut.

2   Right-click the item.

3   Choose Send to from the menu that appears.

4 Select Desktop (Create Shortcut). Windows 7 places a shortcut to the selected resource on the Desktop.

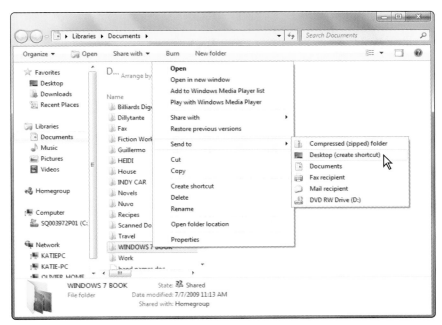

Create a Desktop shortcut.

An even faster way to add a Desktop shortcut for a program is to locate the icon for the program in the Start menu, click it, and drag it to the Desktop.

Customizing a shortcut

If you don't care for the graphic associated with your shortcut icon, you can change it. You can also customize other aspects of the shortcut, such as associating it with a keyboard shortcut. You can then use this keyboard shortcut to launch the resource associated with the shortcut rather than clicking the shortcut icon and specifying whether the resource should launch in a window that's normal, minimized, or maximized. Here's how:

1 Right-click the shortcut you want to customize.

2 Choose Properties.

3 The Shortcut Properties dialog box opens. To set a keyboard shortcut, click in the Shortcut Key text field, then press the key combination you want to use—for example, Ctrl+Alt+B.

4   To specify whether the resource is launched in a window that is normal, minimized, or maximized, choose the desired option from the Run drop-down menu.

5   To change the icon associated with the shortcut, press the Change Icon button.

The Shortcut Properties dialog box.

6   The Change Icon dialog box opens. Click the icon you want to associate with the shortcut.

The Change Icon dialog box.

7   Press OK to close the Change Icon dialog box.

8 Press OK to close the Shortcut Properties dialog box. Windows 7 applies your changes.

The new shortcut icon.

Tidying shortcuts on the Windows 7 Desktop

If your Windows 7 Desktop becomes cluttered with files, folders, and programs you can organize it.

Productivity suffers when your Desktop is cluttered.

Windows 7 makes it easy to tidy up the shortcuts on your Desktop.

1 Right-click an empty area on the Desktop.

2 Choose Sort By from the menu that appears.

3 Select how you want the shortcut icons to be sorted—by name, by size, by type, or by date modified. Windows 7 promptly puts things in their place.

Specify how you want your shortcut items to be sorted; Windows 7 puts your shortcut icons in their place.

  An even easier way to tidy the Desktop is to press and hold down the F5 button on your keyboard.

If you want to tidy your Desktop by deleting shortcut icons, select the icon or icons you want to delete, right-click them, and choose Delete from the menu that appears. Windows 7 asks you to confirm the deletion; press Yes.

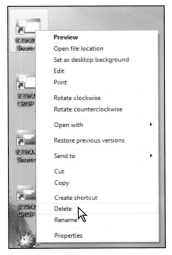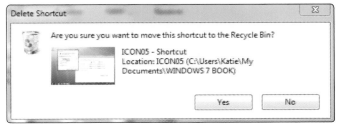

Right-click the icon or icons you want to delete and choose Delete from the menu that appears, then confirm deletion.

 When you delete a shortcut, only the shortcut itself is removed—not the program, folder, file, or other system resource with which it is associated.

Personalizing the Windows 7 startup routine

If you find yourself launching a certain program or tool every time you start Windows 7—for example, WordPad or On-Screen Keyboard—you can personalize your computer to launch that program or tool automatically whenever you start Windows 7. That way, it is available immediately after your computer starts and Windows 7 loads. To do so, add the program or tool to your Windows Startup folder.

 Be aware that every program you add consumes system resources. As a result, you should add only those programs that you really need for every Windows 7 session. If, after you've added programs and/or tools to your System folder, you determine that your system's startup routine takes too long, consider purging your Startup folder of any programs and tools that aren't absolutely necessary.

1 Press the Start button (●).

2 Click All Programs.

3 Right-click the Startup folder.

4 Click Open.

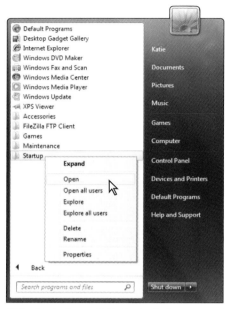

Right-click the Startup Folder icon in the Start menu and choose Open from the menu that appears.

5 The Startup folder's window opens on the Desktop. Open the Start menu and locate the icon for the program you want to add to the Startup folder.

6   Drag the program's icon from the Start menu to the Startup folder. Windows 7 adds the program to the Startup folder; the next time you start Windows 7, the program launches automatically.

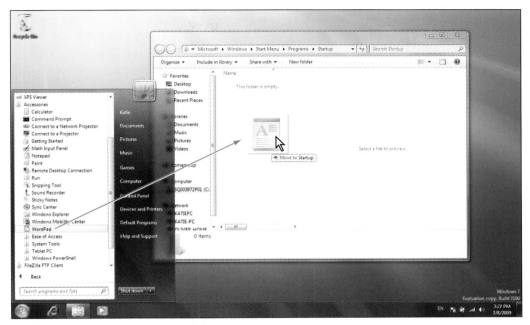

Drag the program's icon to the Startup folder's window.

In addition to adding programs to the Startup folder, you can also add files and folders that you use on a regular basis. To do so, locate the file or folder in Windows Explorer, right-click it, and click Create Shortcut. Windows 7 creates a shortcut to the file or folder in Windows Explorer; drag the shortcut into the Startup folder's window.

Configuring AutoPlay settings

AutoPlay tool lets you select what program to use for various types of media or hardware. For example, you can specify that when you insert a music CD or a movie DVD into your CD/DVD drive, Windows 7 automatically launches Windows Media Player and plays the files on your media; or that media card readers containing image files open in Photo Gallery. You can also configure Windows 7 to prompt you to select the program you want to use on a case-by-case basis when you insert a disc, or you can disable AutoPlay entirely.

1   Open the Control Panel window and Click the Hardware and Sound link.

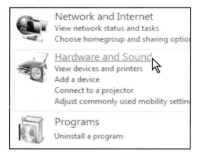

Click the Hardware and Sound link in the Control Panel window.

2   The Hardware and Sound window opens. Click the AutoPlay link.

Click the AutoPlay link in the Hardware and Sound window.

3   The AutoPlay window opens. To enable AutoPlay, click the *Use AutoPlay for All Media and Devices* checkbox to select it. Alternatively, you can disable AutoPlay by clearing the checkbox.

4   To specify what Windows 7 should do when you insert or attach a specific type of media, choose the action you want to occur from the media type's drop-down menu— for example, Play Media Using Program, Open Folder to View Files Using Windows Explorer, Take No Action, and Ask Me Every Time.

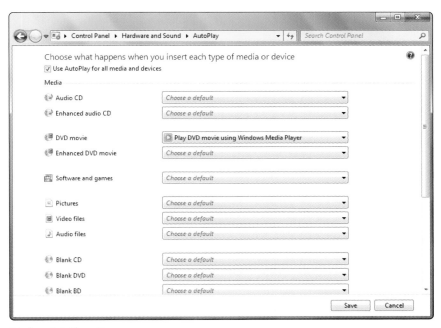

Configure AutoPlay settings.

5   Press Save.

6   Press the Close button ( ) of the Control Panel window to close it.

Self study

1   Set up your Windows 7 Desktop, Start menu, and Taskbar to help you work more efficiently.

2   Add the programs, files, and folders you use most often to the Startup folder. Then reboot your computer to determine whether the addition of these items significantly slows your system's startup routine. If so, delete any items you deem unnecessary from the Startup folder.

Review

Questions

1 Do windows on the Desktop appear larger when your screen resolution is higher.

2 What are gadgets?

3 In Windows 7, what is the difference between the display language and the input language?

4 What are three Windows 7 tools designed to improve accessibility for visually and physically impaired users?

5 What function key do you press to tidy up the Windows 7 Desktop?

Answers

1 No, the higher the screen resolution, the smaller windows appear when open on the Desktop. For example, the windows in a screen with a resolution of 800x600 appear much larger than in a screen with a resolution of 1280x800 or higher.

2 Gadgets are mini-programs on the Windows 7 Desktop that broadcast such information as news headlines, weather conditions, exchange rates, and stock quotes; offer quick access to frequently used tools such as a clock; or are designed to entertain the user.

3 The display language is the language that Windows 7 displays in wizards, dialog boxes, and menus. The input language is the language you use when entering information into your computer.

4 Magnifier, On-Screen Keyboard, and Narrator are three tools designed to improve accessibility.

5 You can press and hold down the F5 key on your keyboard. This is a keyboard shortcut for right-clicking a blank area on the Desktop, choosing Sort By from the menu that appears, and then specifying whether you want shortcut icons to be arranged by name, size, type, or date modified.

Lesson 5

What you'll learn in this lesson:

- Understanding the Internet and the Web
- Connecting to the Internet
- Using Internet Explorer 8
- Customizing Internet Explorer 8
- Exploring Windows Live

Surfing the Web with Internet Explorer 8

In order to access the massive storehouse of information that is the World Wide Web, you need a web browser. Windows 7 is enhanced by the Internet Explorer 8 web browser.

Starting up

Before you start, be sure to download all the files for this lesson from the accompanying DVD to your hard drive. Also make sure that your computer is connected to the Internet.

See Lesson 5 in action!

Use the accompanying video to gain a better understanding of how to use some of the features shown in this lesson. The video tutorial for this lesson can be found on the included DVD.

Understanding the Internet and the World Wide Web

The massive storehouse of information comprising the World Wide Web is presented on web sites, which reside on computers called web servers. A web site is a collection of web pages that relate to a particular person, business, government, school, or organization. A web page, which you download from the web server to your computer and view using a special program called a web browser, such as Internet Explorer 8, can combine text with images, sound, music, and even video to convey information about a particular subject.

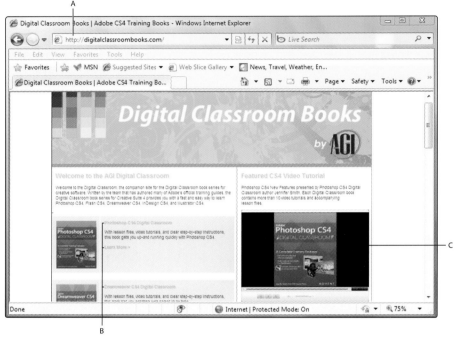

You use a web browser to download and view web pages. ***A****. Web Address.* ***B****. Links.* ***C****. Silverlight video.*

Connecting to the Internet

In order to visit sites on the World Wide Web, you must first connect to the Internet. To do so, you must establish an account with an Internet service provider (ISP). Examples of ISPs in the U.S. include America Online, EarthLink, NetZero, AT&T, Comcast, Verizon, and Time Warner. You'll need appropriate hardware to connect: a dial-up modem if you plan to use your phone line to access the Internet, a cable modem or DSL modem if you plan to use a broadband connection, or a wireless card if you plan to establish a wireless connection. Most computers come with an ethernet connection making it easy to connect to a cable or DSL connection. Your ISP will typically provide the necessary modem or hardware.

A dial-up connection is significantly slower than a broadband one. A dial-up connection transfers data to your computer from a web server on the Internet and back much slower than a broadband connection. A dial-up connection can transfer data at a rate of 56 kilobits per second, a broadband connection can transfer data at speeds greater than 10 times this rate.

1 Using the cable provided by your ISP, connect your cable or DSL modem to your computer. Make sure the modem is also plugged in to a power supply.

2 Press the Start button (⊙).

3 Choose Control Panel.

4 In the Control Panel window, under Network and Internet, click Connect to the Internet.

Click Connect to the Internet in the Control Panel window.

5   Windows launches the Connect to the Internet wizard. Click Broadband.

Click the Broadband option in the Connect to the Internet wizard.

6   In the User Name text field, type the user name for your ISP account (provided by your ISP).

7   In the Password text field, type the password for your ISP account (provided by your ISP).

8   Click the *Remember This Password* checkbox to select it.

9   Type a descriptive name for this connection.

10   If you want this Internet connection to be available to other people who use your computer, click the *Allow Other People to Use This Connection* checkbox to select it.

Some broadband connections are always on and do not require a log-in. For these accounts, connect the ethernet cable to your computer or use the wireless router provided to you. For more information on wireless connections, refer to Chapter 14, "Using Windows 7 on a Laptop Computer."

11 Press Connect. Windows establishes the Internet connection.

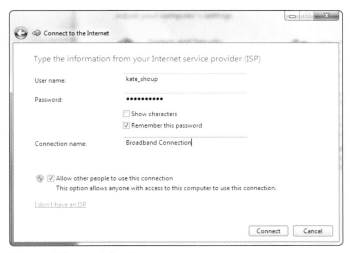

Enter your ISP account information.

Using Internet Explorer 8

As mentioned, a web browser is required to download and view web pages. Fortunately, Windows 7 includes Internet Explorer 8. Start Internet Explorer 8 just as you do any other program in Windows, by clicking the program's icon in the Start menu, in All Programs. Alternatively, you can launch Internet Explorer 8 by clicking the Internet Explorer button ( ) on the Windows Taskbar.

Launch Internet Explorer 8 from the Start menu or from the Windows Taskbar.

If you've used previous versions of Internet Explorer, you'll quickly discover that Internet Explorer 8 operates in much the same way with respect to opening web pages, searching the Web, keeping track of your favorite sites, subscribing to RSS feeds, printing out web pages, and customizing your browser. Internet Explorer 8 did add these new features:

*   **Web slices**. If you frequently visit sites that are updated throughout the day—for example, a news site or a site that displays stock quotes, you may be able to create a Web slice for that site. When you do, Windows displays the Web slice on your Favorites bar; as the site associated with the slice is updated, the Web slice becomes highlighted. You can then click the highlighted Web slice to preview the updated information.

*   **Accelerators**. In the past, mapping an address, translating a word, or performing other routine tasks online meant opening a second web page and copying and pasting information from the original page to the new page. Accelerators speed things up by enabling you to access the information you need without opening additional web pages.

Opening web pages

Although you can open a web page in Internet Explorer 8 using a variety of techniques, the easiest way is to type the URL of the web page you want to visit in the Internet Explorer 8 address bar. As you enter a web page's URL in the Internet Explorer 8 address bar, Internet Explorer 8 displays a list of URLs that include the characters you've typed so far. If the URL for the page you want to visit appears, click it in the list. This is handy if you recently visited a web page but you can't remember the URL. Otherwise, type the entire URL and press Enter.

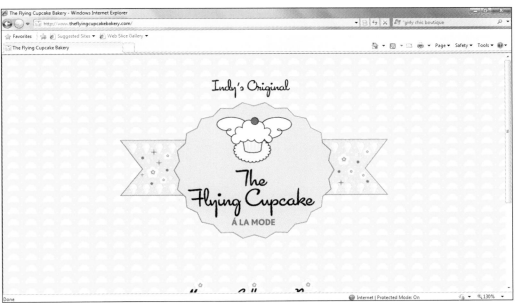

Type the URL for the page you want to visit in the address bar and press Enter; IE 8 displays the page whose URL you entered.

Internet Explorer 8 culls the URLs it displays from your Favorites list, your History list, and any RSS feeds to which you subscribe. You'll learn about the Favorites list, the History list, and RSS feeds later in this lesson.

If the page you want to open is one you've visited before, you may be able to access it from the Internet Explorer 8 jump list on the Windows Taskbar.

1 Right-click the Internet Explorer button (@) on the Windows Taskbar at the bottom of your display. The jump list appears.

2 If the page you want to visit appears in the jump list, click it. Windows opens the page.

You may be able to open the page you want to visit from the Internet Explorer 8 jump list.

Notice that the page opens in a new tab. You'll learn more about tabs in the next section.

3 Another way to open a web page is by clicking a link—that is, a bit of text or an image on a web page that, when clicked, opens a new web page. Often, links are indicated by underlined text or by text that is a different color. To determine whether a link is present, place your mouse pointer over the text or image in question; if the text or image is a link, the mouse pointer will change from an arrow to a pointing hand.

Clicking a link opens a new web page.

4   If, during a web session, you want to reopen a page you viewed previously, you can press the web browser's Back button (⊙). Press the Forward button (⊙) to return to the page on display before you pressed the Back button. Pressing the down arrow to the right of the Forward button displays a list of recently visited sites. To refresh the currently displayed site to ensure that the page you see contains the most up-to-date information, press the Refresh button (⟳); to stop the page-loading process, press the Stop button (✕). Press the Home button (⌂) to return to the page that is displayed by default when Internet Explorer 8 is launched. To print the currently displayed page, press the Print button (⎙).

A. Back button. *B*. Forward button. *C*. Recently visited. *D*. Home button. *E*. Refresh button. *F*. Stop button. *G*. Print button.

 You can change the page that Internet Explorer 8 displays by default when launched, known as the home page. You'll learn how later in this lesson.

Browsing with Quick Tabs

Suppose you are using the Internet to compare the price of flights offered on various airline web sites. In earlier versions of Internet Explorer, you had to open a separate browser window for each site, and switching among open windows. With Quick Tabs, you can open multiple web pages at once within a single browser window. Each page is displayed in a tab; to switch to a different page, click its tab.

1   To launch a page in a new tab, click the blank tab that appears to the right of any populated ones. A blank tab opens.

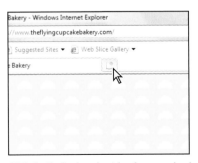 

Click the blank tab to the right of any populated ones; a blank tab opens.

2   Type the URL for the page you want to open in the new tab. The page opens.

There are a few different ways to switch among the various tabs in the Internet Explorer 8 window:

- Click a page's tab to view it. The page whose tab you clicked will appear in the Internet Explorer 8 window.

- Press the Internet Explorer button (⊘) on the Taskbar. You'll see previews of each open page; click the desired page's preview to view it in full-screen mode.

- Press the Quick Tabs button (⊛) to the left of the first tab to view previews of all the pages currently open in your browser; click a preview to view the page in full-screen mode.

- Press the down arrow to the right of the Quick Tabs button to view a list of all open web pages, click a page in the list to view it in the Internet Explorer 8 window.

To view a list of open pages, click the down arrow,
to the right of the Quick Tabs button.

3   If you encounter a link that you want to open in a new tab, right-click the link.

4   A menu appears. Choose Open in New Tab. Internet Explorer 8 opens the page in a
new tab. Notice that this new tab is the same color as the tab containing the link, making
it easy to see which open tabs are related, or part of the same group.

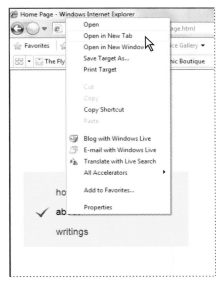

*Open a link in a new tab. Notice that the new tab and the
tab for the page containing the link are the same color.*

*An even faster way to open a link in a new tab is to Ctrl-click the link. That is, click the link
while holding down the Ctrl key on your keyboard.*

5   Right-clicking a tab displays a menu containing several tab-related options. These include the following:

- **Close Tab**. Close the tab you right-clicked.

Another way to close a tab is to click its Close button. To display a tab's Close button, hover your mouse pointer over the tab.

- **Close This Tab Group**. Close the tab you right-clicked as well as any other tabs in the same group.
- **Close Other Tabs**. Leave the tab you right-clicked open, but close all other open tabs.
- **Ungroup This Tab**. If you don't want the tab you right-clicked to be displayed as part of a group, choose this option.
- **Refresh**. If the content in the tab has been updated since the page was displayed, choose this option.
- **Refresh All**. Refresh the content in all open tabs.
- **New Tab**. Open a new, blank tab.
- **Duplicate Tab**. Open a new tab that contains the same page as the tab you right-clicked.
- **Reopen Closed Tab**. If you have closed a tab in error, choose this option. Select it repeatedly to open multiple tabs that have been closed.
- **Recently Closed Tabs**. Choosing this option displays a list of tabs that you closed recently. Choose a tab from the list to reopen it, or select Open All Closed Tabs.

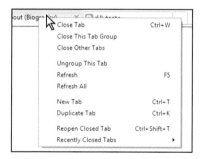

Right-click a tab to view a series of tab-related options.

Browsing in full-screen mode

You may have noticed that the Internet Explorer 8 window contains myriad controls—a title bar, an address bar, toolbar, tabs, status bar, and so on. If you feel that all those controls occupy too much space in the browser window, you can display web pages in full-screen mode—that is, with the various window controls hidden (although the vertical scrollbar remains in place so you can move up and down the page). To switch to full-screen mode, press the Tools button in the Internet Explorer 8 toolbar and choose Full Screen from the menu that appears. Alternatively, press the F11 key on your keyboard. Internet Explorer 8 displays the current page in full-screen mode. To access the window controls, move your cursor to the top of the screen; the controls slide into view. To restore the window to regular view, choose Full Screen from the Tools menu a second time or press the F11 key on your keyboard.

Searching the Web

Internet Explorer 8 features a handy Search box found to the right of the address bar. You use this box much like you would use a Search box in a search engine:

1   Type a keyword or phrase in the Internet Explorer 8 window's Search text field. As you type, Internet Explorer displays a list of suggestions of pages that match your text; click an entry in the list to open a page containing relevant search results. Alternatively, type your text in full and press Enter. Internet Explorer launches *bing*, with the results of your search displayed in list form.

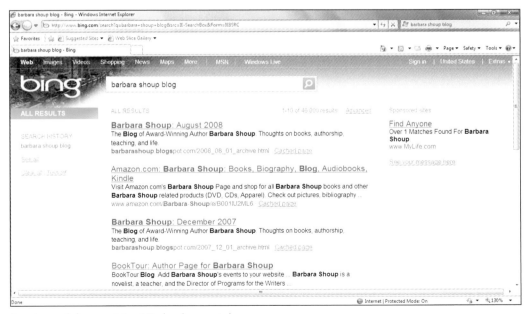

Launch a search from your Internet Explorer browser window.

2　Click an entry in the search-results list. Windows displays the page you clicked.

If you prefer to use a different search tool, for example, Google, you can add it to your list of search providers in Internet Explorer 8. That way, if bing fails to deliver helpful results, you can run the search again using the other provider. Alternatively, you can configure Internet Explorer 8 to use the other provider by default.

You aren't limited to selecting web search engines as search providers. You can also choose search providers that provide results relating to shopping (such as Amazon and eBay), sports (such as ESPN), movies (such as IMDb), and news (such as The New York Times).

Add a search tool to your list of providers

1　Click the down arrow to the right of the Search text field.

2　Choose Find More Providers from the menu that appears.

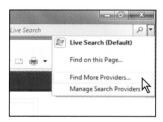

Click the Search box's down arrow and choose Find More Providers.

3　Internet Explorer 8 displays a web page listing several alternative search tools; press the Add to Internet Explorer button for the tool you want to add to your list of available search providers.

Click Add to Internet Explorer to add a search tool.

4   The Add Search Provider dialog box opens. Press the Add button.

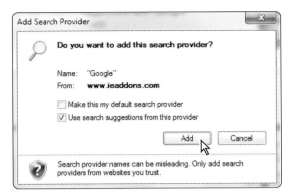

Press the Add button.

If you want this provider to be Internet Explorer 8's default search engine for the Search box, click the Make This My Default Search Provider checkbox in the Add Search Provider dialog box to select it; then press the Add button.

Searching using an alternative provider

1   Type a keyword or phrase in the Internet Explorer 8 window's Search text field, but do not press Enter.

2   Click the down arrow to the right of the Search text field.

3   Choose the desired search provider from the menu that appears (here, Google). Internet Explorer 8 opens the provider's web page, with the results of your search displayed.

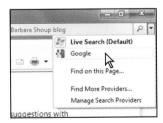

Choose an alternative search provider from the menu.

4   If you want to set an alternative search provider as Internet Explorer 8's default provider, click the down arrow to the right of the Search text field.

5 Choose Manage Search Providers from the menu that appears.

6 The Manage Add-ons dialog box opens. Click the search provider you want to set as the default.

7 Press the Set as Default button.

8 Press the Close button. Internet Explorer 8 establishes the provider you chose as the default.

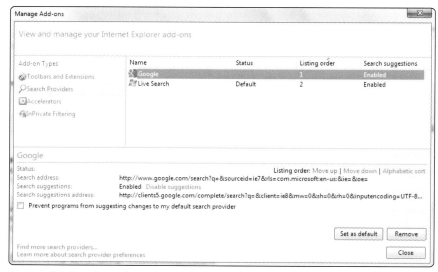

Set a new default search provider.

9 If you decide that you no longer want to use a particular search provider with the Internet Explorer 8 Search text field. You can remove it. Open the Manage Add-ons dialog box.

10 Click the search provider you want to remove.

11 Press the Remove button.

12 Press the Close button. Internet Explorer 8 removes the search provider from the list.

Search tips

If your search fails to yield useful results, try using a more specific keyword or phrase. For example, instead of using the keyword *ski*, try *Volkl Racetiger giant slalom ski*. To search for a specific phrase, surround it with quotation marks, that way, the search will return only those pages containing the exact phrase. Finally, to exclude pages with a certain word from your results, precede the word with a minus sign. For example, if you want to learn about mustang horses, you might use the keyword *mustang* when searching, only to find that many of your results pertain to the Ford Mustang automobile. To omit those results, you could add *-Ford*, note that there's no space between the minus sign and the word, to the search string.

Searching within a web page

In addition to searching the Web for a particular word or phrase, you can also search for that word or phrase within the currently displayed web page.

1   Open the page that contains the word or phrase you want to find.

2   Click the down arrow to the right of the Search text field.

3   Choose Find on This Page from the menu that appears.

Click the down arrow and choose Find on This Page.

4   The Find on Page toolbar appears under the page's tab. Type the text you want to find on the page. As you type, Internet Explorer highlights matching text in yellow.

An even faster way to open the Find on Page toolbar is to press Ctrl+F.

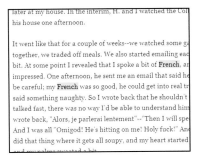

Instances of matching text appear highlighted in yellow.

5   Press the Next button to locate the next match; press the Previous button to find the previous instance.

Keeping track of your favorite pages

With billions of web pages available online, it can be difficult to find the page you need. When you find a page that you will want to revisit, use Internet Explorer 8 to mark that page as a favorite. When you do, Internet Explorer 8 saves the page in a special list, called the Favorites list, located in the Internet Explorer 8 Favorites Center. When you are ready to revisit the page, click the page's entry in the list.

1   Open the page you want to save as a favorite using Internet Explorer 8, then press the Favorites button (⭐).

2   The Favorites Center opens. If necessary, click the Favorites tab to display it.

The Favorites Center appears.

3   Press the Add to Favorites (⭐) button.

4   The Add a Favorite dialog box opens. Here you have the option to type a more descriptive name for the page in the Name text field.

5   By default, favorites are saved in the top-level Favorites folder. To save the page in a different folder, choose the desired folder from the Create in drop-down menu. Alternatively, create a new folder by pressing the New Folder button. This lets you organize your favorites so that related items are stored together.

6   The Create a Folder dialog box appears. Type a name for the new folder in the Folder Name text field.

7   To specify the folder in which this new folder should be saved, choose a folder from the Create in drop-down menu.

8   Press the Create button to close the Create a Folder dialog box.

9   Press the Add button to close the Add a Favorite dialog box. Internet Explorer 8 adds the page to your favorites in the folder you specified.

Save the page as a favorite and create a folder to organize favorites.

Revisiting a favorite

As mentioned, when you save a page as a favorite, it is saved in your Favorites list, located in the Internet Explorer 8 Favorites Center. When you are ready to revisit the page, you can click the page's entry in the list:

1   Open the Favorites Center and click the Favorites tab.

2   A list of pages you've marked as favorites appears. If the page you want to visit has been saved in a subfolder, click the folder.

3 Click the page you want to visit. The page opens in your browser, and the Favorites Center closes.

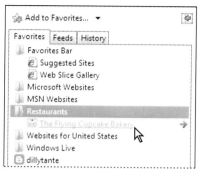

Open a favorite.

To prevent the Favorites Center from closing, press the Pin the Favorites Center button (⊕) before you click the site you want to visit. The Pin the Favorites Center button changes to a Close the Favorites Center button (-); press the Close the Favorites Center button when you are finished using the Favorites Center.

Organizing your favorites

Favorites are saved in the top-level Favorites folder by default. This is fine if you have added only a few pages to your Favorites list. If you add new pages on a regular basis, locating the page you want can become difficult. Internet Explorer 8 lets you organize your favorites by changing the order of your favorites or by grouping related pages into subfolders. For example, you might create one subfolder for news sites, a second subfolder for sites that relate to a favorite hobby, and a third subfolder for travel sites.

1 Click the favorite you want to move in the list.

2   Drag the favorite upward or downward. A line appears indicating where the favorite will be moved in the list; release your mouse button when the line is in the desired spot.

Change the order of the web pages in your Favorites list.

Grouping favorites

To group related pages in a subfolder, you must first create the subfolder.

1   Open the Favorites Center and click the Favorites tab.

2   Click the drop-down menu located to the right of the Add to Favorites button at the top of the Favorites panel.

3 Choose Organize Favorites from the menu that appears.

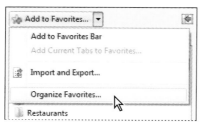

Choose Organize Favorites from the Add to Favorites menu.

4 The Organize Favorites dialog box opens. Press the New Folder button; a new folder appears at the bottom of the favorites list.

5 Type a name for the new folder and press Enter. Internet Explorer 8 renames the folder.

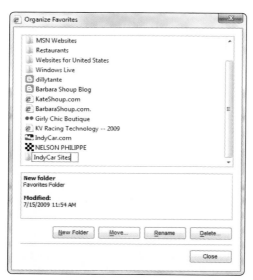

Create a new subfolder.

6 Once you've created a subfolder, you can move favorites into it. Open the Organize Favorites dialog box following the same procedure you used in step 3.

7 Click a favorite that you want to move to the subfolder.

8 Press the Move button.

9 The Browse for Folder dialog box opens. Click the subfolder.

10 Press OK to close the Browse for Folder dialog box.

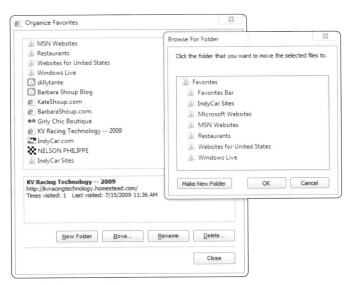

Move a favorite to a subfolder.

11 Repeat steps 2 through 5 to add more favorites to the subfolder.

12 Press Close to close the Organize Favorites dialog box. Internet Explorer moves the favorite into the folder you chose.

Removing a favorite

If you determine that you no longer wish to include a site in your list of favorites, you can easily remove it.

1 Open the Organize Favorites dialog box.

2 Click the favorite you want to delete.

3 Press the Delete button.

4 The Delete Shortcut dialog box appears, asking you to confirm the deletion. Press Yes.

Delete a favorite.

5 Press the Close button to close the Organize Favorites dialog box.

Adding a page to the Favorites bar

If the page you want to save as a favorite is one you access on a daily basis, you might prefer to save it on your Favorites bar. Doing so offers one-click access to the page, bypassing the Favorites Center altogether. To add a favorite to the Favorites bar, open the desired page and press the Add to Favorites Bar button (◉); a button for the page appears under the Internet Explorer 8 address bar.

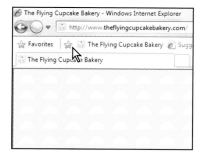

Add a page to the Favorites bar.

Delete pages from the Favorites bar the same way you delete them from the Favorites Center using the Organize Favorites dialog box. Press the Favorites Bar folder in the Organize Favorites dialog box to locate the desired page.

Using the History list

Suppose you want to revisit a page you recently opened, but you can't quite remember its URL. To open the page, try typing as much of its URL as you remember in the Internet Explorer 8 address bar. If Internet Explorer recognizes what you type, it will display the rest of the URL in a list, which you can then click to open the page. Another option might be to select the page from the Internet Explorer jump list in the Windows Taskbar. But what if you don't remember even the first letter of the page's URL, or the page doesn't appear in the jump list? In that case, you can use Internet Explorer's History list to locate the page.

One way to view your History list is to click the down arrow on the right side of the Internet Explorer address bar. When you do, Internet Explorer displays a list of recently visited web pages; if the page you want to open appears in the list, click it to open it.

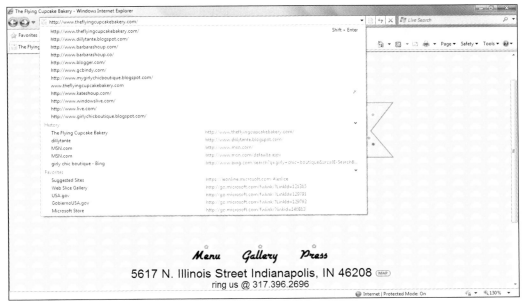

Click the page you want to open in the list; Windows opens the page.

Of course, the list displayed when you click the down arrow to the right of the address bar is limited in scope. You can view even more pages in your History list from the Internet Explorer 8 Favorites Center.

1   Click the Favorites button ( ).

2   The Favorites Center opens. Click the History tab.

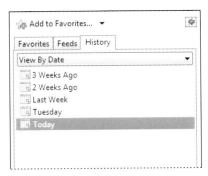

Click the History tab in the Favorites Center.

3 By default, the History list is sorted by date. To sort by a different criterion—site, most visited, or order visited today—choose the desired option from the drop-down menu at the top of the History tab. View By Site was used in this example.

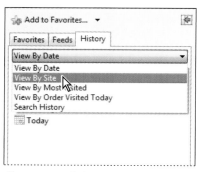

Choose a sort method.

4 Internet Explorer 8 displays a list of the sites you've visited. Click a site in the list.

5 A list of pages you accessed on that site appears. Click the desired page; the page opens in your browser window.

Click a page in the History list to open it in Internet Explorer 8.

Search History

Another way to locate a page from your History list is to search for it.

1 Open the Favorites Center and click the History tab.

2 Choose Search History Click from the drop-down menu at the top of the History tab.

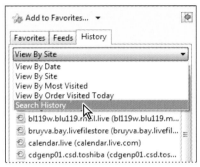

Click the down arrow in the History tab and choose Search History.

3 Type a relevant keyword or phrase in the Search for text field.

4 Press the Search Now button.

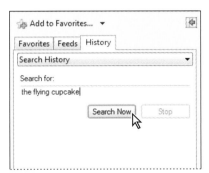

Type a keyword or phrase and press Search Now.

5   Internet Explorer 8 displays a list of pages that match the keyword or phrase you typed; click an entry in the list to launch the page.

Click a page in the History list to open it in Internet Explorer 8.

Deleting History list items

If you like, you can delete the contents of your History list in order to protect your privacy. You might do this if, for example, you have conducted your web session using a public computer, such as one at a library or Internet café and you don't want the next person who uses the computer to see what sites you visited.

1   Press the Safety button near the upper-right corner of the Internet Explorer 8 window.

2   Click Delete Browsing History in the menu that appears.

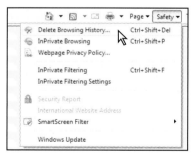

Choose Delete Browsing History from the Safety menu.

3   The Delete Browsing History dialog box opens. If necessary, click the *History* checkbox to select it.

4   Press the Delete button. Internet Explorer 8 deletes your browsing history.

The Delete Browsing History dialog box.

InPrivate browsing

Internet Explorer 8 offers a new feature called InPrivate mode. When you use Internet Explorer 8 in InPrivate mode, the browser does not store information about your browsing history. This is useful if you are using a public computer, or if you are using the family computer to shop for a gift for a family member. To browse the Web using InPrivate mode, press the Safety button in the Internet Explorer 8 toolbar and choose InPrivate Browsing from the menu that appears. Internet Explorer 8 launches a new browser window with a special InPrivate icon (InPrivate) in the address bar and conduct your web session in this browser window. To end the InPrivate session, close the browser window.

Subscribing to RSS feeds

Really Simple Syndication, RSS for short, enables web content such as blogs, podcasts, and news to be syndicated. The content is converted to a web feed, also called an RSS feed, to which you can subscribe. When you subscribe to a web feed, Internet Explorer 8 automatically checks for and downloads feed updates. For example, if you have subscribed to a blog feed, Internet Explorer 8 will automatically download new blog entries. You can access and view all the RSS feeds to which you have subscribed using a special pane in Internet Explorer 8.

When you visit a web page featuring an RSS feed, Internet Explorer 8's Feeds button changes from gray (◙) to orange (◙).

1 With the page containing the RSS feed to which you want to subscribe open in Internet Explorer 8, press the Feeds button (◙).

2 Internet Explorer 8 displays a special page containing information about the feed. Click Subscribe to This Feed.

Click Subscribe to This Feed.

3 The Subscribe to This Feed dialog box opens. Here you can type a more descriptive name for the feed.

4   If you want to be able to access the feed from the Favorites bar, click the *Add to Favorites Bar* checkbox to select it.

The Subscribe to This Feed dialog box.

5   Press the Subscribe button. Internet Explorer 8 subscribes you to the feed.

Viewing a feed

1   Click the Favorites button ( ).

2   The Favorites Center opens. Click the Feeds tab. A list of the feeds to which you have subscribed appears.

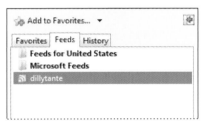

Click the Feeds tab in the Favorites Center.

Internet Explorer 8 includes a few feeds by default, including Microsoft at Home, Microsoft at Work, and MSNBC News.

3   Click the feed you want to view. Internet Explorer 8 opens the web page on which the feed is found.

Deleting a feed

If you decide you no longer wish to subscribe to a feed, you can delete it.

1 Open the Favorites Center and click the Feeds tab.

2 Right-click the feed you want to delete.

3 Choose Delete from the menu that appears.

Right-click a feed and choose Delete.

4 Internet Explorer 8 prompts you to confirm the deletion. Press Yes.

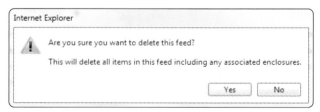

Confirm deletion of an RSS feed.

Using Web slices

If you want to track information on a web page, for example, the status of an online auction, the score of a game, or the value of a stock, but you don't want to repeatedly visit that page, you may be able to create a Web slice for it. When you create a Web slice, Internet Explorer 8 displays the Web slice on your Favorites bar. As the page associated with the slice is updated, the Web slice becomes highlighted; you can click the highlighted Web slice to quickly view the updated information.

1　With the page containing the information you want to save as a Web slice open in Internet Explorer 8, hover your mouse button over the item on the page you want to track.

2　If a Web slice can be created for that item, a Web Slice button (▫) appears. Press the Web Slice button.

3　An Internet Explorer dialog box opens, containing information about the Web slice you are about to create. Press the Add to Favorites Bar button.

Press the Add to Favorites Bar button.

4   A button for the Web slice appears on the Favorites bar. When the Web slice's content has been updated, the button becomes highlighted; press the button to view a preview of the new content.

Click the Web slice to view updated content.

If the slices do not update, be sure that Subscribe to Web Slices is enabled. This is found in the Web Slice Gallery located in the browser tool bar above any Tabs.

Using Accelerators

Have you ever wanted to, say, map an address or translate a word on a web page? Accelerators make it easy to access the information you need without opening additional web pages.

1   Select the text on a page that you want to research further, such as, a street address. An Accelerator button (⬀) appears.

Select the desired text.

2   Press the Accelerator button. A menu appears.

Click the Accelerator button to display a menu.

3   Place your mouse pointer over the desired menu option, select Map with Live Search. Internet Explorer 8 displays a map showing the location of the highlighted street address.

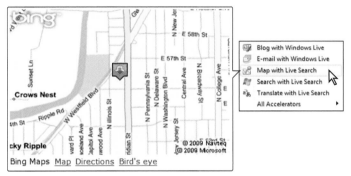

Internet Explorer 8 displays relevant information about the selected text (here, a map).

Customizing Internet Explorer 8

If you like, you can adjust your Internet Explorer 8 settings to direct how it looks and behaves. For example, you can specify which web page loads at startup, reconfigure your browser's toolbars, control the size of the text that your browser displays, and more. Before you adjust a setting, take a moment to note its original state. That way, if you don't like the result of the adjustment, you can change it back.

Changing Your Home Page

If you frequently visit a particular web page, for example, one containing news headlines, the local weather forecast, or an Internet e-mail site, you can direct Internet Explorer 8 to open that page by default anytime you launch the program or press the browser's Home button (⌂). This saves you the trouble of typing the site's URL in the address bar or selecting the site from your Favorites list.

1 With the page you want to set as your home page open in the Internet Explorer 8 window, click the down arrow to the right of the Home button (⌂).

2 Choose Add or Change Home Page from the menu that appears.

Click the Home button and choose Add or Change Home Page.

3 The Add or Change Home Page dialog box appears. Click the *Use this webpage as your only home page* option to select it.

Choose Use this webpage as your only home page *and press Yes.*

4 Press Yes. Windows sets the current page as your home page.

Setting multiple home pages

If you frequently access several sites, for example, a national news site, a local news site, your friend's blog, and a site that contains the latest stock information, you can configure Internet Explorer 8 to launch all these pages whenever you start the browser, or press the browser's Home button ( ).

1   With one of the pages you want to launch at startup open in the Internet Explorer 8 window, click the down arrow to the right of the Home button ( ).

2   Choose Add or Change Home Page from the menu that appears.

3   The Add or Change Home Page dialog box appears. Click the *Add this webpage to your home page tabs* option to select it.

Choose Add this webpage to your home page tabs *and press Yes.*

4   Press Yes.

5   Repeat steps 1 through 4 to add any other pages you want to launch at the startup of Internet Explorer 8.

Remove a home page

1   Click the down arrow to the right of the Home button.

2   Choose Remove from the menu that appears.

3   Internet Explorer 8 displays a list of pages set to launch at startup; click the page you no longer want to launch. Alternatively, press Remove All.

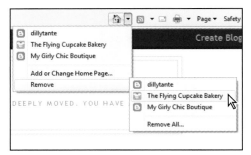

Remove a Home Page.

Personalizing Your Browser Toolbar

The Internet Explorer 8 toolbar has buttons for moving backward and forward through pages you have visited, stopping a page from loading, refreshing a page, printing a page, and more. You can customize this toolbar by adding or removing buttons, rearranging the buttons, and so on.

1   Press the Tools button in the Internet Explorer 8 toolbar.

2   In the menu that appears, click Toolbars.

3   Click Customize.

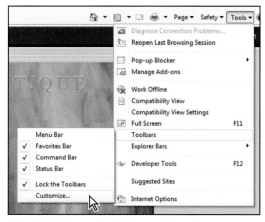

Click the Tools button, click Toolbars, and choose Customize.

4   The Customize Toolbar dialog box opens. In the Available toolbar buttons list, click a button you want to add to your toolbar.

An even faster way to open the Customize Toolbar dialog box is to right-click an empty area of the Internet Explorer 8 toolbar and choose Customize Toolbar from the menu that appears.

5 Press the Add button.

Add a button to the Internet Explorer 8 toolbar.

6 The button appears in the Current toolbar buttons list. To change the order in which the button appears, click it in the Current toolbar buttons list, then press the Move Up or Move Down button as many times as needed to situate the button in the desired order.

7 To remove a button from the toolbar, press the button in the Current toolbar buttons list.

8 Press the Remove button.

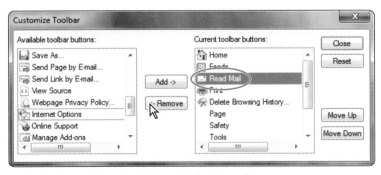

Rearrange and remove buttons in the Current Toolbar Buttons list.

9 The button is removed from the Current Toolbar buttons list and now appears in the Available Toolbar Buttons list. Press the Close button; the Internet Explorer 8 toolbar reflects your changes.

Rearrange and remove buttons in the Current Toolbar Buttons list.

Displaying the menu bar

You can also specify whether the Internet Explorer menu bar should be displayed in the browser window. The menu bar offers an additional way to access various browser tools and commands.

1 Press the Tools button in the Internet Explorer 8 toolbar.

2 In the menu that appears, click Toolbars.

3 Click Menu Bar. A checkmark appears next to the Menu Bar menu option, and Internet Explorer 8 displays the menu bar in the browser window (beneath the address bar).

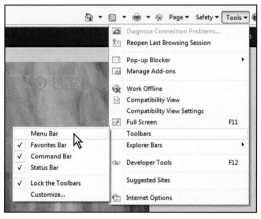
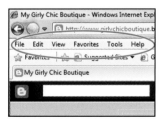

Click the Tools button, click Toolbars, and choose Menu Bar; the menu bar appears in the Internet Explorer 8 browser window.

An even faster way to display the menu bar is to right-click an empty area of the Internet Explorer 8 toolbar and choose Menu Bar from the menu that appears. Notice that a checkmark is added to the menu option. To remove the menu bar, again right-click an empty area of the Internet Explorer 8 toolbar and choose Menu Bar from the menu that appears.

Changing Text size

Instead of indicating a specific size for text, most web pages contain code that specifies the relative size of text on the page. For example, the person who built the page might indicate that text in the web page's title should be larger than the text that appears below it, but not the precise size. Your web browser interprets this code according to its own settings to determine exactly how large the text appears.

You can adjust Internet Explorer 8's Text Size setting to control how large or small text appears onscreen. For example, you might opt to make text appear smaller in order to view more text on the screen without scrolling down.

1 Press the Page button in the Internet Explorer 8 toolbar.

2 In the menu that appears, click Text Size.

3 Click a size option. Internet Explorer 8 resizes the text on the screen.

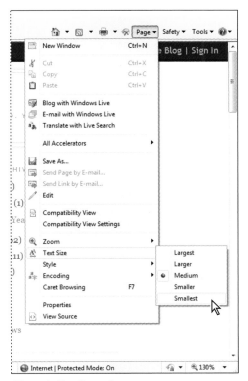

Change the Text Size setting.

Changing Graphics size

The Text Size setting applies to text only; adjusting it will not affect how large or small graphics appear on your screen, even if the graphics contain words. If you want to change how large or small graphics appear, you can use your browser's zoom tools to zoom in and out:

1   Press the Page button in the Internet Explorer 8 toolbar.

2   In the menu that appears, click Zoom.

3   Click a size option. Internet Explorer 8 zooms in on the page.

An even faster way to zoom in on or out of a page is to press Ctrl+(plus sign) or Ctrl+(minus sign).

Installing the Silverlight plug-in

Siliverlight is an increasingly popular platform for viewing video, games, and interactive content on-line. It is used on sites such as NBC Sports for streaming live Olympic video coverage or live football coverage, and by Netflix for subscribers who want to watch movies on-line. Fortunately it takes less than a minute to download and install.

1   With Internet Explorer 8 open, navigate to *www.DigitalClassroomBooks.com.* Click the Get Microsoft® Silverlight™ icon on the right side of the screen.

Click the Get Microsoft® Silverlight™ icon.

If you can see the video, then your browser already has the Silverlight Plug-in installed.

2   A File Download – Security Warning dialog box appears. Press the Run button. The Silverlight.exe file is downloaded from Microsoft's web site.

3   Another security warning dialog box appears asking you if you would like to Run or Don't Run the file. Press Run. If a User Account Control dialog box appears asking if you want to allow the following program to make changes to this computer, press Yes.

4   The Install Silverlight 3 window appears. Press Install now. The plug-in installs. When the installation is successful, a message is displayed. Press Close.

The installation was successful.

5   Quit Internet Explorer 8 by choosing File > Exit.

6   Start Internet Explorer 8 and return to *www.DigitalClassroomBooks.com*. The video tutorial in the upper right corner displays. Click the video to view it and confirm that the Silverlight plug-in has been correctly installed.

The video can now be seen on the web site.

Exploring Windows Live

Windows 7 omits some features that appear in earlier versions of the operating system. Microsoft makes these tools, and others, available from Windows Live, a Microsoft-run web site. Windows Live offers several online services, including the following:

- **Hotmail**. Stay in touch via e-mail using this Web-based e-mail service.
- **Photos**. Share your favorite pictures with friends and family alike.
- **People**. Store information about contacts using this online address book.
- **Calendar**. Coordinate your commitments and share your schedule with others.

Windows Live also offers access to various applications that you can download to your computer, such as the following:

- **Messenger**. Use this program to chat with friends and family.
- **Photo Gallery**. Edit, organize, tag, and share your photos using this robust image program.
- **Mail**. Read and reply to e-mail messages.
- **Writer**. Use Writer to compose posts for your blog.
- **Movie Maker**. Microsoft's Movie Maker makes it easy to create memorable videos and publish them to the Web.

You'll learn how to use all these Windows Live tools throughout the book.

Creating a Windows Live account

Before you can use the various Windows Live offerings, you must first set up an account.

1   Type **www.windowslive.com** in the Internet Explorer 8 address bar.

2   Press the Sign Up button.

Press the Sign up button on the Windows Live web site.

3 When you sign up for Windows Live, you must create a user ID. Type the ID you'd like to use in the Windows Live ID field. To determine whether that ID is available, press the Check Availability button.

4 Type the password you want to use to log on to your Windows Live account in the Create a Password text field.

5 Type the password a second time in the Retype Password text field to confirm it.

6 In the Alternate E-mail Address text field, type the address for an e-mail account you already hold. This is so Windows Live can send you your password in the event you forget it.

7 In the First Name text field, type your first name.

8 In the Last Name text field, type your last name.

9 Select your country or region from the Country/Region drop-down menu.

10 Select your state from the State drop-down menu.

11 Type your ZIP code in the ZIP Code text field.

12 Select your gender from the Male or Female option.

13 Type the year you were born in the Birth Year text field.

14 Type the characters you see in the Characters text field.

15 Press the I Accept button. Windows Live creates your account.

Signing in to Windows Live

Once you have a Windows Live account, you can sign in anytime.

1 Type **www.windowslive.com** in the Internet Explorer 8 address bar.

2 Select your Windows Live ID.

3 Type your password in the text field that appears.

4 If you want Windows Live to remember your password, click the *Save My Password* checkbox to select it. That way, you won't need to retype your password to sign in every time you visit Windows Live.

5   Press the Sign In button to sign in.

Sign in to Windows Live.

Downloading Windows Live applications

Windows Live offers access to applications that you can download to your computer, such as Messenger, Mail, Photo Gallery, and Movie Maker.

1   While signed into Windows Live, click the More link along the top of the page.

2   Choose Downloads.

Click the More link and choose Downloads.

3   The Windows Live Essentials page opens. Press the Download button.

Click the Download button.

4   Press the Run button in the File Download – Security Warning dialog box that appears.

Click the Run button.

5 The Windows 7 User Account Control dialog box prompts you to authorize the download. Press Yes. Windows begins the download process.

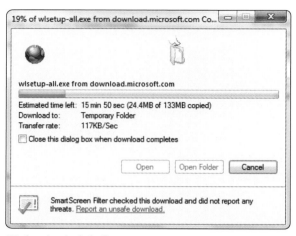

Windows downloads the files.

6 The Windows 7 User Account Control dialog box prompts you again. Press Yes.

7 Windows prompts you to specify what programs you want to install. Ensure that the checkbox next to each desired program is checked. In this example, Messenger, Mail, Photo Gallery, Writer, and Movie Maker are selected.

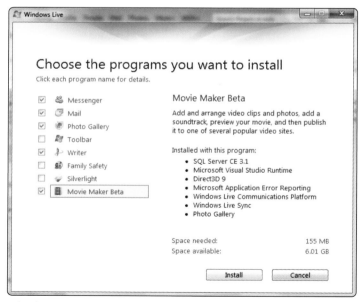

Select the programs you want to install.

8   Press Install. Windows Live installs the selected programs.

Windows installs the programs you selected.

9   After the installation is complete, Windows asks if you want to set Windows Live as your search provider, set MSN as your home page or participate in a program to help improve Windows Live. If so, select the appropriate checkboxes. Then press Continue.

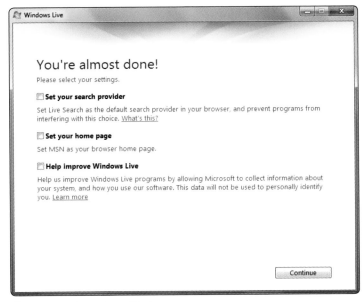

Choose your settings and press Continue.

10 Microsoft welcomes you to Windows Live. Press the Close button.

You'll be introduced to the Windows Live applications in Lessons 12 and 13.

Self study

1 Add those pages you visit most often to your Favorites list, creating subfolders as needed to group related sites together.

2 Determine which tools you use most regularly when browsing the Web with Internet Explorer 8. Then customize the browser's toolbar to include those buttons you use most often, arranging them for easy access.

Review

Questions

1 Name three ways to open a web page in Internet Explorer 8.

2 True or false: You must use Internet Explorer 8's default search provider when using the Search box to the right of the address bar.

3 Where does Internet Explorer 8 save your favorites?

4 What is Windows Live?

Answers

1 You can open a web page in Internet Explorer 8 by typing the page's URL in the address bar, by clicking the page in the Internet Explorer 8 jump list on the Windows Taskbar, or by clicking a link on another page. In addition, you can open a web page by clicking it in your Favorites list or in the History list.

2 False. You can set up the Search text field to use any number of search providers.

3 Favorites are saved in the Favorites list, and are placed in the top-level Favorites folder by default. If you like, however, you can create subfolders for grouping related pages—for example, creating one subfolder for news sites, a second subfolder for sites that relate to a favorite hobby, a third subfolder for travel sites, and so on.

4 Windows Live is a Microsoft-run web site that offers several online services as well as access to various applications that you can download to your computer.

Lesson 6

What you'll learn in this lesson:

- Building your media library with Windows Media Player
- Finding files in Windows Media Player
- Creating and saving playlists
- Syncing a mobile device with Windows Media Player

Enjoying Audio and Video with Windows 7

Using Windows 7, you can listen to music and play videos. Whether from a DVD, CD, or a media file, Windows 7 has the ability to keep you entertained.

Starting up

Before you start, be sure to copy all the files for this lesson from the accompanying DVD to your hard drive.

See Lesson 10 in action!

Use the accompanying video to gain a better understanding of how to use some of the features shown in this lesson. The video tutorial for this lesson can be found on the included DVD.

Windows 7 music software

Windows 7 includes many easy-to-use tools for you to access and share your audio and video files.

- **The Music folder.** The Music folder acts as a central repository for audio files that you download from the Internet, or copy from a CD. The Music folder enables you to see all your audio files in one place and to sort them by name, date, tag, rating, and other file properties. For more information about tagging, rating, and sorting files, refer to Lesson 3, "Working with Files and Folders." Its window contains special toolbar buttons for listening to your audio files, sharing them with others, and burning them to a CD.

  To view the Music folder, press the Start button (⬤) and choose Music. Within the Music folder is a Sample Music folder, double-click this folder to preview the music files.

The Music folder.

- **The Videos folder**. Just as the Music folder acts as a central repository for audio files, the Videos folder is the default location for video files. These might be videos you've downloaded from the Internet, received via e-mail, or imported from your camcorder or phone. You can play back, share, and burn video files to a CD or DVD using the Videos folder's toolbar buttons. You can also sort files by name, date, tag, rating, and other file properties. For more information about tagging, rating, and sorting files, refer to Lesson 3, "Working with Files and Folders."

To access the Videos folder, press the Start button (●), then choose Documents. On the left side of the window that appears, click Videos under the Libraries section. In the Videos folder is a Sample videos folder, double click it to open it, then select the sample file to preview it.

The Videos folder.

- **Windows Media Player.** You can use Windows Media Player to organize your media collection, play back your audio and video files, listen to CDs, watch DVDs, rip music from CDs into your personal library, create playlists of your favorite songs, create mix CDs, and sync your audio and video files to a portable media player. If you are connected to the Internet, you can also use Windows Media Player to shop for music online, listen to Internet radio broadcasts, and access video content such as movie previews. Audio and video files in your Windows 7 Music and Video folders appear in the Windows Media Player library by default. That means any steps you take to manage your music files in your Music and Video folders—for example, editing their names, rating them, or deleting them—will be reflected in Windows Media Player, and vice versa.

Windows Media Player.

- **Windows Media Center**. Like Windows Media Player, Windows Media Center includes support for organizing and playing back your music and video files, listening to CDs, watching DVDs, creating playlists, burning CDs of your favorite songs, watching Internet TV, and listening to Internet radio. It also includes support for watching and recording live TV, if your computer has TV tuner for capturing an incoming TV signal. Unlike Windows Media Player, Windows Media Center is designed to serve as a home-entertainment hub, working in concert with your television, or home-stereo equipment.

Windows Media Center.

This chapter focuses on Windows Media Player, which is Windows 7's default media player, because no additional hardware is required to make it work. You start Windows Media Player just as you do any other program: by clicking its icon in the Start menu. Alternatively, you can click the Windows Media Player button (▶) in the Windows 7 taskbar.

Windows Media Player modes

Windows Media Player enables you enjoy your audio and video content using two different modes:

- **Player Library mode.** This mode offers full control over Windows Media Player, enabling you to access and organize your media collection, create playlists, locate specific media files, and play back your files. The tabs in the top-right corner of the Player Library screen offer access to all the tools you need to play files, burn CDs, and sync a playlist to a portable media player. Simply click the Play, Burn, or Sync tab to view its associated tools; click it a second time to hide the tools.

Player Library mode.

- **Now Playing mode**. If you just want to listen to music, Now Playing mode is ideal. This simplified interface, which offers only playback controls, occupies less space on your desktop, freeing you to work on other tasks. You can also rip music tracks from a CD in Now Playing mode.

Now Playing mode.

To switch from Player Library mode to Now Playing mode, press the Switch to Now Playing button (⸬) in the lower-right corner of the Windows Media Player window. Alternatively, you can press the Alt key and choose View > Now Playing.

To switch back from Now Playing mode to Player Library mode, press Go to Library in the Now Playing screen or press the Switch to Library button (⊞) in the upper-right corner. If this button is not visible, simply move your mouse pointer anywhere in the Now Playing screen to display it.

Building your media library with Windows Media Player

Audio files in your Windows 7 Music folder appear in the Windows Media Player library by default, as do videos in your Windows 7 Videos folder. You can also use Windows Media Player to rip tracks from CDs in your collection or to purchase content online. Note that when you add to your media library in this way, the contents of your Windows 7 Music and Videos folders are duly updated.

Importing content from a video camera

If you want to add content from a digital video camera to your library, connect your camera to your computer and launch Windows Live Photo Gallery. You explored using this program in Lesson 13, "Working with Images."

1 In the Windows Live Photo Gallery window, click File and choose Import from a Camera or Scanner in the menu that appears.

2 The Import Photos and Videos dialog box opens, displaying image-related devices that are connected to your computer; click the device that contains your movie and then click Import.

3 In the next dialog box, click the Review, Organize, and Group Items to Import radio button and then click Next.

4 Windows Live Photo Gallery groups the files on your connected device by date and time. Click Import. Windows Live Gallery imports your video. If your videos are placed in your Pictures folder rather than your Videos folder, you can move them. Click My Pictures in the Windows Live Photo Gallery folder list, locate the video in the file list, and drag it into the My Videos folder in the folder list.

Ripping tracks from a music CD

Windows Media Player makes it easy to rip, or copy, tracks on CDs in your collection and store them on your computer. After you rip a track, you can listen to it on your computer, add it to a playlist, burn it on a mix CD, or sync it to a portable music player. You can access the files you rip from Windows Media Player and from your Music folder.

1 With Windows Media Player open, insert the CD that contains the tracks you want to rip in your computer's CD drive.

2 Windows Media Player displays a list of the CD's tracks in its own window. To rip only certain songs, click the check boxes next to any songs you want to omit to deselect them.

3 Press Rip CD. Windows Media Player copies the selected tracks to your music library.

Rip tracks from a CD

Buying content online

If you are connected to the Internet, you can find music and video content online, right from within Windows Media Player. You have access to numerous online stores, although the stores available to you may vary depending on your location. Some stores offer content to which you can subscribe; in others, you purchase the content outright, downloading it to your computer. You can access the content you purchase online from Windows Media Player and from your Music and Video folders.

Be aware that much of the content available from these stores is protected by media usage rights, which specify what you can do with the content—play it, download it, buy it, burn it to a CD or DVD, and/or synchronize it to a portable device such as an MP3 player.

To access these online stores, select Browse all online stores from the Media Guide or the Online Stores drop-down menu, depending on which one is visible, in the bottom-left corner of the Windows Media Player window. Windows Media Player displays a list of stores; select a store to view it.

Access online stores from Windows Media Player.

To purchase music from an online store, you must first create an account with the store. The ins and outs of using an online store differ depending on which store it is. For information about how to use a specific store, click the Help link on the store's page.

If you plan to visit a particular online store on a regular basis, you can add it to the list that appears when you click the Online Stores button. That way, you won't have to browse all the online stores every time you want to visit this one. To do so, click the arrow beneath the store's logo and choose Add Current Service to Menu.

Add a store to the Online Stores menu.

Creating your own video content with Windows Live Movie Maker

You can use Windows Live Movie Maker to create simple movies in a matter of minutes—complete with audio, video transitions, video effects, and titles—using video or images on your hard drive. You can then share your movies with others by sending them as an e-mail attachment, posting them on a web site, or burning them to a disc. As discussed in Lesson 5, "Surfing the Web with Internet Explorer 8," you download Windows Live Movie Maker from the Windows Live web site. For more details, view the program's help information.

Finding media files in Windows Media Player

If your media collection is particularly large, finding the files you want to listen to or watch can be somewhat difficult. To make it easier to find files Windows Media Player enables you to sort them or search for a particular file.

Rating files in Windows Media Player

You can apply a rating to a file from the Music or Videos folder, as outlined in Lesson 3, or from within Windows Media Player. When you rate a file in Windows Media Player, the program uses the same rating system as your Windows 7 folders, with five stars being the highest rating. To rate a file in Windows Media Player, simply locate it in the Player Library and click the star in the Rating column that represents the rating you want to apply. For example, to give the file a two-star rating, click the second star; to apply a five-star rating, click the fifth star. If no rating column is displayed, right-click the file you want to rate, click Rate in the menu that appears, and then click the appropriate star. Windows Media Player applies your rating.

Sorting files in Windows Media Player

Sorting your music files in Windows Media Player is a snap.

1 Click Music in the folder list.

2 Press the Organize button.

3 Click Sort By.

4 Choose the parameter by which you want to sort—here, Title. Windows Media Player sorts the music files accordingly.

Choose a sort parameter.

You follow the same steps to sort your video files, except instead of clicking Music in the folder list, you click Videos. Then click the Organize button, choose Sort By, and select the parameter by which you want to sort.

Searching for a file in Windows Media Player

In addition to sorting files to locate the one you want, you can also use Windows Media Player's Search text field to search for a file. Simply type a keyword or phrase in the Search text field—say, the name of the song you seek—and press Enter. Windows Media Player displays a list of files that match your criteria in the file list.

Search for files in Windows Media Player.

Listening to music

You can listen to music a couple different ways in Windows Media Player: by playing back the audio files stored on your computer's hard drive or by playing back tracks on a CD you've inserted into your computer's CD drive. You can also use Windows Media Player's Media Guide feature to access Internet radio stations.

Listening to songs and albums in your media library

Assuming you've located the song you want to listen to in Windows Media Player, playing it is as simple as clicking a button. You can opt to hear just the song or the entire album on which the song is found, provided you have the entire album stored on your computer.

1   In the folder list, click Music.

2   In the file list, locate and click the song you want to hear.

3   Press the Play button ( ) in the controls along the bottom of the Windows Media Player screen. The Play button changes to a Pause button ( ) and Windows Media Player plays back the song.

Another way to play a song is to right-click it and choose Play from the menu that appears, or simply double-click the song.

4   Optionally, to confirm that this song—and only this song—will be played back, click the Play tab. The song you chose will be the only one listed in the tab.

5   Drag the Volume slider in the player controls to adjust the volume. To mute the volume, press the Mute button (••); press the Mute button a second time to unmute the volume.

6   Notice that the Seek bar indicates which part of the song is currently playing; to move forward or backward in the song, click the Seek bar's slider handle and drag it to the desired spot on the Seek bar.

A. Seek bar. B. Volume slider.

7   To play back the song more than once, click the Repeat button (○). Windows Media Player will continue repeating the song until you click the Repeat button again to deselect it or you stop playback.

8   To stop playback, press the Stop button (■).

Playback the entire album

1   In the folder list, click Music.

2   In the file list, locate and double-click the album you want to hear. The Play button in the player controls changes to a Pause button and Windows Media Player plays back the song.

3   Optionally, to confirm that the entire album will play back, click the Play tab. All the songs in the album are listed in the tab.

Play back an album.

4   To skip to the next song in the album, press the Next button (▸▸).

5   To skip to the previous song in the album, press the Back button (◂◂).

6   To shuffle the order in which songs in the album are played back, press the Shuffle button (⚡).

7   To repeat playback of the entire album, press the Repeat button (○). Windows Media Player will continue repeating the album until you click the Repeat button again to deselect it or you stop playback.

8   To stop playback, press the Stop button (▪).

Sometimes, you may opt to minimize your Windows Media Player window in order to focus on other work while listening to your music. If so, you can control playback from the Windows Media Player thumbnail preview on your taskbar—playing or pausing the current song, advancing to the next song, or skipping to the previous one. To do so, simply hover your mouse pointer over the Windows Media Player taskbar button (▣). A thumbnail image of the Windows Media Player window appears; click the appropriate control.

Control Windows Media Player from the taskbar.

Playing a music CD

If you have a vast collection of CDs, you can play them on your computer using Windows Media Player). To play back a CD, open Windows Media Player and then insert the CD into the CD drive. Windows Media Player displays an entry for the disc in the folder list and the contents of the disc in the file list, and the disc begins playing. You use the same controls—the Volume slider, the Mute button (•), the Seek bar's slider handle, the Shuffle button (•), the Repeat button (◦), the Back button (◂◂), the Next button (▸▸), and the Stop button (■)—when playing a music CD as you do when playing back music files on your hard drive. You can also control playback of the CD by hovering your mouse pointer over the Windows Media Player taskbar button and using the buttons that appear.

If you only want to hear certain songs on the CD, simply click the checkboxes next to any songs you want to omit to deselect them. Windows Media Player will skip unchecked songs during playback.

Listening to Internet radio with Windows Media Player

The Windows Media Player Media Guide is an online resource that is updated regularly to provide links to a variety of Internet content, such as music and video clips. Access to Internet radio stations is also available here.

1   Press the Media Guide button in the bottom-left corner of the Windows Media Player window. If this button is not visible, choose Media Guide from the Online Stores drop-down menu.

2   Click the Internet Radio link. The Windows Media Guide displays a list of genres, as well as editors' picks. To find a station in a particular genre, click the genre. If the genre you seek is not shown, click the Show All Genres link.

The Internet Radio screen in the Windows Media Player Media Guide.

3   The Media Guide displays a list of stations in the genre you chose. Click a station's Listen link to listen.

Click the Listen link to listen to a station.

If you know the name or call letters of the station you seek, you can search for it. Click the Search for Radio Stations link in the main Internet Radio screen and enter your search criteria in the Radio Station Search screen that appears.

Watching videos

As with audio, you can watch videos in a couple different ways in Windows Media Player: by playing back the video files stored on your computer's hard drive or by playing a DVD you've inserted into your computer's DVD drive. You can also use Windows Media Player's Media Guide feature to access video content such as movie previews.

Watching videos in your media library

Like listening to music files, watching a video stored on your computer's hard drive is a snap: Simply click the Video entry in the folder list, locate and click the video you want to watch in the file list, and then click the Play button (▶) in the controls along the bottom of the Windows Media Player screen. The Play button changes to a Pause button (⏸) and Windows Media Player plays back the video. You can also play back a video by right-clicking it in the Player Library and choosing Play from the menu that appears or by simply double-clicking the video.

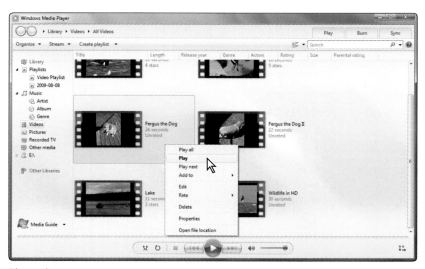

Play a video.

When you play a video, Windows Media Player automatically switches to Now Playing mode; to view the player controls, simply place your mouse over the Now Playing window. As you probably guessed, you use the same controls—the Volume slider, the Mute button (••), the Seek bar's slider handle, the Shuffle button (ᴠ), the Repeat button (ᴏ), the Back button (••), the Next button (••), and the Stop button (•)—to play back videos as you do to play back music.

To view the video in Full screen, press the View full screen button (▣) in the lower right corner of the window. Press this button again to exit Full screen mode.

Windows Media Player switches to Now Playing mode when you play back a video.

Once the video has ended, you can return to the Library by pressing the Switch to Library button (⊞) in the upper right corner of the window.

Playing a DVD

In addition to watching videos you've stored on your hard drive, you can also use Windows Media Player to watch a DVD. To play a DVD, simply insert it into your computer's DVD drive.

1   If it doesn't automatically display the DVD's menu, in Windows Media Player, click the icon for the DVD in the folder list.

2   Right-click the movie in the file list and choose play.

Launch the menu screen.

3   The DVD menu appears. Press Play. Windows Media Player plays the DVD. To enlarge
the window, click its Maximize button (▣).

Windows Media Player plays back the contents of the DVD.

Accessing video content online with the Windows Media Guide

As mentioned, the Windows Media Player Media Guide is a regularly updated online resource
that offers links to Internet content, including video clips. To view a video clip featured in the
Media Guide, follow these steps:

1   Press the Media Guide button in the bottom-left corner of the Windows Media Player
window. If this button is not visible, choose Media Guide from the Online Stores
drop-down menu.

2   Click one of the pictures on the main page to view its associated content. Alternatively,
click the Movies or TV link.

3   Choose an option from the menu that appears.

Choose an option from the menu.

4   Click one of the pictures in the page that appears to view its associated content.

Click a picture to view its associated content.

Creating and saving playlists

If you want to listen to more than just a single song or a single album or watch multiple videos in a row, you can stack up files in a playlist. Windows Media Player then plays the songs or videos in your playlist in the order you specify.

Creating a playlist

1   Click the Play tab to display it.

2   If the Play tab already contains other items, press the Clear List button to remove them.

3 Locate an audio or video file you want to include in your playlist, click and drag it to the Play tab. Windows Media Player adds the item to the playlist and begins playing it back.

Add a file to your playlist.

4 Continue adding files to the playlist until it contains everything you want to hear or watch.

5 To rearrange the order of the contents of the playlist, click a file you want to move and drag it to the desired location in the list.

Change the file order.

6   To sort the contents of the playlist, press the List Options button (⊟·), choose Sort List By from the menu that appears, and select a sort parameter (for example, Title).

Sort files in the playlist.

7   To remove a file from the playlist, right-click it and choose Remove from List from the menu that appears. Note that removing a file from a playlist simply deletes it from the list. It does not remove it from your Windows Media Player library.

Remove a file from the playlist.

Saving a playlist

If you develop a playlist you particularly like, you can save it. When you save a playlist, you can then open it in a later session to listen to the set of songs or view the videos it contains. To save a playlist, simply press the Save List button in the Play tab, type a name for the playlist, and press Enter.

Save a playlist.

Playing back a playlist

To play back a saved playlist, click the right arrow next to Playlists in the left pane of Windows Media Player, right-click the playlist you want to play back, and choose Play in the menu that appears.

Play back a saved playlist.

When you play back files in a playlist, you use the same controls as when you play back a single video, a single song, or an album: the Volume slider, the Mute button (•)), the Seek bar's slider handle, the Shuffle button (⋈), the Repeat button (↻), the Back button (◄◄), the Next button (►►), and the Stop button (■).

Deleting a playlist

If you no longer wish to keep a playlist, you can easily delete it. Right-click the playlist in the left pane of the Windows Media Player window and choose Delete from the menu that appears. When prompted, specify whether the playlist should be deleted from your library only, or from your library and your computer, then press OK.

Burning CDs and DVDs

You can create an audio CD for playback on your car stereo or burn your favorite media files to a DVD for a friend so they can view them on their own computer. In order to burn a CD or DVD using Windows Media Player, you need a blank recordable CD or DVD as well as a CD or DVD drive that is capable of recording to disc.

You cannot use Windows Media Player to create DVDs for playback on a standard DVD player like you might have attached to your home television. Windows 7 does include a program called Windows DVD Maker that enables you to do just that.

One way to specify which content you want to include on the disc is by creating and saving a playlist, as discussed in the previous section. Alternatively, you can click the Burn tab in the Player Library window and drag the files you want to burn to the disc into the tab.

Burning an audio CD

You can use Windows Media Player to burn audio CDs, which you can play back using any standard CD player. You might burn a CD if, for example, you are planning to take a long road trip and you would like to listen to your music while in the car. When you burn an audio CD, Windows Media Player converts the files in your library, which are compressed to save space, into an uncompressed format meant for playback on an audio CD.

1   In the left pane of the Windows Media Player window, right-click the playlist you want to burn to a CD.

2   Choose Add To.

3 Select Burn List.

Right-click the playlist, choose Add To, and select Burn List.

4 Windows Media Player opens the Burn tab, with the contents of the playlist displayed. Insert a blank audio CD.

 Another way to populate the Burn tab is to simply drag items from your music library into it.

5 If the AutoPlay dialog box opens, press its Close button (▬) to close it.

6 Press Start Burn. Windows Media Player burns the contents of your playlist onto the blank CD. This may take several minutes.

 If your playlist is too long to fit on a single CD, Windows Media Player will give you the option of burning the remaining items on a second blank CD.

Burn the CD.

7 When the burn is complete, click Clear List to remove the playlist from the Burn tab.

Burning audio and video files to a data CD or DVD

In addition to burning audio CDs, which can be played back using any standard CD player, you can also burn your music as data files to a CD. That is, you can burn them to a CD in their original, data format, such as MP3 or WMA, rather than converting them to a format for playback on a standard CD player. In addition to burning audio files as data, you can also burn video files this way; these video files can then be played back on any computer with Windows Media Player or similar software.

When you burn your music files as data files, you can fit many more files on a disc—to the tune of several hours of music. The drawback: These CDs can only be played back on a computer or on a stereo system that supports the format in which the music files have been stored.

1. Repeat steps 1 to 3 in the section "Burning an Audio CD," right-clicking the playlist you want to burn to a CD, choosing Add To, and selecting Burn List. Windows Media Player opens the Burn tab, with the contents of the playlist displayed. Another way to populate the Burn tab is to simply drag items in your media library into it.

2. Press the Burn Options button (⌐) and choose Data CD or DVD from the menu that appears.

Burn a data CD or DVD.

3. Insert a blank CD or DVD.

4. If the AutoPlay dialog box opens, click its Close button (▬) to close it.

5. Click Start Burn. Windows Media Player burns the contents of your playlist onto the blank CD or DVD. This may take several minutes.

6. When the burn is complete, click Clear List to remove the playlist from the Burn tab.

Syncing a mobile device with Windows Media Player

Depending on its manufacturer, you may be able to sync your portable media player or mobile phone with Windows Media Player. You can also sync some types of storage cards. To do so, you simply connect the device to your computer; Windows Media Player will assess the device's storage capacity and the size of your Windows Media Player library to determine whether an automatic or a manual sync is required.

What portable devices are supported?

Windows Media Player cannot sync Apple's iPod, iPhone, or Microsoft Zune. However, several Sony devices are compatible, as are devices by Samsung and SanDisk, and various types of Windows Mobile devices.

If, the first time you attach your device, Windows Media Player determines that the device has a storage capacity of more than 4 gigabytes and that your entire Windows Media Player library can fit on the device, it will sync your device automatically now and in the future. That is, each time you connect your computer to the device while Windows Media Player is running, Windows Media Player will automatically update the contents of the device to match the contents of your Windows Media Player library, copying any files you've ripped or purchased and removing any files you've deleted from your library. All you need to do is click the Finish button that appears when the sync is complete.

If you don't want to sync your whole library during an automatic sync, you can sync only certain playlists. Only the playlists you select will sync each time you connect your portable device to your computer. To do so, follow these steps:

1   With Windows Media Player open, turn on your portable device and connect it to your computer.

2   Click the Sync tab.

3   Press the Sync Options button (⊞·).

4   Choose Set Up Sync from the menu that appears.

*Press the Sync Options **button and** choose Set Up Sync.*

5 The Windows Media Player Device Setup dialog box appears. In the Playlists to Sync list on the right side of the screen, click a playlist you want to omit from the sync.

6 Press Remove. The playlist is removed from the list of playlists that will be synced.

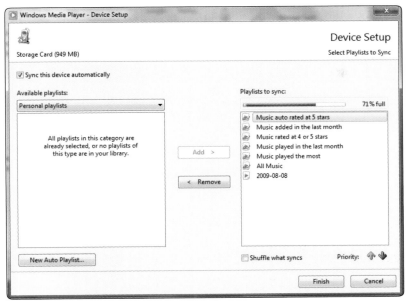

The Windows Media Player Device Setup dialog box.

If you change your mind about omitting a playlist from the list of playlists that will be synced, you can return it to the list by clicking it in the Available Playlists list and pressing the Add button.

7 Click Finish.

Specifying which files to sync

If, after you connect your portable device to your computer, Windows Media Player determines that it stores less than 4 gigabytes or that your Windows Media Player library can't fit in its entirety on the device, then a manual sync is required. In that case, you specify which files you want synced with the device and launch the sync operation yourself.

1 With Windows Media Player open, turn on your portable device and connect it to your computer.

2 Click the Sync tab.

3 Drag any playlists and/or song files you want to copy to your device to the Sync tab.

4 Press Start Sync.

Create a list of items to sync and click Start Sync.

Self study

1 Pick several of your favorite CDs and use Windows Media Player to rip their tracks to your computer.

2 Use Windows Live Movie Maker to create a movie using video clips in your personal media library.

Review

Questions

1 What are the two available modes in Windows Media Player.

2 What are three criteria you can use to sort files?

3 What program do you use to import video from a video camera?

4 Can you control playback in Windows Media Player from the program's taskbar button?

5 Can you sync your iPhone, iPod, or Zune player with Windows Media Center?

Answers

1 Windows Media Player offers two modes: Player Library mode and Now Playing mode.

2 Audio files can be sorted in Windows Media Player by artist, album, album artist, genre, song title, release date, date taken, file name, or rating

3 Rather than using Windows Media Player to import video from a video camera, you use Windows Live Photo Gallery.

4 Yes, you can control playback of Windows Media Player by hovering your mouse pointer over the Media Player taskbar button; doing so displays buttons for playing or pausing the current song, advancing to the next song, or skipping to the previous one.

5 No, Windows Media Player cannot sync with the iPhone, iPod, or Microsoft Zune player. However, several Sony devices are compatible, as are devices by Samsung and SanDisk, and various types of Windows Mobile devices.

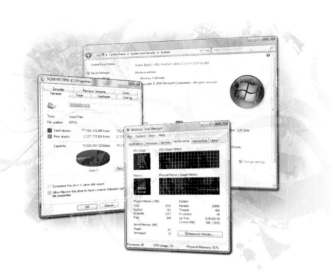

What you'll learn in this lesson:

- Exploring the Windows 7 Control Panel
- Updating your Windows 7 system
- Backing up
- Troubleshooting and repairing

Maintaining Windows 7

Periodic housecleaning helps to keep Windows 7 running smoothly on your computer. This lesson covers critical monitoring and maintenance methods as well as helpful troubleshooting techniques.

Starting up

Before you start, be sure to copy all the files for this lesson from the accompanying DVD to your hard drive.

See Lesson 7 in action!

Use the accompanying video to gain a better understanding of how to use some of the features shown in this lesson. The video tutorial for this lesson can be found on the included DVD.

Exploring the Windows 7 Control Panel

When it comes to maintaining your system, the Windows 7 Control Panel acts like a master console, providing direct access to your computer's hardware, settings, and services. It serves as a launching point for performing many system-maintenance tasks, such as troubleshooting common problems, viewing system information, setting up Windows Update, backing up your data, scheduling system tasks, adding hardware devices, and more. To open the Control Panel, simply click its icon in the Start menu.

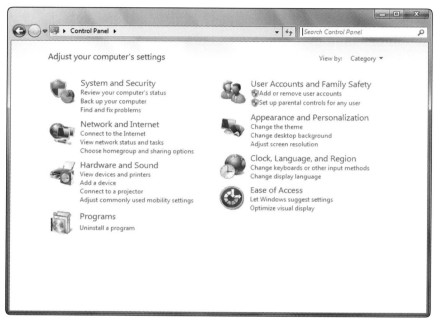

The Windows 7 Control Panel window.

The main Control Panel window features several links. Click a link to display information about a device or service or, in some cases, to launch a tool or wizard. To access many of the tools covered in this lesson, click the System and Security link.

Click the System and Security link to access many of the tools you'll use in this lesson.

If you know the name of the tool you need to access but aren't sure which series of links to click to access it, you can type the tool's name or a relevant keyword in the Control Panel window's Search text field located in the upper right hand corner of the window. Windows 7 displays a list of tools that match what you typed; click a tool to launch it.

Use the Control Panel's Search text field to locate a tool.

Updating your Windows 7 system

Windows 7 is a complex operating system and may require updates or patches or additions to the operating-system software that are designed to prevent or fix problems or to enhance security or performance. Microsoft regularly develops and publishes updates for Windows 7; one of the most important maintenance tasks you can perform is to make sure that your system is up-to-date.

By default, Windows 7 automatically checks for system updates and installs those it deems essential. But there are additional, optional updates that Windows 7 does not install by default; you should make it a habit to view these updates and install those that you feel will improve your Windows 7 experience on a regular basis. You can also perform a manual update if you discover that Microsoft has released a new patch but your system has not yet run its automatic update operation. In order to perform an update, whether it is automatic or manual, Windows 7 must be connected to the Internet.

Performing a manual update

1   In the Control Panel's System and Security window, click the Windows Update link.

2   The Windows Update window opens, indicating whether any updates are available. In this case, one important update is available, as are 32 optional updates. Click the Optional Updates Are Available link.

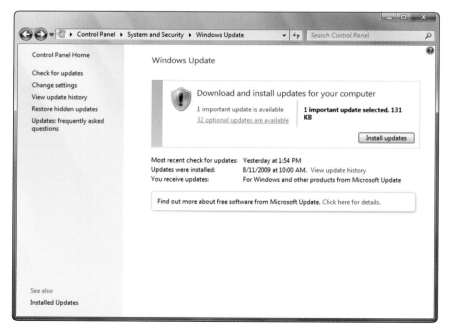

Click the Optional Updates Are Available link.

3   The Select the Updates You Want to Install screen appears, displaying a list of optional updates. Click the checkbox next to any optional updates you want to install to select them.

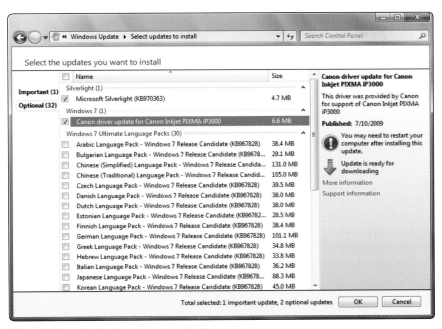

Choose which **optional** *updates you want to install.*

4   To view the updates Microsoft has deemed essential, click the Important link along the left side of the screen. Notice that the checkboxes next to any important updates are selected by default.

5   Press OK.

6 Press the Install Updates button. Windows 7 downloads and installs the important update as well as any optional updates you chose and informs you when the operation is complete. In the event an important update cannot be installed, Windows Update will notify you.

You may be prompted to restart your computer for the updates to take effect.

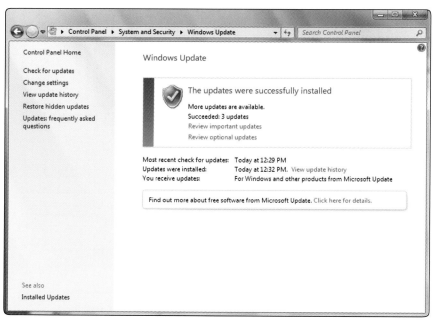

Install the updates; Windows 7 notifies you when the operation is complete.

Changing automatic update settings

If you want to change the automatic update settings—for example, change the time of day when Windows 7 performs automatic updates or specify that no updates be installed until you've had the opportunity to review them—you can easily do so. Here's how:

1 Click the Change Settings link along the left side of the Windows Update window.

2 Under Important Updates, choose the desired option from the Install Updates Automatically drop-down menu. For a bit more control over the update process, choose Download Updates but Let Me Choose Whether to Install Them; for still more control over the update process, choose Check for Updates but Let Me Choose Whether to Download and Install Them.

3 From the Install New Updates drop-down menus specify the day(s) on which updates should occur and at what time.

4   Review the remaining options and make your selections.

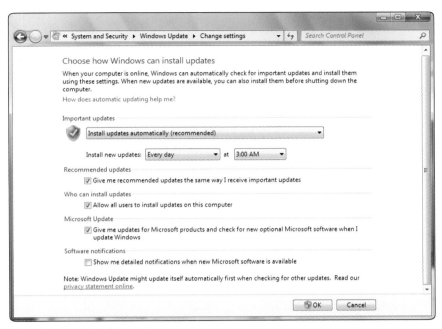

*Change the automatic **update** settings.*

5   Press OK.

Undoing an update

If you notice any problems with your system immediately after an update, the update itself may be the culprit. If you suspect this is the case, you can undo the update.

You should not undo an update unless you are certain it is the root of your system's problems. Be aware, too, that some updates, such as ones that relate to the security of Windows 7, cannot be removed.

1 Click the Installed Updates link in the bottom-left corner of the Windows Update window.

Click the Installed Updates link.

2 A list of installed updates appears. Click the update you want to undo.

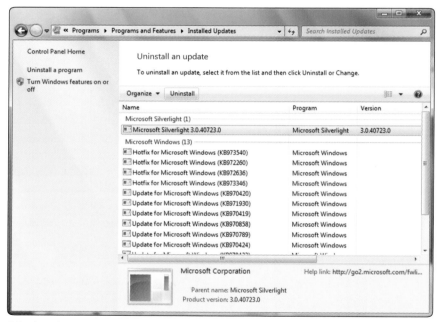

Select the update you want to undo and press Uninstall.

3 Press Uninstall.

4 Windows 7 asks you to confirm the operation; press Yes.

5 If you are prompted for an administrator password or confirmation, type your password or press **Allow**. Windows uninstalls the update.

Hide an update

If Windows 7 automatically reinstalls the update you removed, remove it again, and then follow these steps to hide it. This ensures that Windows 7 won't continue reinstalling it. You can also follow these steps to prevent Windows 7 from repeatedly suggesting an update you don't want to install.

1   In the Select the Updates You Want to Install screen, right-click the update you don't want to install. For help opening the Select the Updates You Want to Install screen, refer to the steps in the section "Performing a Manual Update" earlier in this lesson.

2   Click Hide Update in the list that appears. The update is hidden.

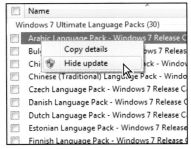

Hide an update.

If you realize you've hidden an update in error, you can restore it. To do so, click the Restore Hidden Updates link in the left side of the Windows Update screen, click the update you want to restore, and press Restore.

Backing up

Imagine if a disaster—such as theft, loss, breakage, or virus attack—were to befall your computer. No doubt, certain files, such as digital pictures, would be impossible to replace; others, such as files used for work, would be at best extremely difficult to reconstruct. For this reason, you should back up your files—that is, copy them to an external hard drive, a Flash drive, a CD, or a DVD. You can also save your backed up files on a network resource. Wherever you save your backup, you should keep it in a safe, separate location from your computer.

You'll learn more about networking your Windows 7 computer in Lesson 9, "Networking Your Computer."

You can set up Windows 7 to perform backups automatically, which is highly recommended. In addition, you can run manual backups. You might run a manual backup if, for example, you're about to make a system change, such as adding new hardware; by backing up beforehand, you ensure your data will remain safe in the event a problem occurs.

Setting up automatic backup

To set up Windows 7 to perform automatic backups, connect the drive on which you want to save your backup to your computer, insert the necessary media, or connect to the appropriate network, then follow these steps.

1   In the Control Panel's System and Security window, click the Backup and Restore link.

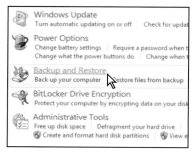

Click Backup and Restore.

2   The Backup or Restore Your Files screen appears. Click the Set Up Backup link.

Click Set Up Backup.

3   Windows 7 launches the Set Up Backup Wizard's first screen, the Select Where You Want to Save Your Backup screen. If the drive you want to use to store your backup is displayed, click it, and skip to step 9. If you want to back up to a network location, press Save on a Network.

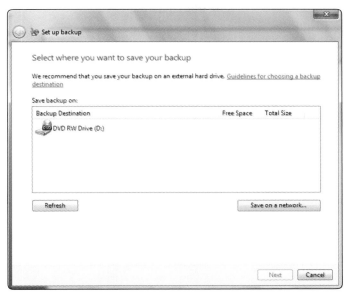

Choose the desired drive or choose Save on a Network.

4   If you pressed Save on a Network, the Set Up Backup Wizard displays the Select a Network Location screen. If you know the network location's file path, enter it in the Network Location field. Otherwise, press Browse.

5   If you pressed Browse, Windows 7 will launch the Browse for Folder dialog box. Locate and select the folder on the network in which you want to save your backup.

Indicate the network folder in which the backup should be saved.

6 Press OK to close the Browse for Folder dialog box.

7 Enter the appropriate user name and password to access the network in the Username and Password text fields.

If you're not sure what user name and password to use, click the Which Credentials Should I Enter link above the Username text field.

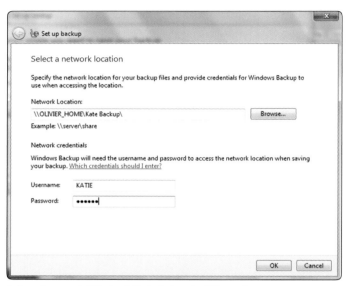

Indicate the network folder in which the backup should be saved.

8 Press OK to close the Select a Network Location screen.

9 In the Select Where You Want to Save Your Backup screen, make sure the appropriate drive or network folder is selected, and press Next.

10 The Set Up Backup Wizard displays the What Do You Want to Back Up? screen. If you want to specify which folders should be included in the backup, click the *Let Me Choose* radio button. Otherwise, stick with the default, *Let Windows Choose.*

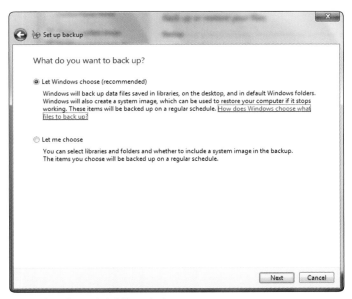

Let Windows choose which folders to back up.

11 Press Next.

12 The Review Your Backup Settings screen summarizes your settings, including when and how often backups will occur. To change the backup schedule, click the Change Schedule link.

13 In the How Often Do You Want to Back Up screen, make sure the Run Backup on a Schedule check box is selected.

14 From the How Often drop-down menu, choose whether backups should occur daily, weekly, or monthly.

15 If you chose Weekly or Monthly in the How Often list, from the What Day drop-down menu, choose the day on which backups should occur.

16 From the What Time drop-down menu, specify the hour on which backups should occur.

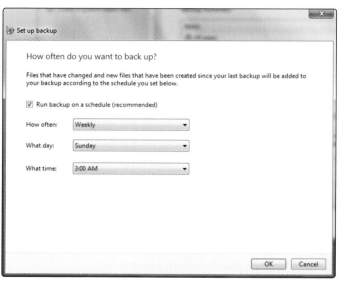

Set the backup schedule and launch the backup operation.

17 Press OK to close the How Often Do You Want to Back Up? screen.

18 Press Save Settings and Run Backup in the Review Your Backup Settings screen. Windows launches the backup operation. Subsequent backups will occur on the schedule you specified.

Running a manual backup

You might choose to run a manual backup if you're about to make a system change or install new software. Alternatively, you might run a manual backup if for some reason your automatic backup did not occur as scheduled. To run a manual backup, follow these steps:

1   In the Control Panel's System and Security window, click the Backup and Restore link.

2 The Backup or Restore Your Files screen appears. Press Back Up Now. Windows 7 launches the backup operation.

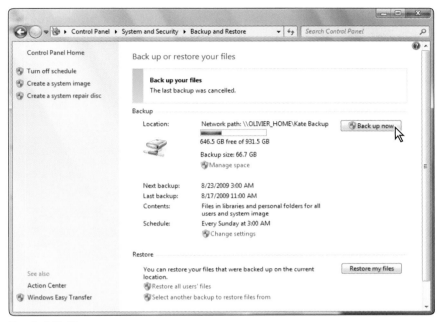

Press Back Up Now.

Restoring backed-up files

If you used Windows 7's Backup tool to back up the files and folders on your computer, you can restore your backed up files and folders in the event of system failure or some other disaster. To restore the files, you need the medium on which the backed up files are stored. For example, if you stored the backed up files and folders on a CD or DVD, you need to insert the disc in your drive. Alternatively, if you saved the backed up files and folders on an external hard drive or a Flash device, you must connect it to your computer.

1 In the Control Panel's System and Security window, click the Backup and Restore link.

2 The Backup or Restore Your Files screen appears. Press Restore My Files.

3 Windows 7 launches the Restore Files Wizard. To restore all folders and files in your system, press Browse for Folders.

If you only need to restore certain files, you can do so. Simply press Browse for Files instead of Browse for Folders; then locate and select the files you want to restore.

4   A Browse dialog box appears. Select the folder containing the backup of your hard drive.

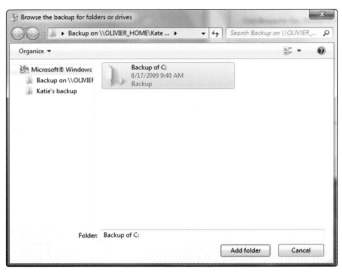

Choose the folder for your hard drive.

5   Press Add Folder.

6   The folder is added to the Restore Files Wizard's list of items to restore. Press Next.

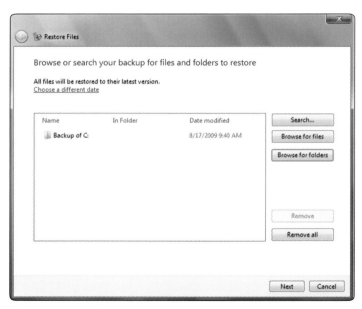

The folder appears in the Restore Files Wizard screen.

7   Click the *In the Original Location* radio button to restore the folder to its original location on your hard drive.

8   Press Restore. Windows 7 restores the files.

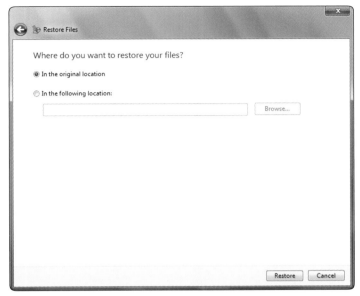

Press Restore.

9   Windows 7 notifies you when the restore operation is complete. Press Finish.

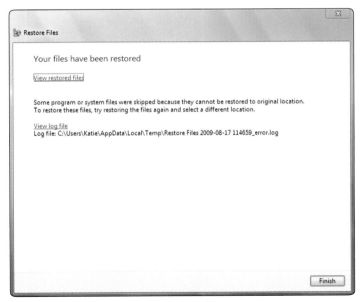

Press Finish.

Managing the hard drive

Your computer's hard drive houses all the programs and files on your computer—all of which can consume considerable space. Sometimes it may be necessary to free up space—for example, by deleting unnecessary files. You can also defragment your hard drive to make it operate more efficiently. And if you experience problems with your hard drive, you can also check it for errors.

Viewing free space and other disk information

Windows 7 makes it easy to determine whether you are running low on hard-drive space: You simply open the Computer folder. For additional information and to access various tools that relate to managing your hard drive, you can view its Properties dialog box.

1   Press the Start button (⊕). Select Computer.

2   The Computer folder opens, listing the various drives associated with this computer, the size of each drive, and how much space remains on each drive. Right-click the disk's icon in the Computer folder to access additional information about the hard drive as well as tools and options for improving the hard drive's performance.

3   Choose Properties. The hard drive's Properties dialog box opens with the General tab displayed. This tab includes a pie chart illustrating how much free space is available, indexing and compression options, and access to Disk Cleanup, a utility for deleting temporary files that are created as you work in a program, files that are left over from web browsing, and setup files that remain after the installation of some applications. The utility also empties the Recycle Bin. You'll learn how to use Disk Cleanup in the next exercise.

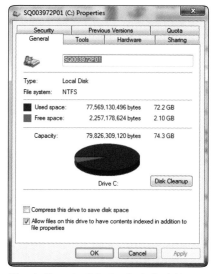

View the Properties dialog box for the hard drive.

The Properties dialog box

As you can see the Properties dialog box includes multiple tabs, some of which you will explore in this and later lessons:

- **The Tools tab.** This tab offers access to tools for checking errors, defragmenting the drive, and backing it up.

The Tools tab.

- **The Hardware tab.** Click the Hardware tab to see information about various disk–related hardware components.

The Hardware tab.

• **The Sharing tab.** This tab indicates the sharing status of the drive and provides access to various share-related features.

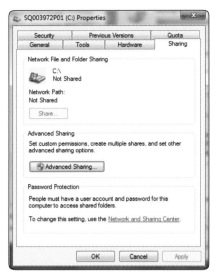

The Sharing tab.

• **The Security tab**. Click the Security tab to view and change permissions.

The Security tab.

- **The Previous Versions tab**. Use this tab to enable access to previous versions of your disk. Any file or folder modified since the last restore point is made available as a previous version. These previous versions can be used to restore files that have been damaged or that have been changed or deleted by accident. You'll learn more about restore points later in this lesson.

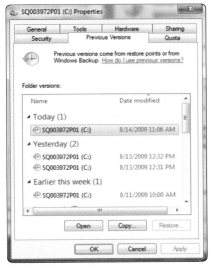

The Previous Versions tab.

- **The Quota tab**. If multiple users have accounts on your computer, you can set a disk–space limit for each user via the Quota tab. You'll learn how to establish user accounts in Lesson 8, "Setting Up User Accounts."

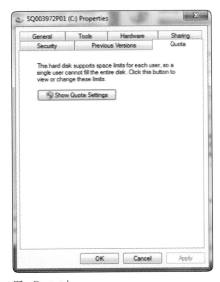

The Quota tab.

Deleting unnecessary files

Your hard drive stores many files that are created, changed, and saved automatically by Windows 7. Some of these files, called temporary files, are the result of web browsing; others are created by applications to store the contents of open files before they are saved to disk; still others are setup files that remain after the installation of some applications. Over time, you can end up with a gigabyte or more of unneeded files, consuming valuable space on your hard drive.

If your hard drive is low on free space, you can use the Disk Cleanup tool to find and remove these temporary files, which are scattered throughout your hard drive and stored with various filename extensions (such as .bak and .tmp). This utility also empties the Recycle Bin. In fact, it's wise to run the Disk Cleanup tool regularly as part of standard disk management. To run Disk Cleanup, follow these steps:

1   In the Computer folder, right-click the disk you want to clean and choose Properties from the menu that appears. The hard drive's Properties dialog box opens with the General tab displayed.

2   Press the Disk Cleanup button. Windows 7 launches Disk Cleanup.

Another way to launch Disk Cleanup is to click the Free Up Disk Space link under Administrative Tools in the System and Security Control Panel window.

3   Disk Cleanup conducts a scan of your system to determine how much space can be freed. When the scan is complete, it displays the Disk Cleanup dialog box, indicating how much space can be freed. Click the checkbox next to each type of file you want to delete.

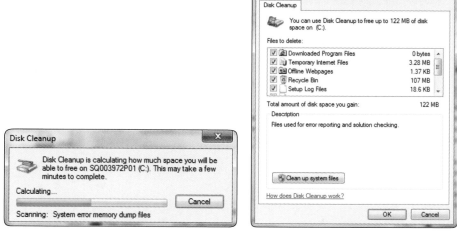

After Disk Cleanup scans your disk, click the checkbox next to each type of file you want to delete.

4   Press OK. Disk Cleanup prompts you to confirm the cleanup operation; press Delete Files. Disk Cleanup deletes the unnecessary files, freeing up disk space.

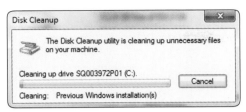

Disk Cleanup frees up space on your hard drive.

Defragmenting your hard drive

When Windows 7 saves information to your hard drive, it's a little bit like pouring water into an empty ice-cube tray—one space is filled in the tray, then the next, then the next. When you save a file, Windows *pours* the data into an empty space on the hard drive. If the space, called a sector, is too small to hold the entire file, the bits that don't fit will be saved in the next available space on the disk. When you open the file, Windows 7 must then access all the various bits of the file from the sectors in which they were saved in order to reconstruct it.

Over time, you may find that you files become more and more fragmented—with bits spread over more and more sectors on the disk—which means it takes Windows longer to reconstruct them. To solve this problem, you can run the Windows 7 Disk Defragmenter utility. When you do, Windows 7 attempts to reassemble the files on your hard drive such that each one occupies as few sectors as possible.

1   In the Computer folder, right-click the disk you want to clean and choose Properties from the menu that appears. The hard drive's Properties dialog box opens with the General tab displayed.

2   Click the Tools tab.

3   Press Defragment Now. Windows 7 launches the Disk Defragmenter utility.

Another way to launch Disk Defragmenter is to click the Defragment Your Hard Drive link under Administrative Tools in the System and Security Control Panel window.

4   Before defragmenting your disk, you should analyze how fragmented it is. Click the disk you want to analyze, then press Analyze Disk.

5   If a large percentage of the disk is fragmented, click the disk you want to defragment and then click Defragment Disk. Windows defragments your disk.

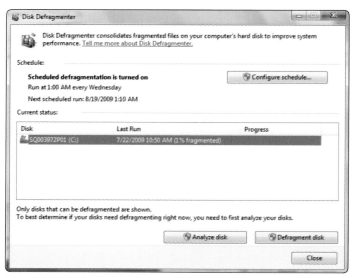

Click Defragment Disk

Schedule the Disk Defragmenter

You can configure Disk Defragmenter to run automatically on a schedule you specify.

1   In the Disk Defragmenter window, press Configure Schedule. The Disk Defragmenter: Modify Schedule dialog box opens.

2   Click the *Run on a Schedule* checkbox.

3   From the Frequency drop-down menu, choose whether Disk Defragmenter should run daily, weekly, or monthly. Most users will benefit from weekly defragmentation of their disk drive.

4   If you chose Weekly or Monthly in the Frequency list, choose the day on which Disk Defragmenter should run from the Day drop-down menu.

5   Specify the hour on which Disk Defragmenter should run from the Time drop-down menu.

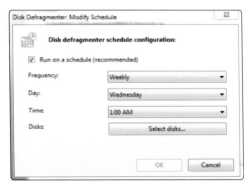

Set a defrag schedule.

6   Press Select Disks. The Disk Defragmenter: Select Disks for Schedule dialog box opens.

7   Click the disks you want to defragment.

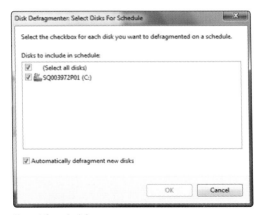

Set a defrag schedule.

8   Press OK to close the Disk Defragmenter: Select Disks for Schedule dialog box.

9   Press OK to close the Disk Defragmenter: Modify Schedule dialog box.

Checking your hard drive for errors

Hard-drive errors can cause files to become corrupted, which may prevent you from running a program or opening a document. You can use Windows 7's Check Disk program to look for and fix hard-drive errors.

Check Disk runs two different types of checks: a basic hard-drive check and a more thorough bad sector check. You should perform the basic check about once a week; perform the more thorough bad sector check once a month. A bad sector is one that through physical damage or some other cause can no longer be used to reliably store data.

1 In the Computer folder, right-click the disk you want to clean and choose Properties from the menu that appears. The hard drive's Properties dialog box opens with the General tab displayed.

2 Click the Tools tab.

3 Press Check Now.

4 The Check Disk dialog box appears. If you want Check Disk to fix any errors it finds, press Automatically Fix File System Errors.

5 If you want Check Disk to look for bad sectors, check Scan For and Attempt Recovery of Bad Sectors.

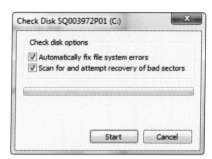

The Check Disk utility.

6 Press Start.

7 Windows notifies you that it cannot check the disk while the disk is in use. Press Schedule Disk Check to run the check the next time you start your computer.

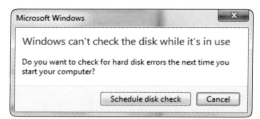

Press Schedule Disk Check.

8 Restart your computer by pressing the Start button (), clicking the right arrow next to the Shut Down option, and choosing Restart. Before restarting your computer, Windows 7 runs the Disk Check utility.

Managing programs and devices

Over time you will want to install additional programs and devices. Windows 7 is designed to make this as easy as possible.

The specifics of installing a program differ by program. Some programs are downloaded from the Internet, others from a CD. The precise steps required are a different as the programs themselves. In the event you need to install a new program, all you need to know how to do is download it from the Internet or insert the necessary media into your computer's CD or DVD drive; Windows 7 will guide you step by step the rest of the way.

The same goes for connecting devices, such as a printer, an external hard drive, or a mouse, to your computer. In most cases, Windows 7 will access the software it needs to interact with the device, called drivers, with no input from you after you connect the device to your computer. In the event Windows 7 is unable to install a device, it will generally notify you and offer suggestions on what steps to take next. If it fails to do so, follow these steps:

1 Press the Start button (⊙).

2 Select Devices and Printers. The Devices and Printers window opens.

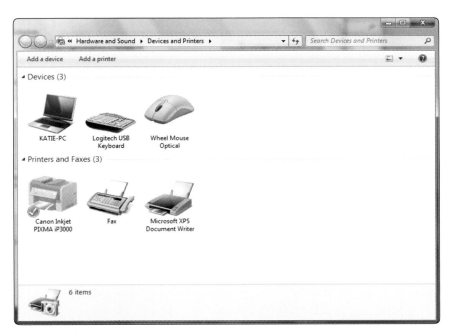

The Devices and Printers window.

3 If you want to add a printer, press Add a Printer to launch the Add a Printer Wizard; then follow the onscreen instructions. If you want to add some other type of device, click Add a Device to launch the Add a Device Wizard; then follow the onscreen instructions.

Uninstalling a program

Removing devices is also easy: Disconnect a device from your computer to remove it. Removing a program, however, is a bit more involved. You might remove a program if, for example, you no longer use it and you want to free up space on your computer.

1 In the main Control Panel window, click the Uninstall a Program link under Programs.

2 The Programs and Features window opens. Click the program you want to remove.

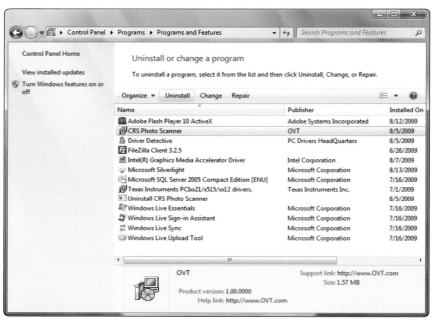

Choose the program you want to remove and click Uninstall.

3 Press Uninstall.

4 Windows 7 prompts you to confirm the removal of the program. Press Yes. The program is removed. You may be prompted to restart your computer.

You can also change a program's configuration or repair a program in the event it becomes damaged from within the Programs and Features window. Not all programs can be changed. Any program that does not have a Change or Repair button listed cannot be changed or repaired.

Assessing your computer's performance

There may be times when you need to view information about your system—for example, to determine whether it is compatible with a particular type of software, to see what type of processor or how much RAM you have, or to troubleshoot. You can find general information about your computer, its manufacturer, the amount of memory installed, its processor type and speed, and details about the operating system in the Control Panel's System screen. To access this screen, press the Start button (⬤) and choose Control Panel. In the Control Panel window, click the System and Security link, then click the System link in the System and Security screen. Alternatively, you can right-click the Computer link in the Start menu and choose Properties from the menu that appears.

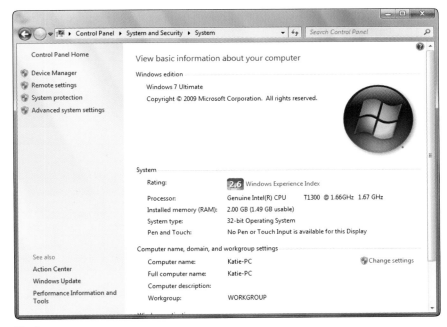

The System screen.

In the event you are required to call Microsoft for assistance, you may be asked to open the System screen to provide the information it contains to the technician on the other end of the line. Knowing how to find it will come in handy!

The System screen also displays your computer's Windows Experience Index base score. This score gauges the performance and overall capability of your computer's hardware configuration. To determine the base score, Windows evaluates your computer's RAM, CPU, hard disk, and graphics capabilities, giving each a sub score. Windows then uses the lowest sub-score to establish your system's base score. A computer whose base score is 2 or lower can handle general applications such as ones for word processing or Internet browsing but not more complex programs such as certain games. In contrast, a computer with a base score of 4 or 5 can support programs using high-end graphics, 3D gaming, and even HDTV. If your base score is insufficient for the types of programs you are running, causing your computer to seem sluggish or to crash, you can upgrade your hardware components. To determine which components need upgrading, view their sub-scores by clicking the Windows Experience Index link in the System screen.

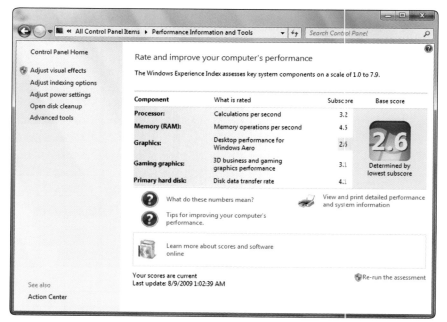

View your Windows Experience Index sub-scores.

Another place to view information about your computer's performance is in the Windows Task Manager dialog box's Performance tab. To view it, right-click the Taskbar at the bottom of the screen, then select Start Task Manager from the menu that appears and click the Performance tab in the Task Manager window. At the top of this tab are graphs that illustrate the percentage of the CPU in use (a higher percentage means that more CPU resources are being consumed) as well as how much RAM (that is, physical memory) is being used. Below the graph is a series of tables that provide more information about your computer's consumption of CPU and RAM.

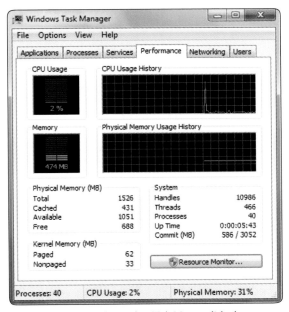

The Performance tab in the Windows Task Manager dialog box.

For an even more detailed view, open the Windows 7 Resource Monitor by clicking the Resource Monitor button in the Performance tab of the Windows Task Manager dialog box. Resource Monitor offers a detailed view of the CPU, hard disk, network, and RAM with respect to resource consumption. You can use this window to monitor the various processes and services currently running on your computer; if any of these are using more than their fair share of resources, you'll be able to see that here, and to end, suspend, or resume these processes and services as needed. Right-click a process and choose the appropriate option from the menu that appears to end, suspend, or resume it. Only use these options with the guidance of an experienced technical resource.

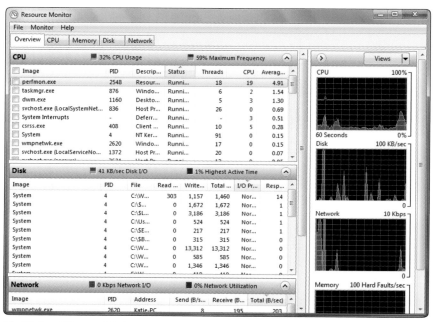

The Windows 7 Resource Monitor.

Troubleshooting and repairing

As reliable as the Windows 7 is, there may be times when you encounter problems with your system. Fortunately, the operating system offers several tools for detecting and repairing problems.

Reviewing alerts in the Action Center

Windows 7 displays alerts in a window called the Action Center, which offers direct access to tools for resolving any issues that Windows 7 has detected. For example, if Windows 7 has determined that your system is in need of a backup or that your system lacks virus-protection software, it displays notifications in the Action Center window. When the Action Center window contains items that require your attention, Windows 7 displays an Action Center icon in your Taskbar's notification area; you can click the icon at your leisure to see a menu of options for addressing whatever problems Windows 7 is experiencing as well as a link to the Action Center window. You can also open the Action Center window by clicking the Action Center link in the Control Panel's System and Security window.

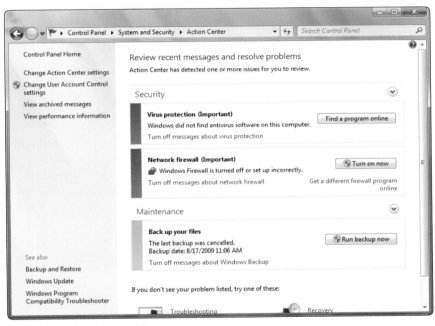

The Windows 7 Action Center window.

Accessing troubleshooting tools

If your system is experiencing problems beyond those cited in the Action Center window, for example, problems with networking, hardware, program compatibility, or using the Internet. You can use one of any number of troubleshooting tools to automatically pinpoint and resolve the issue. Of course, troubleshooters can't fix every problem your Windows 7 system may encounter, but they are a good starting point and can solve numerous common problems that may occur, saving you significant time and effort in the process.

To access these tools, click the Troubleshooting link at the bottom of the Action Center window. The Troubleshooting screen appears; click the category that best describes the type of problem your system is having to view troubleshooting tools in that category. Alternatively, click the View All link in the left side of the Troubleshooting screen to view all available troubleshooting tools.

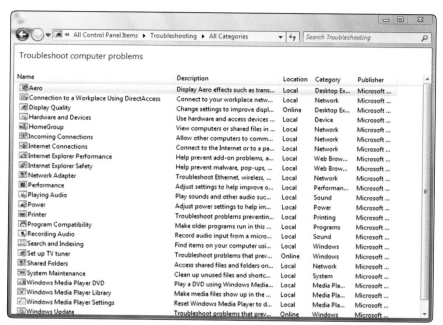

View troubleshooting tools

Then click a tool to launch it.

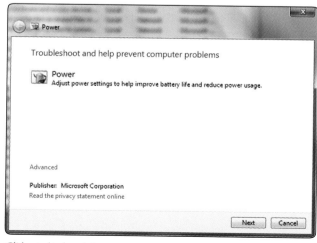

Click a tool to launch it.

In the event none of Windows 7's troubleshooting tools neither find nor fix your problem, you can use the operating system's Problem Steps Recorder. This screen-capture tool enables you to *record* the problems you're experiencing. You can then send this recording, which is an HTML file saved in a ZIP folder, to Microsoft or a friend.

1   Click Get Help from a Friend in the left side of the Troubleshooting screen.

2   The Remote Assistance screen opens. Click the Problem Steps Recorder link.

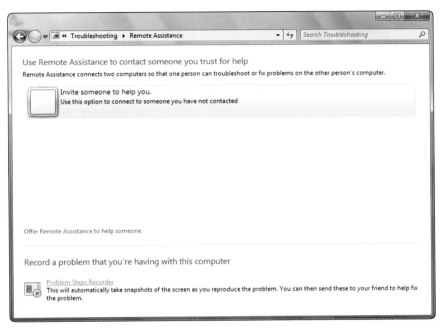

Click the Problem Steps Recorder link.

3   Windows 7 launches the Problem Steps Recorder. Press Start Record.

Press Start Record.

4   Follow the steps necessary to re-create the problem. As you do, you can add comments to clarify what problems you're experiencing; simply press Add Comment, highlight the area of the screen that you are commenting on, type your comment in the Highlight Problem and Comment dialog box, and press OK.

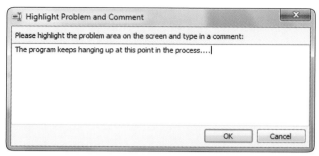

Re-create the problem.

5   When you're finished recording, click Stop Record. Windows 7 launches a Save As dialog box. Locate the folder in which you want to save your recording.

6   Type a name for your recording.

7   Press Save. Windows 7 saves the recording in the folder you chose.

8   To close Problem Steps Recorder, press its Close button (▬).

Getting help via Remote Assistance

Another way to resolve a computer problem is to invite someone you trust to help you via Remote Assistance—regardless of his or her physical location. During a Remote Assistance session, you and your helper can communicate via chat. In addition, your helper can view your computer screen and, with your permission, use his or her mouse and keyboard to make changes to your system.

Your helper will have access to your personal files and information during the Remote Assistance session. For this reason, although all Remote Assistance sessions are encrypted and password-protected, you should engage in a Remote Assistance session only with someone you trust. You should also close any sensitive files before initiating the connection.

1   Click Get Help from a Friend in the left side of the Troubleshooting screen.

2   The Remote Assistance screen opens. Click Invite Someone to Help You.

3   Windows 7 launches the Windows Remote Assistance Wizard. Choose how you want to invite your friend to help—in this example, Use E-mail to Send an Invitation.

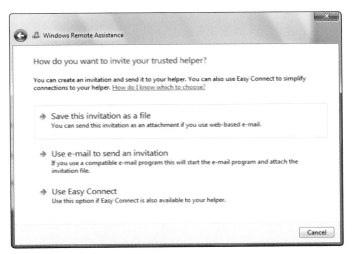

*Choose how you want to invite your **helper**.*

4   Windows 7 launches your e-mail program and opens a New Message screen containing a standard form message. Enter the message recipient in the To text field.

5   Add to the standard message as needed.

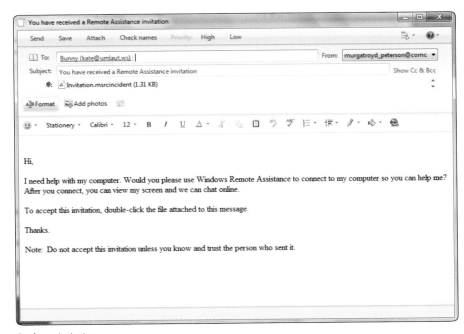

Send your invitation.

6 Press Send. Windows 7 sends your message.

7 A Windows Remote Assistance window containing a password appears. Your friend will need this password to connect to your Remote Assistance session. Send the password to your friend via e-mail after he or she replies to your original message to accept your invitation.

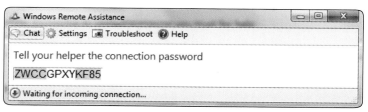

Send this password to your friend.

8 Windows Remote Assistance prompts you to allow your friend to connect. Press Yes. Your friend will now be able to see the contents of your desktop, and to use his or her own mouse and keyboard to make changes to your system. To chat with your helper, press the Chat button in the Windows Remote Assistance window, type your message, and press Enter.

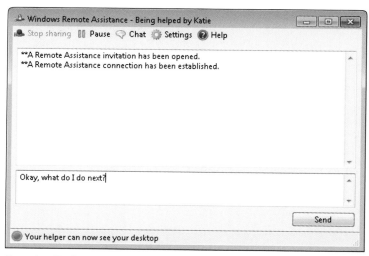

Engage in a Windows Remote Assistance session.

9 To stop your helper from sharing control over your system, press Cancel, press Stop Sharing, or press the Esc key. Close Windows Remote Assistance by pressing the its Close button (▭).

Working with restore points

If you encounter problems and want to return to a point in time when your system functioned properly, you can use System Restore to restore your system to the way it worked before the problem emerged. For example, you might use System Restore to revert to the setup you had before your system was exposed to a virus.

System Restore takes a sort of snapshot, called a restore point, of all the details about your setup and files as they exist at a given point in time. If you need to revert to a last-known-good configuration—that is, the configuration your computer had before problems emerged—you can simply choose to roll back to the most recent restore point from before the problem began. Choosing a very old restore point may result in your system failing to reflect the more recent changes you have made.

System Restore only restores your system to a known-good state. It does not affect your personal files. If you delete a personal file, running System Restore cannot restore it for you. That's why you should also run a backup utility such as Windows Backup.

Windows 7 creates restore points automatically—usually on a daily basis, as well as before significant system events such as the installation of a new program or hardware device. You can, however, create a restore point manually. Here's how:

1 Click the Advanced System Settings link in the left side of the Control Panel's System screen. To access this screen, click the System link in the Control Panel's System and Security screen.

2 The System Properties dialog box opens. Click the System Protection tab.

3 If necessary, click the disk for which you want to create a restore point.

4 Press the Create button.

5 The System Protection dialog box opens. Type a description to help you identify the restore point. Note that the date and time are included automatically.

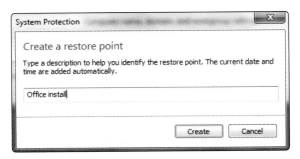

Create a restore point.

6   Press Create.

7   Windows notifies you when the restore point has been created. Click Close.

System Restore using a restore point

If you find that a system update or newly installed application or hardware device has wreaked havoc on your machine, you can attempt to roll back your computer to the most recent restore point from before the problem began.

1   Click the Advanced System Settings link in the left side of the Control Panel's System screen. To access this screen, click the System link in the Control Panel's System and Security screen.

2   The System Properties dialog box opens. Click the System Protection tab.

3   Press System Restore.

4   Windows launches the System Restore wizard.

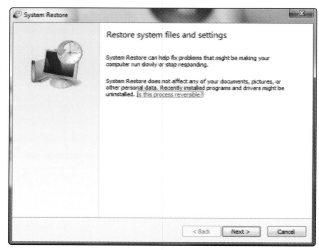

Launch the System Restore wizard.

5　Press Next. Choose the restore point you want to revert to.

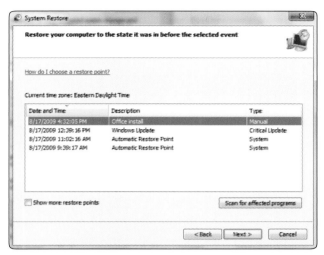

Choose a restore point.

6　Press Next.

7　Select the disk you want to restore.

8　Press Finish.

Choose a disk.

9   Windows 7 notifies you that restoring your system may take some time. Press Yes. Windows restores your system to the earlier state.

10 Windows 7 notifies when the restore operation is complete. Press Close.

If, after you follow these steps, the problem remains, try undoing the restore operation. Press Undo System Restore in the first screen of the System Restore wizard and press Finish. Then run System Restore again—this time choosing a different restore point.

Previous Versions

If you've ever saved changes to a file or folder only to later wish you hadn't, then Previous Versions is for you. With Previous Versions, you can revert to an earlier version of a file or folder—also handy in the event a file or folder becomes damaged. When reverting to an earlier version of a file or folder, Previous Versions uses either a backup copy (a copy created with Windows Backup) or a shadow copy (a copy created by Windows automatically between restore points). To revert to a previous version of a file or folder, right-click the file or folder in Windows Explorer, and choose Restore Previous Versions from the menu that appears. The file or folder's Properties dialog box opens with the Previous Versions tab displayed; click the backup or shadow file or folder that you want to revert to and click Restore. Note that when you revert to a previous version of a file or folder, the more recent version will be deleted—an operation that cannot be undone.

System recovery options

If the problem you are experiencing is that your computer will not start, then obviously you will not be able to run System Restore as outlined here to attempt to roll back to a known-good configuration. You may, however, be able to access various system-recovery options—including System Restore—when you attempt to start Windows 7. To find out, remove all media such as CDs or DVDs from your computer's disk drives and press your computer's power button to start it. As your computer attempts to boot, press the F8 key on your keyboard. Note that you must press this key before the Windows logo appears. When the Advanced Boot Options screen appears, use the arrow keys on your keyboard to highlight the Repair Your Computer option and press Enter. Next, select a keyboard layout; then, in the System Recovery Options screen, choose the recovery tool you want to use. Choices include Startup Repair, which automatically fixes problems that are preventing Windows from starting; System Restore, which restores your Windows system to the settings used in an earlier point in time; System Image Recovery, which you can use to recover your computer using a system image. This works only if you've created a system image—a task that is beyond the scope of this book; Windows Memory Diagnostic, which checks your computer for memory hardware errors; and Command Prompt, which opens a command-prompt window.

Self study

1 Run Disk Cleanup to free up disk space on your computer.

2 Use Windows 7's various tools, such as the System screen in the Control Panel, the Windows Task Manager dialog box's Performance tab, and the Windows 7 Resource Monitor, to assess your computer's performance.

Review

Questions

1 What is a patch?

2 Why is it important to back up your files and folders?

3 Where does Windows 7 display alerts?

4 When restoring your computer, should you choose a very old restore point?

5 What keys do you press to access Windows 7's various system-recovery options during a system boot?

Answers

1 A patch, or update, is an addition to the operating-system software that is designed to prevent or fix problems or to enhance security or performance.

2 If a disaster—such as theft, loss, breakage, or virus attack—were to befall your computer, certain files, such as digital pictures, would be impossible to replace and others, such as files used for work, would be at best extremely difficult to reconstruct.

3 Windows 7 displays all alerts in a new window called the Action Center, which offers direct access to tools for resolving any issues that Windows 7 has detected.

4 No, you should roll back to the most recent restore point from before the problem began. Choosing a very old restore point may result in your system failing to reflect the more recent changes you have made.

5 As your computer attempts to boot, press the F8 key on your keyboard. Note that you must press this key before the Windows logo appears. When the Advanced Boot Options screen appears, use the arrow keys on your keyboard to highlight the Repair Your Computer option and press Enter.

What you'll learn in this lesson:

- Understanding user accounts
- Creating a user account
- Setting up Windows 7 parental controls
- Setting space quotas
- Enabling the Guest account

Setting Up User Accounts

If more than one person uses your computer, you can create accounts for each user. This enables each user to set up Windows 7 in whatever way he or she likes, and to create his or her own set of folders and files.

Starting up

Before you start, be sure to copy all the files for this lesson from the accompanying DVD to your hard drive.

See Lesson 8 in action!

Use the accompanying video to gain a better understanding of how to use some of the features shown in this lesson. The video tutorial for this lesson can be found on the included DVD.

You can create user accounts if more than one person uses your computer and you want to customise the appearance and settings for each user. You can also set up user accounts to limit capabilities of certain users which can be beneficial if you've provided a computer to a child or if you're managing computers in a small office.

Understanding user accounts

If you share your computer with others, you can create a separate user account for each user. Each user can create his or her own set of folders and files, and personalized desktop.

There are three types of user accounts, each giving the user a different level of control over the computer:

- **Administrator.** An Administrator account allows the most control over the computer, enabling you to change security settings, install and remove software and hardware, access all files on the computer, or create and make changes to other user accounts. There must be at least one Administrator account on a Windows 7 computer.

- **Standard.** Users with Standard accounts can do almost anything an Administrator account can do—but they may be prompted to provide the Administrator password before installing hardware or software or changing security and other settings.

- **Guest.** The Guest account is for people who need temporary access to the computer, such as a house guest or an office visitor. People using the Guest account can't install software or hardware, change settings, or create a password, and they cannot gain access to your personal files.

In general, you should use an Administrator account only to perform computer-management tasks. For your everyday computing tasks, such as word-processing or Internet browsing, you should set up and use a Standard account. This will make your computer more secure, as users in the Administrators group can see everyone's files, change anyone's password, and install any software they want.

Creating a user account

Creating a user account is a simple matter—although to do so, you must be logged in to a Windows Administrator account.

1   Press the Start button (⊙) and choose Control Panel to open the Control Panel window.

2   Under User Accounts and Family Safety, click the Add or Remove User Accounts link

Click the Add or Remove User Accounts link.

3   The Manage Accounts window opens. Click the Create a New Account link.

Click the Create a New Account link.

4 The Create New Account window opens. Type a name for the new account. Choose an account type.

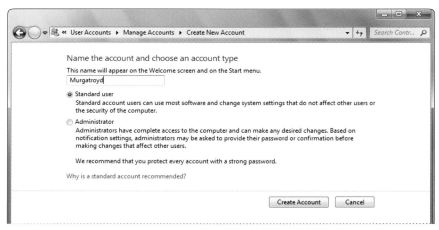

Create the new account.

5 Press Create Account. Windows 7 creates the account.

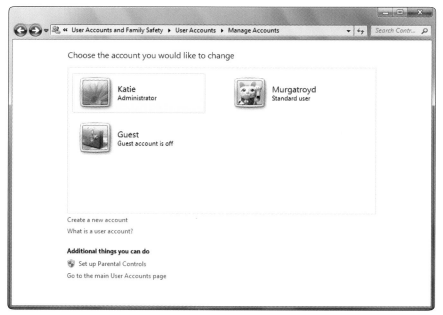

The new account is created.

Logging in to a user account

When you start Windows 7, the operating system displays a Welcome screen with clickable icons for each account on the system. To log on to an account, simply click its icon.

If Windows 7 is already running, switch user accounts by pressing the Start button (⊙), clicking the right arrow to the right of the Shut Down button, and choosing Switch User from the submenu that appears.

Switch accounts.

Windows 7 displays the Welcome screen; simply select the account you want to use. Before you switch accounts, be sure to save any open files in the current account. If you've set a password for the account you want to switch to, you are prompted to enter the account's password when you click the account in the Welcome screen; simply type the password and press the Enter key on your keyboard to log in. You'll learn about setting passwords in Lesson 10, "Securing Your Computer."

Changing a user's picture

When you create a user account, Windows 7 assigns a picture to the account. This picture is displayed on the Windows 7 Welcome screen and along the top of the Start menu. You can assign a different picture—either one supplied by Windows 7 or one that you've saved on your computer's hard drive.

To change the picture associated with a user account, first log on to the account.

1   In the main Control Panel window, click the User Accounts and Family Safety link.

2   The User Accounts and Family Safety window appears. Under User Accounts, click the Change Your Account Picture link.

Click Change Your Account Picture.

3   The Change Your Picture screen appears. Click the picture you want to use, then press Change Picture. Alternatively, to apply one of your own pictures to the account, click the Browse for More Pictures link. An Open dialog box appears. Locate and select the picture you want to use and press Open.

Choose a picture and press Change Picture or click the Browse for More Pictures link.

4   Windows 7 applies the picture you selected to the account.

Windows 7 applies it to your account.

Changing the picture from the Administrator account

From the Administrator account, change the picture associated with an account while logged in to the account.

1   Select the account to which you want to apply a new picture in the Manage Accounts window. To open the Manage Accounts window, click the Add or Remove User Accounts link under User Accounts and Family Safety in the main Control Panel window.

2   The Change an Account screen opens. Click Change the Picture.

3   The Change Your Picture screen appears. Click the picture you want to use, then press Change Picture. Alternatively, to apply one of your own pictures to the account, click the Browse for More Pictures link. An Open dialog box appears. Locate and select the picture you want to use and press Open.

4   Windows 7 applies the picture you selected to the account.

Changing the username

If you want to change that account's username after you create an account, you can do so if you have administrative privileges. For example, you might need to update the user's name to reflect a name change.

One approach is to update the username using the computer's Administrator account. Alternatively, if the account is a Standard account, you can change its name while logged in to it, provided you know the password for the Administrator account. You'll explore both methods here:

1   In the main Control Panel window, click the User Accounts and Family Safety link.

2   The User Accounts and Family Safety window appears. Click the User Accounts link.

3   In the User Accounts window, click the Change Your Account Name link.

Click Change Your Account Name.

4   Windows 7 prompts you to enter the Administrator password. Type it and press Yes.

5   The Change Your Name window opens. Type the name you want to apply to the account.

Change the account name.

6   Press Change Name. Windows 7 applies the name you typed.

Changing the account name from the Administrator account

You can change the name associated with an account while logged in to the account from the Administrator account.

1   In the main Control Panel window, click the Add or Remove User Accounts link under User Accounts and Family Safety.

2   Click the Account you wish to rename.

3   The Change an Account screen opens. Click Change the Account Name.

4   Follow steps 5 and 6 above to change the name.

Changing the account type

An important aspect of user-account management is ensuring that users have the type of account they need—Administrator or Standard. An Administrator account can be used to create, modify, and delete any account, as well as to specify how users log in. A Standard account cannot be used to perform any changes to other user accounts, nor can it be used to configure the system without first supplying the Administrator account's password.

One approach to changing the account type is to update it using the computer's Administrator account. Alternatively, if the account is a Standard account, you can change its type while logged in to it, provided you know the password for the Administrator account. Here's how:

1 In the main Control Panel window, click the User Accounts and Family Safety link.

2 The User Accounts and Family Safety window appears. Click the User Accounts link.

3 In the User Accounts page, click the Change Your Account Type link.

Click Change Your Account Type

4 Windows 7 prompts you to enter the Administrator password. Type it and press Yes.

5   The Change Your Account Type window opens. Click the *Administrator* radio button to change a Standard account to an Administrator account; alternatively, click the *Standard User* radio button to change an Administrator account to a Standard account.

Change the account type.

6   Press Change Account Type. Windows 7 applies the change.

Changing the account type from the Administrator account

In addition to changing the account type while logged in to the account, you can do so from the Administrator account.

1   From the Control panel window, click the Add or Remove User Accounts link under User Accounts and Family Safety.

2   Click the account whose type you want to change.

3   The Change an Account screen opens. Press Change the Account Type.

4   Follow steps 5 and 6 above to change the account type.

Setting up Windows 7 parental controls

If you share your computer with children, you can set up the Windows 7 parental controls to limit their use of the computer to certain hours of the day on certain days of the week. You can also use parental controls to block users from playing games on the computer or to restrict access to games by age rating or content rating. And if your computer has programs installed on it that you'd prefer to keep private—you can use Windows 7's parental controls to prevent unauthorized access. To implement the Windows 7 parental controls, each child who uses your computer must have his or her own Standard user account.

In addition to using the Windows 7 parental controls to limit access to games and programs, you can also use the parental controls included with Internet Explorer 8. Called Content Advisor, these controls prevent exposure to inappropriate subject matter, such as violent or sexually explicit Internet content. You'll learn more about Content Advisor in Lesson 10, "Securing Your Computer."

To set up parental controls for an account, first log on to an Administrator account.

1   In the main Control Panel window, under User Accounts and Family Safety, click the Set Up Parental Controls for Any User link.

2   The Parental Controls window opens. Click the Standard user account to which you want to apply parental controls.

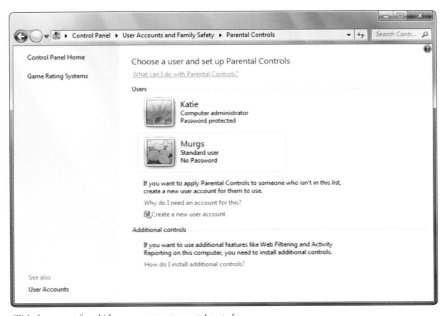

Click the account for which you want to set parental controls.

3 The User Controls window opens. Under Parental Controls, click the *On, enforce current settings* radio button to select it.

4 Click the Time Limits link.

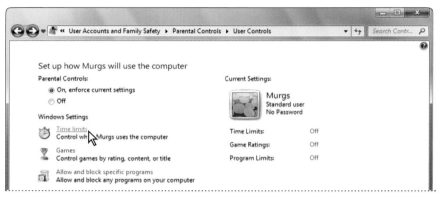

Enable parental controls; then click the Time Limits link.

5 The Time Restrictions window opens. Click and drag to indicate the hours during which you want to block or allow computer use for this account.

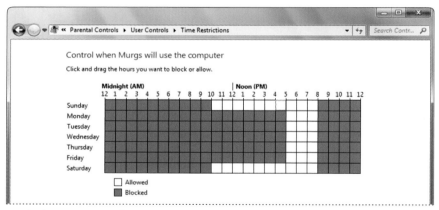

Specify when computer use is blocked and when it is allowed.

6 Press OK to return to the User Controls window.

7 In the User Controls window, click the Games link.

8 The Game Controls window opens. Under Can *{username}* Play Games?, click Yes or No.

9   If you selected Yes, click the Set Game Ratings link. If you clicked No, skip to step 15.

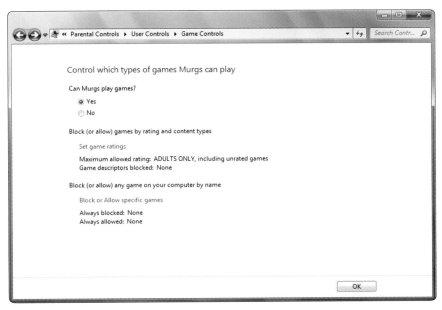

Specify whether the user can play games.

10   The Game Restrictions window opens. Scroll down to view the various settings, clicking the desired radio buttons to allow or block certain types of games.

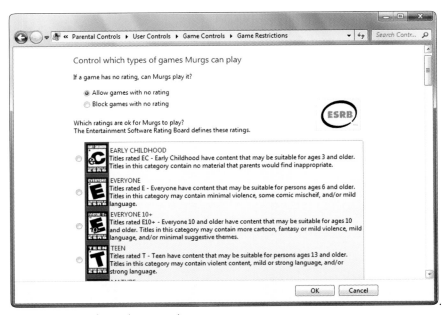

Control which types of games the user can play.

11 Press OK to return to the Game Controls window.

12 In the Game Controls window, click the Block or Allow Specific Games link.

13 The Game Overrides window appears. Click the *User Rating Setting, Always Allow, or Always Block* radio button for each game, as desired.

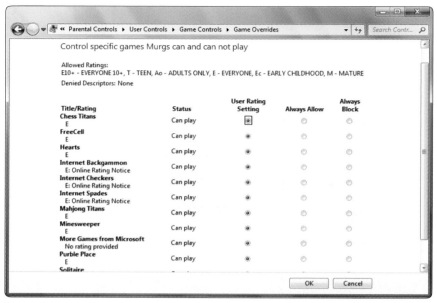

Control which types of games the user can play.

14 Press OK to return to the Game Controls window.

15 Press OK to return to the User Controls window.

16 In the User Controls window, click the Allow and Block Specific Programs link.

17 The Application Restrictions window opens. To limit the programs available to this user, click the *{username} Can Only Use the Programs I Allow* radio button to select it.

18 Windows 7 displays a list of programs installed on the computer. Click the checkbox for each program you want to allow.

If you want this user to be able to use most—but not all—programs installed on the computer, press the Check All button in the Application Restrictions window, and then uncheck those programs you want to block.

19 Press OK to return to the User Controls window.

20 Press OK to return to the Parental Controls window.

Setting space quotas

To prevent one user from consuming more than his or her fair share of disk space, you can establish space limits for each user.

1 Open the Computer folder by clicking the Start button (⊕) and choosing Computer from the menu that appears.

2 Right-click the icon for the computer's hard drive.

3 Choose Properties.

Right-click the hard drive and select Properties.

4 The hard drive's Properties dialog box opens. Click the Quota tab.

5 Click Show Quota Settings.

6 The Quota Settings dialog box opens. Click the *Enable Quota Management* checkbox to select it.

7 Optionally, click the *Deny Disk Space to Users Exceeding Quota Limit* checkbox to select it.

8 To automatically limit disk space available to new users, click the *Limit Disk Space* radio button to select it.

9 In the Limit Disk Space To text field, type the number of kilobytes (KB), megabytes (MB), gigabytes (GB), terabytes (TB), petabytes (PB), or exabytes (EB) new users will be allotted.

10 Choose the desired unit, KB, MB, GB, TB, PB, or EB, from the Limit Disk Space To drop-down menu.

11 In the Set Warning Level To text field, type the number of kilobytes, megabytes, gigabytes, terabytes, petabytes, or exabytes that the user must consume before being warned that they are reaching their disk-space limit.

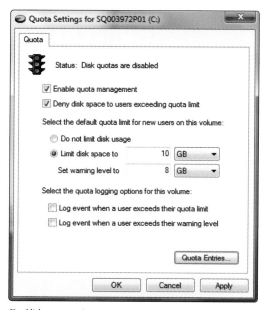

Establish quota settings.

12 Press OK to close the Quota Settings dialog box.

13 Windows 7 prompts you to confirm that you want to enable space quotas. Press OK.

14 Press OK to close the hard drive's Properties dialog box.

Enabling the Guest account

You can allow others to temporarily share your computer with limited access and control. This limited account, allows the user to browse the Internet, play computer games, and use applications such as WordPad but restricting the user's ability to view advanced settings or to modify the Windows 7 configuration or support files.

Enabling the Guest account reduces overall Windows 7 system security because it allows someone without a user account on the computer to use the system and open files. For this reason, the Guest account is disabled by default. Nonetheless, there are legitimate reasons for enabling the use of the Guest account—for example, if you have a house guest or an office visitor who needs temporary access to a computer—although you should disable the account anytime it isn't being used.

1   From the Control panel window, click the Add or Remove User Accounts link under User Accounts and Family Safety.

2   Select the Guest account in the Manage Accounts window.

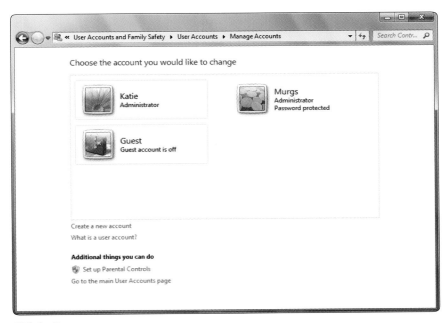

Click the Guest account.

3   The Turn On Guest Account screen opens. Press Turn On. Windows 7 enables the Guest account.

Press Turn On.

Disabling the Guest account

Disable the Guest account after your guest has finished using it. Start by logging on to an Administrator account:

1   Select the Guest account in the Manage Accounts window.

2   The Change Guest Options window appears. Click the Turn Off the Guest Account
link. Windows 7 turns off the Guest account.

Disable the Guest account.

Deleting an account

If a user no longer shares your computer, you should remove his or her account from the
system. You cannot delete the account that you are currently using, however. This ensures that,
in the event there is only one Administrator account on the computer, the person who uses that
account does not delete it.

1   Open the Control panel and click the Add or Remove User Accounts link under User
Accounts and Family Safety.

2   Select the account you want to delete in the Manage Accounts window.

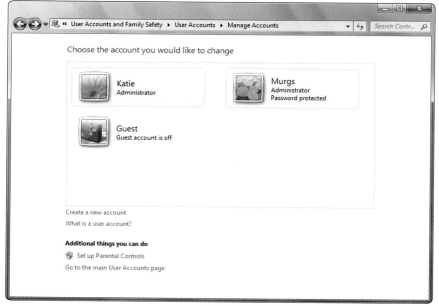

Click the account you want to delete.

3   The Change an Account screen opens. Click the Delete the Account link.

Click Delete the Account.

4   The Delete Account screen appears. To delete the account and all files the account contains, press Delete Files. To delete the account but save the files in the account, click Keep Files. If you opt to keep the files, Windows 7 will save the contents of the account's desktop, Documents, Favorites, Music, Pictures, and Videos folders in a new folder named after the account on your desktop.

Keep or delete files associated with the account.

5   The Confirm Deletion screen appears. Press Delete Account. Windows 7 deletes the account.

Confirming deletion of the account.

Self study

1   Choose a picture for your user account.

2   Enable and then disable the Guest account.

Review

Questions

1   What is the difference between a Standard account and an Administrator account?

2   Should you use an Administrator account for general computing tasks.

3   For what type of user is the Guest account appropriate?

4   How do you access the Manage Accounts window in the Control Panel?

Answers

1   Users with Standard accounts can do anything users with an Administrator account can do—but they may be prompted to provide the Administrator password before installing hardware or software or changing security and other settings.

2   No, its best to use an Administrator account only to perform computer-management tasks. For your everyday computing tasks, such as word-processing or Internet browsing, you should set up and use a Standard account.

3   The Guest account is for people who need temporary access to the computer, such as a house guest or an office visitor.

4   To open the Manage Accounts window, click the Add or Remove User Accounts link under User Accounts and Family Safety in the main Control Panel window.

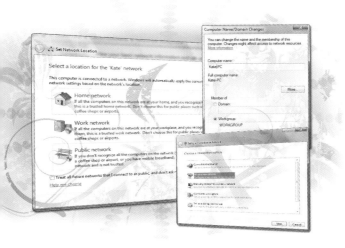

Lesson 9

What you'll learn in this lesson:

- Setting up your network
- Sharing files and folders
- Using the Share With menu
- Sharing a printer
- Troubleshooting your network

Networking Your Computer

Find out how Windows 7 makes it easy to share documents, music, photos, and other files by creating a home or office network. See how you can use a network to also share hardware resources such as printers.

Starting up

Before you start, be sure to copy all the files for this lesson from the accompanying DVD to your hard drive.

See Lesson 9 in action!

Use the accompanying video to gain a better understanding of how to use some of the features shown in this lesson. The video tutorial for this lesson can be found on the included DVD.

Setting up a wireless network

You can set up a wireless network which offers mobility as it transmits data between computers using radio waves rather than wires or cables. Here is what you'll need:

• **A wireless network adapter.** Also called a wireless card. A wireless network adapter enables computers to connect to the network and communicate with each other. You'll need a wireless network adapter for each computer you want to connect to your wireless network. Most laptops and many desktop computers come with a wireless adapter already installed; if yours doesn't, you can buy one from your local computer or electronics store. If you're not sure whether your computer features a wireless network adapter, open Windows 7 Device Manager.

1 Press the Start button (⊙), then click Control Panel.

2 In the Control Panel window, click the Hardware and Sound link, then click the Device Manager link under Devices and Printers.

3 Double-click the Network Adapters entry in the list of devices, and look for a network adapter whose name includes the word *wireless*.

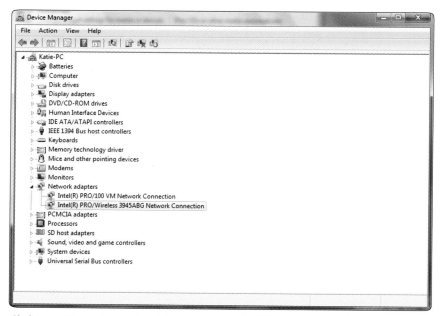

Check Device Manager to determine whether your computer already has a wireless network adapter.

- **A wireless router.** The router connects the computers to each other and to the Internet. Wireless routers connect computers and transmit information between them via radio signals instead of wires or cables. There are a few different types of wireless network technologies: 802.11a, 802.11b, 802.11g, and 802.11n. The 802.11g and 802.11n offer the fastest data-transmission speeds and strongest wireless signals. Your wireless network adapter must be compatible with the network technology used by your wireless router.

- **An Internet connection.** If you want the computers on your wireless network to access the Internet via a shared connection, you'll need an Internet connection—preferably a broadband variety, such as cable, DSL, or fiberoptic.

Other types of networks

Wireless networks are not the only types of networks you can create. Other types of networks include the following:

- **Ethernet networks.** Ethernet networks use data cables to transmit information between computers. To set up an Ethernet network, you need Ethernet cables between each computer and a router. If your home or office is already wired for Ethernet, you can plug the computers on your network into the Ethernet jacks in your home or office.

- **HomePNA.** HomePNA networks use your existing telephone wires to transmit information between computers. To set up a HomePNA network, you'll need a phone jack in each room where you have a computer. You'll also need a HomePNA network adapter for each computer on the network.

- **Powerline.** Powerline networks use your home's or office's existing electrical wires to transmit information between computers. To set up a powerline network, you'll need an electrical outlet in each room where you have a computer. You'll also need a powerline network adapter for each computer on the network. Interference and *noise* on the line can affect powerline networks.

Some of these types of networks also require additional hardware, such as a router, hub, or switch.

This lesson focuses on setting up a wireless network. For information about setting up other types of networks, see the Windows 7 Help files.

Setting up the router

If you see the Windows 7 logo or the phrase, "Compatible with Windows 7," on your router, you can use Windows Connect Now (WCN) to set up your router automatically. Start by plugging the router into a power outlet; then, on your computer, click the wireless networks icon in the Windows 7 taskbar's notification area. Windows 7 displays a list of available networks, including an entry for your router. Click the network, and press Connect, then follow the onscreen instructions.

 If your router doesn't support WCN, then use the setup CD that came with your router.

Once your router is up and running, locate it where it will have the strongest signal with the least amount of interference. Choose a central location, position it off the floor and away from walls and from metal objects such as filing cabinets. If you are running an 802.11g wireless network, it uses a radio frequency that may be interrupted if you turn on the microwave or use a cordless phone.

Securing the router

Your wireless signal may extend beyond the boundaries of your home or office, so you should make it a point to secure it so that outsiders cannot access information on your network or use your Internet connection.

Although WCN turns on security automatically, it uses the manufacturer's default username and password. To prevent someone who has this information from modifying your router, you should change the default username and password to ones that will be difficult for others to guess. The exact procedure for changing usernames and passwords varies by manufacturers so, refer to the documentation that came with your wireless router.

Install firewall software on each of your networked computers to protect your computer and network from hackers or malicious software. Windows 7 includes its own firewall software, called Windows Firewall; you'll learn more about it in Lesson 10, "Securing Your Computer."

You also want to set up a security key for your network to lock it in the same way you might use a real key to lock a filing cabinet. Anyone who attempts to log on to your network will require this security key to gain access.

Next you will see how to connect to a new wireless network.

1 Press the Start button (⬤) and choose Control Panel.

2 In the Control Panel window, under Network and Internet, click the View Network Status and Tasks link.

Click View Network Status and Tasks.

3 The Network and Sharing Center opens. Under Change Your Networking Settings, click the Set Up a New Connection or Network link.

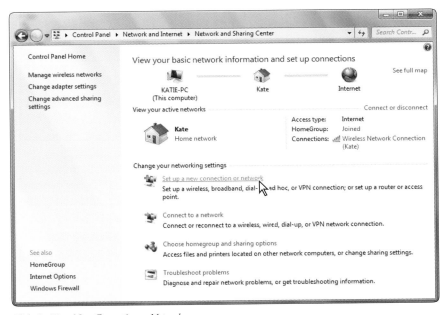

Click Set Up a New Connection or Network.

4 The Set Up a Connection or Network Wizard opens. In the Choose a Connection Option screen, click Set Up a New Network.

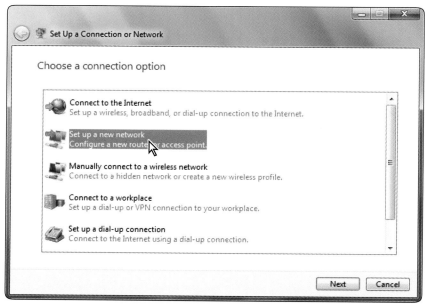

Click Set Up a New Network.

5 Press Next. Click the router you want to configure in the list that appears.

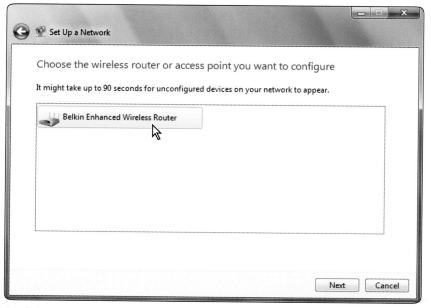

Specify the router you want to configure.

6   Press Next. Type the router's PIN, located on the bottom or back of the router, in the
PIN text field.

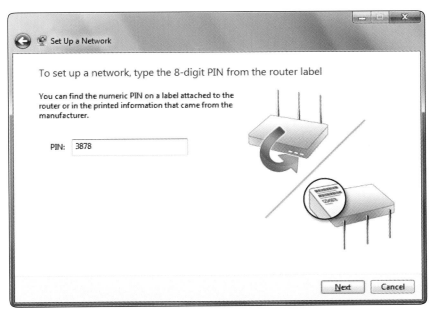

Enter the router's PIN.

7   Press Next. Type a name for your network in the Type Your Network Name text field.
Type a security key for your network in the Security Key text field. If your network
supports the use of WPA2- or WPA-level security, your security key can be a passphrase
rather than a cryptic sequence of numbers.

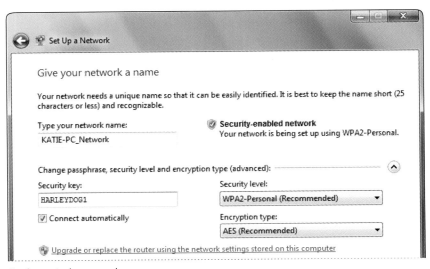

Set the security key or passphrase.

Be sure to select a passphrase or security key that will be difficult for others to guess, but that you will be sure to remember. If necessary, write down your security key or passphrase and store it in a safe place.

8   Click Next. Windows 7 applies your changes to the network.

Connecting the router to the Internet

Once you have your router set up, you're ready to connect it to the Internet. Doing so will enable every computer on your network to go online. First plug one end of an Ethernet cable into the Internet port on your router and the other end into your broadband modem.

Connecting computers to the router

The exact procedure for connecting your computer to your new wireless network depends on the operating system the computer is running and whether your router supports WCN or another technology called Wi-Fi Protected Setup (WPS).

1   Log on to the computer you want to add.

2   If you are using Windows 7, click the wireless networks icon in the Windows 7 taskbar's notification area. If you are using Windows Vista, press the Start button (⊕) and choose Connect To.

3   Windows displays a list of available networks, including one for your router. Click your network to select it.

4   Press Connect.

5   When Windows prompts you to enter a security key or passphrase, press the power button on your router; when you do, your router automatically sets up the computer to connect to your network.

Add a Windows 7 computer that does not support WCN or WPS

These steps show you how to add a computer running Windows 7 to a wireless router that does not support WCN or WPS.

1   Log on to the computer you want to add.

2   If you are using Windows 7, click the wireless networks icon in the Windows 7 taskbar's notification area. If you are using Windows Vista, press the Start button (⊕) and choose Connect To.

3   Windows displays a list of available networks, including one for your router. Click it to select it.

4   Press Connect.

5   If prompted, enter your network security key or passphrase.

6   Press OK.

Testing your network

To make sure the computers you added to your network are accessible, press the Start button
(●) and click your username in the Start menu. In the left pane of the window that opens, click
Network. Windows displays icons for the computer you are using and for all other computers
connected to the network. Be aware that it might take a few minutes for computers running
earlier versions of Windows to appear in the list.

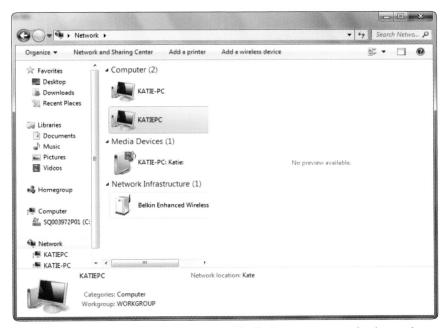

Windows displays icons for the computer you are using and for all other computers connected to the network.

Sharing files and folders via Public folders

Windows 7 offers special folders, called Public folders, which you can use to share files and folders with other users. There are four Public folders: Public Documents, Public Music, Public Pictures, and Public Videos. These folders are subfolders of the main Documents, Music, Pictures, and Videos folders, respectively. Move or copy the file or folder you want to share to the relevant Public folder to make it accessible to others. When you do, others can open and view the file or folder as if it were stored on their own PC. And if you give them permission to make changes to files you place in a Public folder, then any changes they make will be reflected in the version stored on your PC.

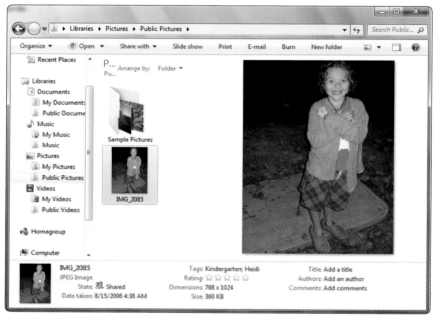

Notice the Public folders in the folder list.

When you place an item in a Public folder, any other person with a user account on that same computer can view the item. To make items in your Public folders accessible to others on your network, you must take a few extra steps:

1   Press the Start button ( ) and choose Control Panel to open the Control Panel window.

2   Under Network and Internet, click the View Network Status and Tasks link.

3   In the Network and Sharing Center, click the Change advanced sharing settings link in the left side of the Network and Sharing Center.

4   The Advanced sharing Settings screen opens. If necessary, click the down arrow to the right of your current profile to expand it.

An even faster way to open the Advanced Sharing Settings screen is to open one of your Public folders in Windows Explorer, click Share With, and choose Advanced Sharing Settings.

5   Under Public Folder Sharing, click the *Turn On Sharing* radio button to select it.

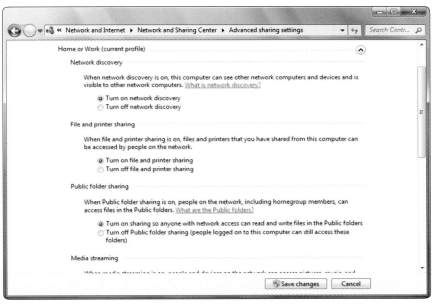

Enable Public folder sharing.

6   Press Save Changes.

Sharing files and folders with homegroups and workgroups

Sharing your files and folders using Windows 7's Public folders is one way to go; another is to create a homegroup or a workgroup. This links together the computers on the network in such a way that pictures, music, videos, documents, and even printers can be shared. Other people can't change the files you share unless you give them permission to do so.

You'll learn about setting permissions later in this lesson. When you create or join a group, you specify which of your items you want to share and which should remain private.

Setting up a homegroup

If all the computers on your network run Windows 7, you can create a homegroup. When you do, **Windows 7** works behind the scenes to configure the appropriate settings.

You can create a homegroup in all versions of Windows 7 except for Windows 7 Starter and Windows 7 Home Basic. Computers running these two versions can join homegroups, but cannot create them.

1 Press the Start button (⬤) and choose Control Panel to open the Control Panel window.

2 Under Network and Internet, click the View Network Status and Tasks link.

3 In the Network and Sharing Center, under View Your Active Networks, click the link to your network type. This is usually the default: Unidentified.

4 The Set Network Location window appears. Click Home Network.

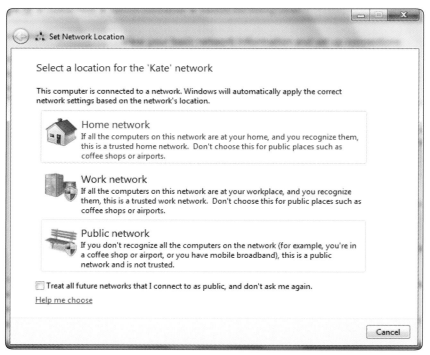

Click Home Network in the Set Network Location window.

5   The Create a Homegroup Wizard starts. Click the checkbox next to each folder you
     want to share—Music, Documents, or Pictures.

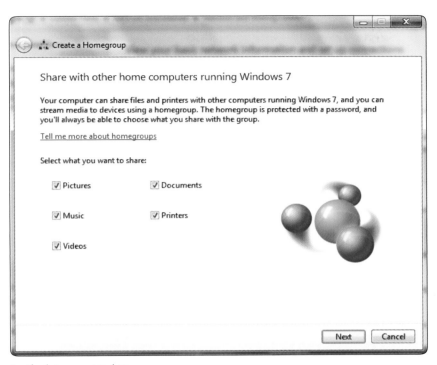

Specify what you want to share.

6   Press Next.

7 The Create a Homegroup Wizard generates a password. Write it down. You'll need it to add additional Windows 7 computers to the homegroup.

Write down the password.

8 Press Finish. Windows 7 creates the homegroup.

Connecting a computer to a homegroup

Once you've set up your homegroup, other computer on your network running Windows 7 can join it, enabling users to easily share files and access shared resources such as printers. You'll learn more about sharing printers later in this lesson.

1   In the main Control Panel window, under Network and Internet, click the Choose Homegroup and Sharing Options link.

2   Windows 7 launches a wizard, asking whether you want to join the homegroup. Press Join Now.

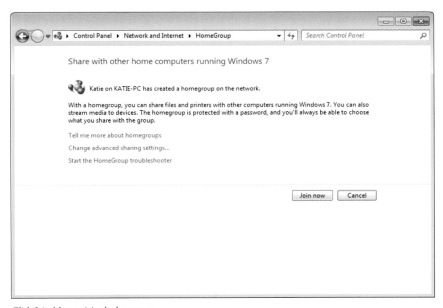

Click Join Now to join the homegroup.

3   Click the checkbox next to each folder you want to share—Music, Documents, Pictures, etc.

4   When prompted, type the password required to join the homegroup. This is the password you obtained in step 5 in the previous exercise.

5   Press Join Now.

6 Windows 7 notifies you that you have joined the homegroup. Press Finish.

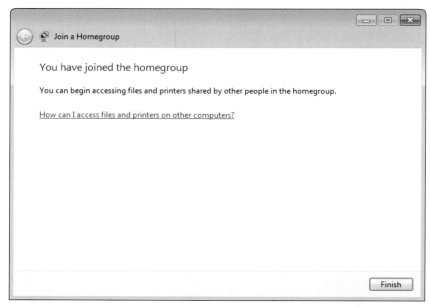

When Windows 7 notifies you that you have joined the homegoup, click Finish.

 If you forgot the password required to join the network, you can easily retrieve it. To do so, return to the computer you used to set up the network and, in the Network and Sharing Center, under Change Your Network Settings, click Choose Homegroup and Sharing Options. Next, click View Other Homegroup Options, then click View or Print the Homegroup Password.

View files and folders that other users in your homegroup have shared

1 Press the Start button (⊙).

2 Click your username.

3 In the navigation pane on the left side of the window that opens, click Homegroup.

4   In the file list, double-click the username of the person whose files you want to access.

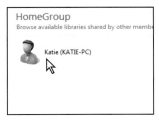

Double-click a user name to see that person's files and folders.

If the user's computer is turned off, hibernating, or asleep, it won't appear in the Homegroup list in the navigation pane.

5   Windows 7 displays the files and folders shared by that user in the file list. Double-click the file or folder you want to open.

Double-click the file or folder you want to open.

Setting up a workgroup

If your network is composed of computers running different versions of Windows—for example, Windows 7, Windows Vista, and Windows XP—you should not create a homegroup. You can share files and folders among the computers using different operating systems by adding them to the same workgroup.

If all the computers on your netowrk are using Windows 7, you can skip this section and jump ahead to "Using the Share With menu" section.

Windows creates a workgroup and gives it a name when you set up a network. In order to share files and folders among the various computers on the network, you must ensure that the workgroup name listed for each computer is the same.

1   If you are using Windows 7, click the System and Security link in the Control Panel window. If you are using Windows Vista, click the System and Maintenance link.

2   In the System and Security window (Windows 7) or System and Maintenance window (Windows Vista), click the System link.

3   The System window opens, listing the name of the workgroup in the Computer Name, Domain, and Workgroup Settings section. To change the name of the workgroup, click the Change Settings link.

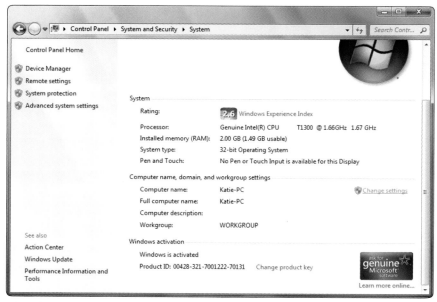

Click Change Settings under Computer Name, Domain, and Workgroup Settings.

4   The System Properties dialog box opens with the Computer Name tab displayed. Press the Change button.

5   The Computer Name/Domain Changes dialog box opens. Under Member Of, click the *Workgroup* radio button.

6   Type the name you want to use for the workgroup.

Set the workgroup name.

7   Press OK to close the Computer Name/Domain Changes dialog box.

8   Windows alerts you that you must restart your computer to apply the change. Press OK.

9   Press Close to close the System Properties dialog box.

10   Windows prompts you to restart your computer. Click Restart Now.

Changing the workgroup name on a Windows XP computer

These step show you how to find and change the workgroup name on a Windows XP computer if your network features a computer running Windows XP:

1   Press the Start button (⊙).

2   Right-click the My Computer entry in the Start menu.

3   Choose Properties.

4   The System Properties dialog box opens. Click the Computer Name tab.

5   Press the Change button.

6   Type the same workgroup name as the one used on your Windows 7 and Windows Vista computers.

7   Press OK.

Establishing the network location

Your next step is to establish the network location of all computers running Windows Vista or Windows 7. You have three network location choices:

- **Home**. Choose this option if your network is a home network, with known and trusted computers.

- **Work**. Choose this option if your network is a work network—for example, a small business—again, with known and trusted computers.

- **Public**. Choose this option if the network is available for public use—for example, one found in an airport, library, or coffee shop.

When you set the network location, Windows automatically applies security settings tailored to the network location you chose and opens the appropriate firewall ports on your computer, assuming you use Windows Firewall. For example, if you choose Home or Work, Windows enables the following: a setting called Network Discovery, which enables the computer to detect other computers on the network; file sharing, which enables you to share your files and folders; and Public folder sharing.

If you use a firewall other than Windows Firewall, you will need to configure it to allow file and printer sharing. For more information, see the Windows 7 Help files.

1   To change the location of your network, press the Start button (⊙) and click Control Panel.

2   In the Control Panel window, click the Network and Internet link. When the Network and Internet window appears, click the Network and Sharing Center link.

3   In the Network and Sharing Center window, under the View your active networks section, click current network location link located under the Network title. In this example, Public network is listed.

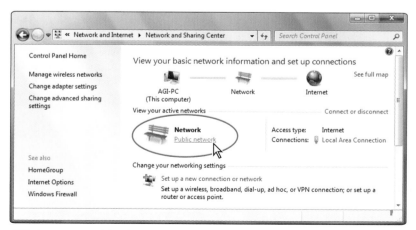

Click the current network location.

4   The Set Network Location dialog box appears. Select an alternate location: Home or Work. In this example, Work is selected.

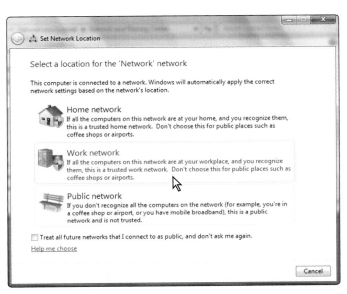

Select a new network location.

After selecting the new network location, the next screen may vary. For example, after selecting the Home network location, the next screen offers you the option to set up homegroups.

5   The new Work location is confirmed in the next screen. Press Close.

6   The new network location is also updated in the Networking and Sharing center. Press the Close button in the upper right corner of the Networking and Sharing Center window to close it when finished.

Using the Share With menu

If you want to share a file or folder on your Windows 7 computer that is not shared automatically when you set up a homegroup or workgroup, then you can use the Share With menu to do so. This menu enables you to select an individual file or folder to share with others. If you belong to a homegroup, you can opt to share the file or folder with Read permissions with everyone in your homegroup, with Read/Write permissions with everyone in your homegroup, or with specific individuals in your homegroup. If you belong to a workgroup, you can share with specific individuals in the workgroup.

Sharing with your homegroup

Next you will learn how to share a file or folder on your Windows 7 computer with homegroup users,

1 In Windows Explorer, locate and select the file or folder you want to share.

2 Click Share With.

3 Choose Homegroup (Read) or Homegroup (Read/Write) to share the file or folder with everyone on your homegroup. Alternatively, click Specific People to share the file or folder with specific people in the homegroup.

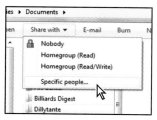

The Share With menu.

4 Windows 7 launches the File Sharing Wizard. Click the down arrow in the Type a Name text field.

5 Select the name of the user with whom you want to share the file or folder.

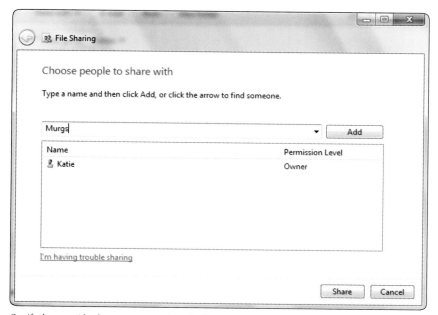

Specify the user with whom you want to share the file or folder.

6   Press Add.

7   Windows 7 adds the user you selected to the list of users with whom the file or folder is shared. To set the permission level, choose Read or Read/Write from the Permission level drop-down menu for that user.

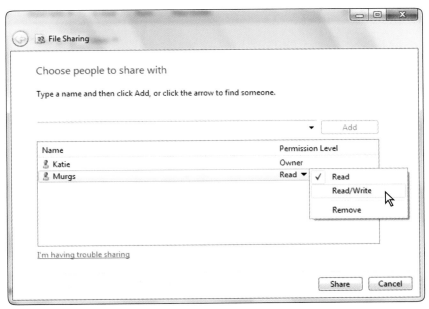

Specify the user with whom you want to share the file or folder.

8   Press Share.

9   The File Sharing Wizard notifies you that the file or folder you selected has been shared. To notify the user that he or she can access the shared file or folder, click the e-mail link.

10 Windows 7 launches your mail program, with a New Message window pre-addressed to the user, the Subject line filled in, and a link to the file or folder in the message body. Click Send to send the message.

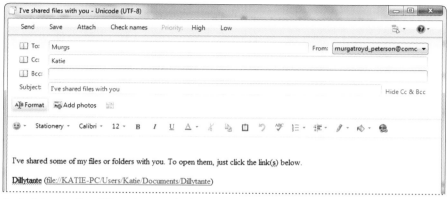

Send a link to the file or folder to the user with whom you have shared it.

11 Press Done.

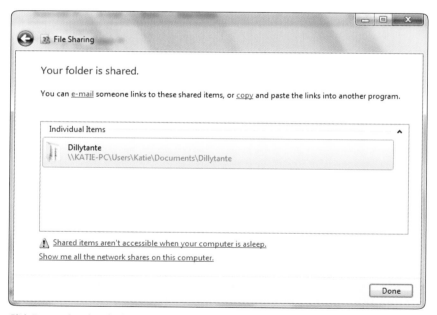

Click Done to close the File Sharing Wizard.

Sharing with your workgroup

To share a file or folder on your Windows 7 PC with workgroup users, simply choose Specific People from the Share With menu and follow steps 4 to 11 in the preceding section.

Un-sharing a file or folder

What if you've shared a folder, but you want to prevent certain files in that folder from being shared? For example, maybe you've shared your Documents folder, but you want to prevent others from reading the daily journal you keep on your PC. To keep an item private, follow these steps:

1   In Windows Explorer, right-click the file or folder you want to keep private.

2   Choose Share With.

3   Select Nobody. Windows 7 blocks access to the file or folder to others on your homegroup or workgroup.

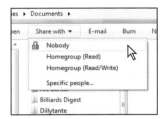

Un-share a file or folder.

Applying permissions to files and folders

To specify what users who share your computer or your network can do with files and folders you make available to them, you can apply permissions. Permissions are like rules that specify the level of access—if any—a particular user has to a file or folder. Access levels include the following:

- **Full control**. When this level of access is applied, users can see the contents of a file or folder, make changes to files and folders, create new files and folders, and run any programs in folders.

- **Modify**. Users with this level of access can make changes to files and folders but cannot create new ones.

- **Read and execute**. When this level of access is applied, users can see the contents of files and folders and can run any programs in folders.

- **Read**. Users with this level of access can view the contents of folders and open files and folders.

- **Write**. When this level of access is applied, users can make changes to files and folders and create new ones.

You cannot adjust permissions for files or folders shared in Public folders.

1   In Windows Explorer, right-click the file or folder for which you want to set permissions.

2   Select Properties.

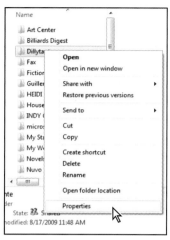

Right-click the file or folder in Windows Explorer and choose Properties.

3   The file or folder's Properties dialog box opens. Click the Security tab.

4   Press the Edit button.

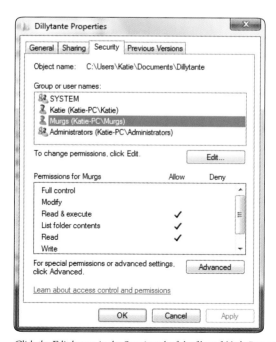

Click the Edit button in the Security tab of the file or folder's Properties dialog box.

5 The file or folder's Permissions dialog box opens. To change a user's permissions, click the name of the user in the Group or User Names area.

If the user for which you want to set permissions does not appear in the Group or User Names area, click Add, type the name of the user for which you want to set permissions, then press OK.

6 Under Permissions for {username}, allow or deny a permission by clicking the appropriate check box to select or deselect it.

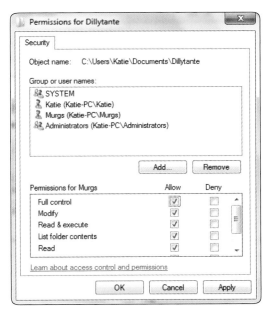

Set permissions for a user.

7 Press OK to close the Permissions dialog box.

8 Press OK to close the Properties dialog box.

Creating a user group

If several users have access to your computer, and if you want those users to have the same level of permission to a certain file or folder, you may find it arduous to apply those permissions one user at a time. Instead, you can create a user group for those users, and then grant that group permission to a file or folder. Then, simply select the group name in the file or folder's Permissions dialog box in the Group or User Names area. If necessary, refer to step 5 in the preceding instructions.

Windows 7 includes two user groups by default: the Administrator group and the Standard group. These groups include all users who have Administrator accounts and all users who have Standard accounts, respectively.

To create a user group, you use a tool called Microsoft Management Console (MMC).

1   Click the Start button ( ).

2   In the Start menu's Search text field, type **MMC**.

3   Windows 7 displays an entry for Microsoft Management Console in the Start menu; click it.

Search for MMC.

4   Windows 7 prompts you to confirm that you want to use Microsoft Management Console. Press Yes.

5   A Microsoft Management Console window opens. Before you can create a group, you must install the Local Users and Groups snap-in. A *snap-in* is a tool or a set of tools that can be added to Microsoft Management Console to help manage a computer. To begin, click the File menu.

6   Click Add/Remove Snap-In.

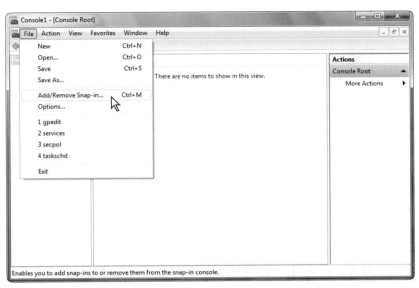

Choose Add/Remove Snap-In from the File menu.

7   The Add or Remove Snap-Ins window opens. In the Available Snap-Ins pane on the left, click Local Users and Groups. Press Add.

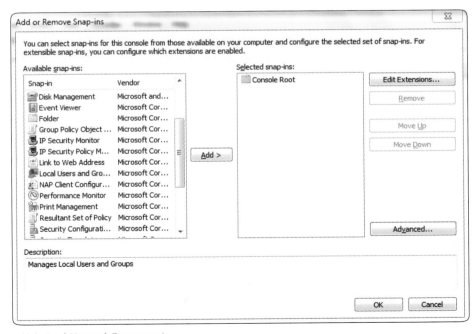

Add the Local Users and Groups snap-in.

8   The Choose Target Machine window opens. Click the Local Computer radio button.

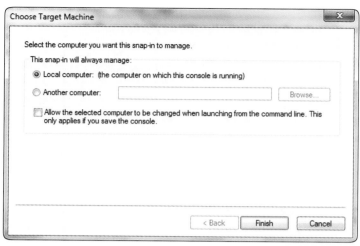

Specify the target computer.

9   Press Finish.

10 The snap-in is added to the Selected Snap-Ins pane on the right side of the Add or Remove Snap-Ins window. Press OK.

11 The snap-in appears in the Microsoft Management Console window. In the left pane, click the snap-in.

12 In the middle pane, double-click the Groups folder.

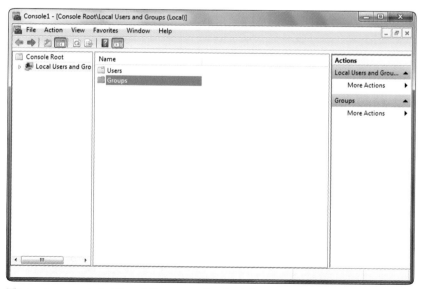

The snap-in appears in the Microsoft Management Console window.

13 In the right pane, click More Actions.

14 Choose New Group from the menu that appears.

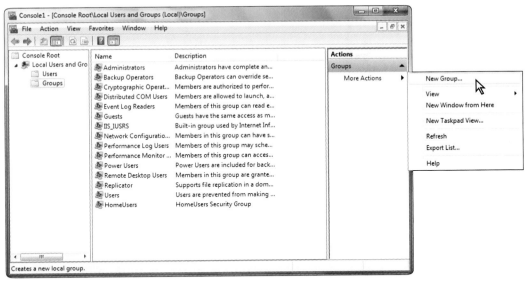

Click More Actions and then choose New Group.

15 The New Group dialog box opens. Type a name for the group.

16 Type a description for the group.

17 Press the Add button.

18 The Select Users dialog box opens. Type the name of the user you want to add.

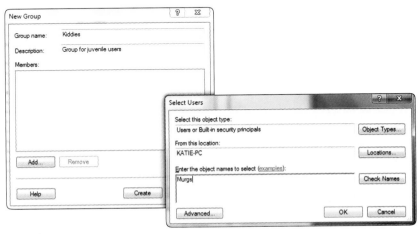

Create the group.

19 Press OK. Windows 7 adds the user to the group.

20 Repeat steps 18 to 20 for each user you want to add to the group.

21 Press Create to create the group. The group is added to the list in the middle pane of the Microsoft Management Console window.

22 Press Close to close the New Group dialog box.

Adding a user to an existing group

To add a user to an existing group, right-click the group in the Microsoft Management Console window and choose Add to Group from the menu that appears. The group's Properties dialog box opens; press Add, repeat steps 19 and 20 from the preceding instructions, then press OK.

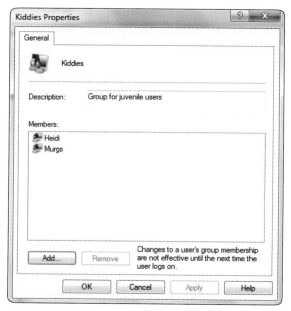

Adding a user.

Connecting to a printer

You may need to let Windows 7 know which printer or printers you plan to use. This let's Windows 7 create a connection that all programs can use for printing, and Windows 7 can take advantage of any features that might be unique to your printer, such as printing on both sides of the paper or printing in color. You'll indicate whether the printer is connected directly to your computer, or connected to a network.

1   From the Start menu, choose Devices and Printers. The Devices and Printers
     window opens.

Choose Devices and Printers from the Start menu.

2   In the Devices and Printers window, press the Add a Printer button.

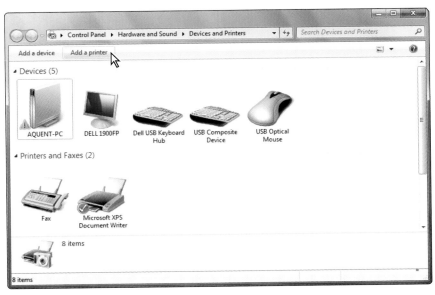

Press the Add a printer button.

3   Select Add a network, wireless, or Bluetooth printer if you have a networkable printer. Windows locates available printers on your network.

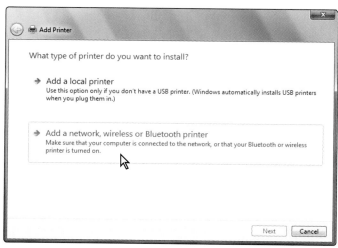

Choose the network, wireless or Bluetooth printer option.

4   From the list of printers that appears, select the printer you wish to add and press Next. If you wish to change the name of the printer within Windows 7, you can name it in the next window. For example, you can name it Home Office printer. Otherwise, press Next.

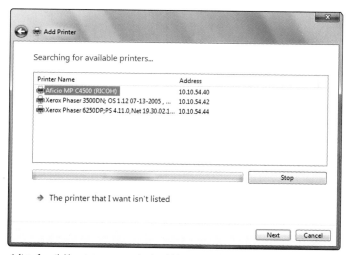

A list of available printers appears in the Add a printer dialog box.

5   A window appears when the printer is successfully added. You can print a test page or press Finish.

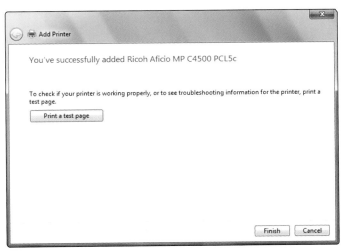

The printer has been successfully added.

Sharing a printer

Suppose you share your network with several other users, but you have only one printer. If so, you can set up Windows 7 to share that printer with the other computers on your network. When you do this, the other computers on the network can access the printer through the Print dialog box.

Sharing a printer with a homegroup

To share a printer with a homegroup, first connect it to your Windows 7 PC.

1   In the main Control Panel window, under Network and Internet, click the Choose Homegroup and Sharing Options link.

2 The HomeGroup screen appears. Under Share Libraries and Printers, click the Printers check box to select it.

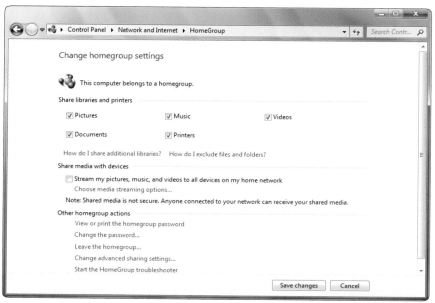

Share a printer.

3 Press the Save Changes button.

Setting up each computer on a homegroup to print

Next, set up each computer on the homegroup to print from that printer.

1 Log in to a computer in the homegroup from which you want to be able to print.

2 In the main Control Panel window, under Network and Internet, click the Choose Homegroup and Sharing Options link.

3 The HomeGroup screen appears. Press Install Printer.

4 If you don't already have the appropriate printer drivers installed on this computer, click Install Driver in the dialog box that appears. Windows 7 configures the computer to print via the network.

A driver is a special kind of software that enables your computer to communicate with an external device such as a printer. For more information about adding a printer, see the section, "Connecting to a printer," earlier in this lesson.

Sharing a printer with a workgroup

To share a printer with a workgroup rather than a homegroup, first connect it to your Windows 7 computer.

1   Press the Start button (⦿) and choose Control Panel to open the Control Panel window.

2   Under Network and Internet, click the View Network Status and Tasks link

3   On the left side of the Network and Sharing Center, click the Change Advanced Sharing Settings link.

4   The Advanced Sharing Settings screen opens. If necessary, click the down arrow to the right of your current profile to expand it.

5   Under File and Printer Sharing, click the *Turn On File and Printer Sharing* radio button to select it.

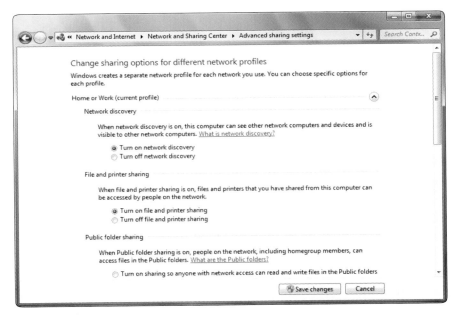

Enable printer sharing.

6   Press the Save Changes button.

Troubleshooting your network

If you experience a problem with your network, you can use the Windows 7 Network Troubleshooter to diagnose the problem, suggest fixes for the problem, and potentially repair the problem itself.

After you run Network Troubleshooter, it generates a report about the problem for future reference. This report can help a technical-support person identify and solve your problem in the event that Network Troubleshooter fails to do so.

1 Click the Start button (●) and choose Control Panel to open the Control Panel window.

2 Under Network and Internet, click the View Network Status and Tasks link.

3 In the Network and Sharing Center, under Change Your Networking Settings, click the Troubleshoot Problems link.

4 The Troubleshooting Problems – Network and Internet screen appears. Click the entry in the Network or Printer list that best reflects the problem you are experiencing with your network.

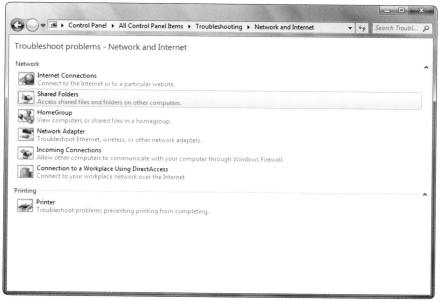

Click the entry that best reflects the problem you are experiencing.

5   Windows 7 launches a special troubleshooting wizard to help you solve the problem.
    Simply follow the onscreen instructions, pressing Next to advance from screen to screen.

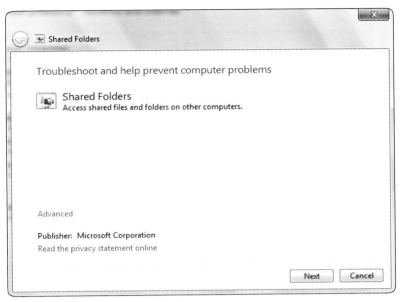

Windows 7 launches a troubleshooting wizard.

Self study

1   Set up a wireless network for your home or office.

2   Apply the appropriate permissions to any files or folders you want to share.

Review

Questions

1   What is required to set up a wireless network?

2   Besides wireless networks, name two other types of networks.

3   What is the difference between a homegroup and a workgroup?

4   What types of permissions can be applied to files and folders?

5   Can you apply permissions to files and folders in a Public folder?

Answers

1   To set up a wireless network, you need a wireless network adapter for each computer you want to add to the network, a wireless router, and optionally, an Internet connection.

2   In addition to wireless networks, there are Ethernet networks, which use special cables called Ethernet cables to transmit information between computers; HomePNA networks, which use your home's or office's existing telephone wires to transmit information between computers; and Powerline networks, which use your home's or office's existing electrical wires to transmit information between computers.

3   You set up a homegroup if all the computers on your network run Windows 7. If the computers on your network run different versions of Windows, you must set up a workgroup.

4   The following permissions can be applied to files and folders: Full Control, Modify, Read and Execute, Read, and Write.

5   No, you cannot apply permissions to files and folders shared in Public folders.

What you'll learn in this lesson:

- Password-protecting your computer

- Encrypting your data

- Thwarting intruders with Windows Firewall

- Guarding against spyware with Windows Defender

Securing Your Computer

If your computer is connected to the Internet, it may be vulnerable to threats from hackers, Internet worms, or viruses. Even a computer that isn't connected can be compromised by someone who gains physical access to it. This lesson covers ways to secure your computer and keep your data private.

Starting up

Before you start, be sure to copy all the files for this lesson from the accompanying DVD to your hard drive.

See Lesson 10 in action!

Use the accompanying video to gain a better understanding of how to use some of the features shown in this lesson. The video tutorial for this lesson can be found on the included DVD.

Password-protecting your computer

When you set a password for your user account, you prevent anyone who does not know the password from logging on to your account and accessing your files. If you care about keeping your files private, then creating a password and keeping it confidential is crucial. This is especially true with your Administrator account, as anyone with access to an administrative account can change virtually anything on your system.

The most frequently used password is the word *password*. Pet names and birthdates are also common. These are weak passwords, since they can be easily guessed by anyone who knows you. When choosing a password, select one that is at least eight characters long, does not contain your username, your real name, or your company's name, does not contain a complete word, differs from passwords you have used in the past, and contains a mixture of uppercase letters, lowercase letters, numbers, symbols, and spaces. You should also change your password periodically.

Creating a password

To create a password for your account, first log on to the account.

1   Press the Start button (⊙) and choose Control Panel.

2   In the Control Panel window, click the User Accounts and Family Safety link.

3   The User Accounts and Family Safety window opens. Under User Accounts, click the Change Your Windows Password link.

Click the Change Your Windows Password link.

4   The User Accounts screen opens. Click the Create a Password for Your Account link.

Click the Create a Password for Your Account link.

5   The Create Your Password screen opens. Type the string of characters you want to use as your password in the top–most text field.

6   Type the characters a second time in the next text field to confirm it.

7   If you want Windows 7 to supply a password hint in the Windows 7 Welcome screen in the event you forget your password, type the hint in the next field. Be aware that the hint you type will be visible to anyone who attempts to log in to your computer.

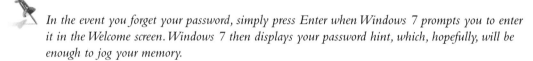

In the event you forget your password, simply press Enter when Windows 7 prompts you to enter it in the Welcome screen. Windows 7 then displays your password hint, which, hopefully, will be enough to jog your memory.

8   Click Create Password. Windows 7 password–protects the user account.

Create the password.

Although setting a password hint is helpful, if you are truly worried about forgetting your password, you should write it down—but make sure you store it somewhere safe and private. If you forget your password and you haven't written it down, it will need to be reset by the Administrator—in which case you may lose access to certain files. If you forget the password for your computer's Administrator account and there are no other user accounts on the computer, your only option is to reinstall Windows 7—which means you may lose your files.

Changing the password

Changing your password is similar to creating one. First. log on to the account.

1   Press the Start button (⬤), and click Control Panel.

2   Click the User Accounts and Family Safety link in the Control Panel window.

3   In the User Accounts screen, click the Change Your Password link.

4   The Change Your Password screen appears. In the top-most text field, type your current password.

5   In the next text field, type your new password.

6   Retype the new password in the next text field. Optionally, enter a new password hint.

Change the password.

7   Press Change Password.

Removing the password

If you decide you no longer want to password-protect your account, you can remove your password. First log on to the account, and then do the following:

1   Press the Start button (⊙), and click Control Panel.

2   Click the User Accounts and Family Safety link in the Control Panel window.

3   In the User Accounts screen, click the Change Your Password link.

4   The Remove Your Password screen appears. Type your current password.

Remove the password.

5   Press Remove Password. Windows 7 removes the password from the account.

Using the Administrator account to set and change passwords

You can also set an account password from the Administrator account. You might do this if your users are not in the habit of password-protecting their own accounts, or if a user has forgotten his or her password and you need to reset the account. Here's how:

1 Press the Start button (⊕), and click Control Panel.

2 Click the User Accounts and Family Safety, then click the Add or Remove User Accounts link.

3 Click the account for which you want to set a password in the Manage Accounts window.

Click the account for which you want to set a password.

4 The Change an Account screen opens. Click the Create a Password link.

Click Create a Password.

5   The Create Password screen opens. Follow steps 5 to 8 in the section, "Creating a Password," to create a password for the user account.

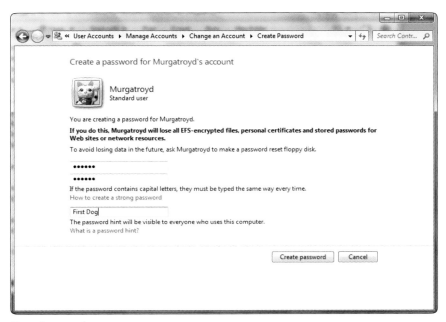

Create the password.

To use the Administrator account to change the password of another user account, click the Change the Password link in the Change an Account screen; then follow steps 4 to 7 in the section, "Changing the Password." Remove a password by clicking the Remove the Password link and following steps 4 and 5 in the section, "Removing the Password."

Password-protecting your screen saver

You can also set up your system to prompt you for that same password when your computer *wakes* from Sleep mode.

1   Press the Start button (●) and choose Control Panel.

2   In the Control Panel window, click the Hardware and Sound link.

3   The Hardware and Sound screen appears. Under Power Options, click the Require a
    Password When the Computer Wakes link.

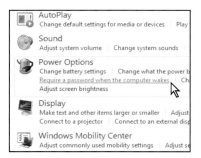

Click Require a Password When the Computer Wakes.

4   The System Settings screen appears. Click the *Require a Password* radio button to select it.

Click Require a Password.

5   Press Save Changes.

Encrypting your data

In the event a hacker in a remote location cracks your system password and gains access to your files, you can prevent that person from viewing their contents by encrypting them. Windows 7 offers two encryption tools: Encrypting File System and BitLocker. Only perform these steps if you need to encrypt your data. Failure to follow the instructions can result in the permanent encryption of your data, making it inaccessible.

Encrypting files and folders with Encrypting File System

You can use Windows 7's Encrypting File System, or EFS, to encrypt any files or folders that you store on your drive. With EFS, you choose which files and folders you want to encrypt. When you encrypt an entire folder, you automatically encrypt all the files and folders within.

Not all files and folders can be encrypted. For example, files and folders that are not stored on an NTFS drive cannot be encrypted, nor can compressed files or folders, or certain other types of files such as system files that support your operating system.

When you encrypt a folder or file using EFS, Windows 7 issues a certificate with an associated file encryption key, which EFS uses to encrypt and decrypt your data. Windows 7 does all this encryption and decryption work behind the scenes; you can work with the encrypted file or folder as you normally would. Someone attempting to infiltrate your system from the outside, however, is unable to unscramble any encrypted files or folders because that person does not have access to the certificate containing the encryption key.

1   In Windows Explorer, right-click the file or folder you want to encrypt. Click Properties.

2   The file or folder's Properties dialog box opens. In the General tab, click Advanced. The Advanced Attributes dialog box opens. Click the *Encrypt Contents to Secure Data* checkbox.

Encrypt the file or folder.

3   Press OK to close the Advanced Attributes dialog box.

4   Press OK to close the file or folder's Properties dialog box.

5   If you are attempting to encrypt a folder, the Confirm Attribute Changes dialog box opens, asking you to specify whether the encryption should be applied to the folder only, or to subfolders and files in the folder.

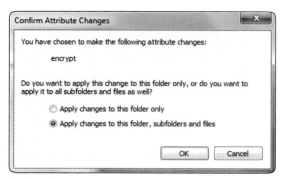

Confirm the encryption.

If you are attempting to encrypt a file, the Encryption Warning dialog box opens, asking if you want to encrypt the file and its parent folder (that is, apply the encryption to every file in the same folder as the one you selected) or just the file.

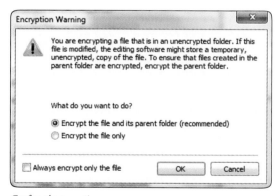

Confirm the encryption.

Select the desired option and press OK.

If you decide you no longer want to encrypt a file or folder, you can decrypt it. Simply clear the Encrypt Contents to Secure Data check box in the Advanced Attributes dialog box.

Backing up your encryption key

After you encrypt a file or folder, it's critical that you back up your encryption key, and store the backup file on removable media—such as a USB flash drive, a CD or DVD, or an external hard drive—and store this removable media in a safe place. Otherwise, if your keys are deleted or corrupted, your data will be virtually impossible to recover.

1   Press the Start button (⊕), and click Control Panel. Click the User Accounts and Family Safety, then click the Change Your Windows Password link.

2   Click the Manage Your File Encryption Certificates link on the left side of the User Accounts screen

Click the Manage Your File Encryption Certificates link.

3   Windows 7 launches the Encrypting File System Wizard. Press Next.

Press Next in the first screen of the Encrypting File System Wizard.

4   The Select or Create a File Encryption Certificate screen appears. Click the Use This Certificate radio button to select it.

Select Use This Certificate and click Next.

5   Press Next.

6   The Back Up the Certificate and Key screen appears. Click the Back Up the Certificate and Key Now radio button to select it.

7   Press Browse.

8   Windows 7 opens a Save As dialog box. Locate and select the folder on the external media in which you want to save the backup key—for example, a flash or other type of external drive you've connected to your computer, or a CD or DVD you've inserted into the computer's disc drive, or even another computer on your network.

9   Type a name for the backup key in the File Name text field.

10 Press Save.

11 In the Back Up the Certificate and Key screen, type a password for the backup in the Password text field.

12 Retype the password in the Confirm Password text field.

Enter a password for the backup.

13 Press Next.

14 In the Update Your Previously Encrypted Files screen, locate and click the check box next to any drives and folders that already contain encrypted files or folders. This associates these previously encrypted items with the most recent encryption key.

15 Press Next.

16 Windows 7 creates a backup of your encryption key and stores it on the media you selected. Press Close. This process may take up to two minutes to complete, depending upon the speed of your computer.

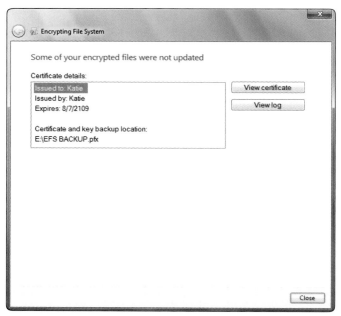

Windows 7 stores a backup key on the media you selected.

Encrypting your system with BitLocker

The process of encrypting your computer files using BitLocker should only be attempted if you absolutely need to have your files secured and if you are an experienced computer user. You should not attempt this process for the first time with the computer you use as your primary system.

To further secure your system, consider using BitLocker. Unlike Windows 7's EFS feature, which you use to encrypt certain documents or folders on your system, BitLocker encrypts all files stored in the system drive on a computer's hard disk—including those used for startup and logon. Any files you save to the encrypted drive will also be encrypted automatically. BitLocker prevents others from uncovering your password or accessing your system remotely, or from being able to access your information in the event they remove your hard drive from your computer and install it in a different computer.

To use BitLocker, your system hardware must include a special microchip called a Trusted Platform Module (TPM). This chip stores the BitLocker encryption keys, wrapping them in its own storage root key for added security. It then releases these keys during the boot process to unlock your system unless certain conditions are detected, such as disk errors, changes to various startup components, or indications that the hard disk is being accessed by a different computer. If such conditions are detected, BitLocker locks down the system drive and enters recovery mode; only after the recovery password is entered can it again start normally.

If your system does not include a TPM, you can still use BitLocker. For this to work, you must use either a removable USB memory device, such as a flash drive, or a hard drive that you connect using a USB cable to store BitLocker's encryption keys. You will need to insert the device into a USB port on your computer every time you start it. The first step is to use Microsoft Management Console (MMC) to configure Windows 7 to use BitLocker without a TPM. First, install the Local Computer Policy snap-in. Refer to Lesson 13 for help with opening MMC and installing snap-ins.

1   In the left pane of the Microsoft Management Console window, click Local Computer Policy.

2   Under Local Computer Policy, click Administrative Templates.

3   Under Administrative Templates, click Windows Components.

4   Under Windows Components, click BitLocker Drive Encryption.

5   Under BitLocker Drive Encryption, click Operating System Drives.

6   In the middle pane of the Microsoft Management Console window, double-click Require Additional Authentication at Startup.

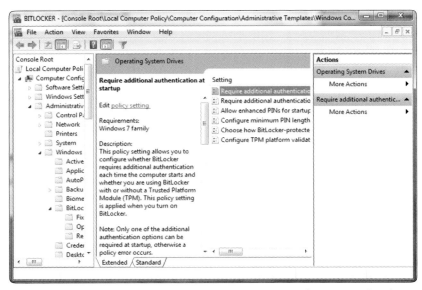

Navigate to the Require Additional Authentication at Setup setting in Microsoft Management Console.

7 The Require Additional Authentication at Startup dialog box opens. Click the *Allow BitLocker Without a Compatible TPM* checkbox to select it.

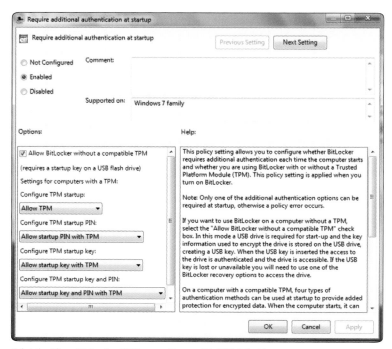

Select the Allow BitLocker Without a Compatible *TPM checkbox.*

8 Press OK.

9 Click the Microsoft Management Console window's Close button (▬) to close the window.

Enabling BitLocker

Before you enable BitLocker, you should back up your computer. For help backing up, refer to Lesson 7, "Maintaining Windows 7." Only enable BitLocker if you require you entire hard drive to be encrypted. If you key is lost, you may lost access to you drive's contents.

1 Click the Start button (⬤) and choose Control Panel.

2 In the Control Panel window, click the System and Security link.

3   In the System and Security screen, under BitLocker Drive Encryption, click the Protect Your Computer by Encrypting Data on Your Disk link.

Click Protect Your Computer by Encrypting Data on Your Disk.

4   The BitLocker Drive Encryption screen appears. Click the Turn On BitLocker link.

Click Turn On BitLocker.

If your system has a TPM but it has not yet been initialized, the Initialize TPM Security Hardware Wizard opens after you click Turn On BitLocker. Follow the onscreen instructions to initialize the TPM and reboot your computer. Then, click Turn On BitLocker on the system volume again.

5   BitLocker scans your system to ensure that it meets your requirements. When the scan is complete, the BitLocker Drive Encryption Setup screen appears, informing you that Windows 7 will first prepare your drive for BitLocker and will then encrypt the drive. To proceed, press Next.

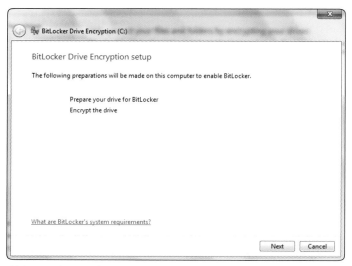

Click Next after BitLocker scans your system.

6   The Preparing Your Drive for BitLocker screen appears. Press Next.

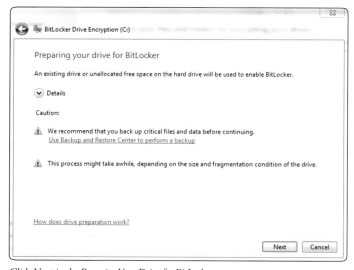

Click Next in the Preparing Your Drive for BitLocker screen.

7   Windows 7 prepares your drive for use with BitLocker.

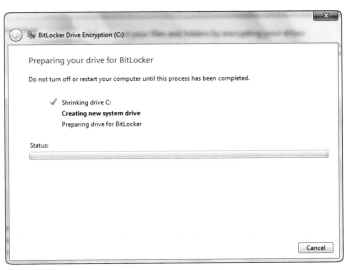

Preparing your drive for BitLocker.

8   Windows 7 notifies you when preparations are complete. Press Restart Now.

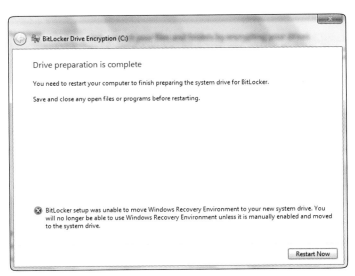

Press Restart Now.

9   Windows 7 restarts. After the operation is complete, the BitLocker Drive Encryption Setup screen reappears; click Next to launch the encryption process.

10 In the Set BitLocker Startup Preferences screen, click the desired startup option. In this example, Require a Startup Key at Every Startup is selected because a USB drive is being used to store the BitLocker encryption keys.

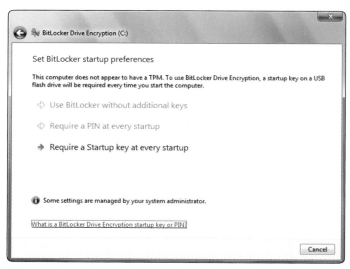

Choose a startup option.

11 If you selected Require a Startup Key at Every Startup in step 10, then you see the Save Your Startup Key screen. Insert your USB drive into your computer's USB port. (If you selected one of the other two options in step 9, simply follow the onscreen instructions and skip to step 13.)

12 Select the drive and press Save.

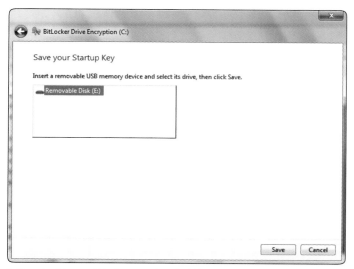

Indicate the drive on which the startup key should be stored.

13 Windows 7 prompts you to save your recovery key in the How Do You Want to Store Your Recovery Key? screen. This key is different from your startup key; it's the key you use in the event BitLocker detects a problem at startup and locks your system. Specify whether this key should be saved to a USB flash drive or to a file. This file should be stored on an unencrypted drive or printed out. Here, Save the Recovery Key to a USB Flash Drive is selected.

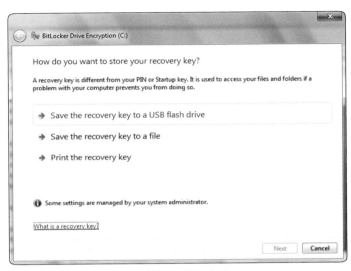

Indicate where the recovery key should be saved, or print it out.

14 If you selected Save the Recovery Key to a USB Flash Drive in step 13, then you see the Save a Recovery Key to a USB Drive window. Insert the USB drive on which you want to save the key into your computer's USB port. If you selected one of the other two options in step 13, follow the onscreen instructions and skip to step 16.

15 Click the drive and press Save.

Indicate the drive on which the recovery key should be stored.

16 In the How Do You Want to Store Your Recovery Key? screen, click Next.

17 The Are You Ready to Encrypt This Drive? screen appears. Click the *Run BitLocker System Check* checkbox to select it.

18 Press Continue.

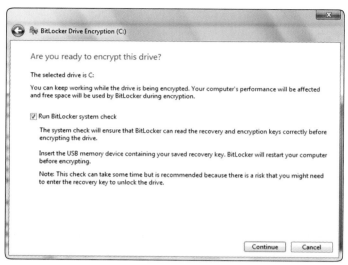

Select the Run BitLocker System Check *checkbox and press Continue.*

19 Windows 7 prompts you to restart your computer. This is so that BitLocker can confirm that your computer is encryption-compatible. Press Restart Now. Assuming your machine can be encrypted, BitLocker begins the encryption process automatically. This procedure can take some time to complete.

If you decide you no longer want to encrypt your drive, you can turn off BitLocker Drive Encryption. To do so, click Turn Off BitLocker Drive Encryption next to the appropriate volume in the Control Panel's BitLocker Drive Encryption screen and follow the onscreen instructions. To access the BitLocker Drive Encryption screen, open the Control Panel, click the System and Security link, and then click the BitLocker Drive Encryption link.

Encrypting external media

In addition to using BitLocker to encrypt your computer's hard drive, you can also encrypt removable storage devices, such as USB flash drives and external hard drives, using Windows 7's BitLocker To Go feature. To enable BitLocker To Go, connect the removable storage device to your computer. Then open the Control Panel's BitLocker Drive Encryption screen (open the Control Panel, click the System and Security link, and then click the BitLocker Drive Encryption link) and click the Turn On BitLocker link next to the icon for the removable device.

Thwarting intruders with Windows Firewall

Anytime you are connected to the Internet, you are subject to system intrusions, such as hackers, who may try to access your files or other confidential information, or Internet worms, which are computer viruses that can, among other things, leave behind files to create an opening for hackers or send copies of themselves to people listed in your address book. To protect your system from such intrusions and other problems, you can enable Windows Firewall. As its name implies, a firewall creates a barrier between your private computer files and outside connections.

When you enable Windows Firewall, it monitors all programs that access the Internet from your computer or try to communicate with you from an external source, and moves to block programs that may compromise the security of your system. When this happens, Windows Firewall displays a message asking what you want to do; you can choose to either continue blocking the software or stop blocking it.

You should not use more than one firewall on your system at any given time.

1   Press the Start button (⬤) and choose Control Panel.

2   In the Control Panel window, click the System and Security link.

3   In the System and Security screen, click the Windows Firewall link.

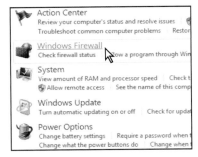

Click Windows Firewall.

4   In the left panel of the Windows Firewall screen, click the Turn Windows Firewall On or Off link.

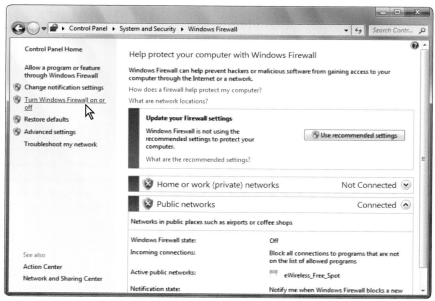

Click Turn Windows Firewall On or Off.

5   The Customize Settings screen appears. Under Home or Work (Private) Network Location Settings, click the *Turn On Windows Firewall* radio button.

6   Make sure the *Block All Incoming Connections* checkbox is unchecked.

7   Make sure the *Notify Me When Windows Firewall Blocks a New Program* checkbox is checked.

8   Under Public Network Location Settings, click the *Turn On Windows Firewall* radio button.

9   Make sure the *Block All Incoming Connections* checkbox is unchecked.

10 Make sure the *Notify Me When Windows Firewall Blocks a New Program* checkbox is checked.

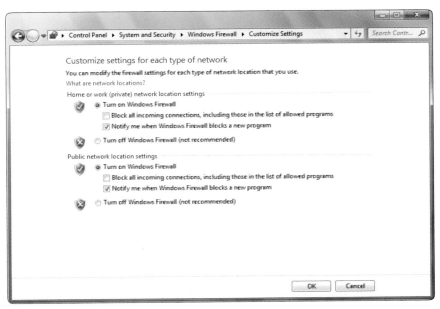

Enable Windows Firewall.

11 Press OK. Windows 7 enables Windows Firewall.

Managing exceptions

Sometimes, Windows Firewall works a little too well, blocking a program or connection that you know to be safe. For example, the firewall may block the short-term connection that is made when you attempt to instant-message with someone. One way to deal with this is to temporarily disable the firewall. But disabling the firewall increases your system's exposure to various security threats. A better approach is to allow the network connection or program as an exception. An exception is a program or connection that you want to allow so that it does not limit your ability to work or communicate.

1   Press the Start button (⊙) and click Control Panel.

2   Click the System and Security link, then click the Windows Firewall link

3   In the left pane of the Windows Firewall screen, click the Allow a Program or Feature Through Windows Firewall link.

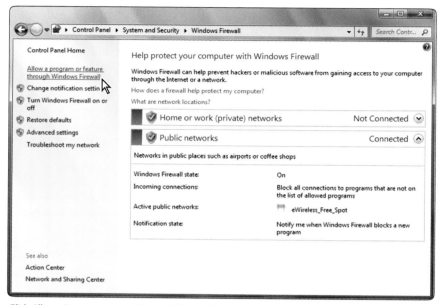

Click Allow a Program or Feature Through Windows Firewall.

4   The Allow Programs to Communicate Through Windows Firewall screen appears. Click Change Settings.

5   To allow a program or feature, locate it in the Allowed Programs and Features list and then click its checkbox to select it.

You can also use this screen to block them. Simply uncheck the checkbox next to the program or feature you want to block.

6 Select or deselect the program or feature's Home/Work (Private) and Public checkboxes to indicate whether the program or feature should be allowed on both types of networks.

If the program or feature you want to allow (or block) is not in the list, click the Allow Another Program button. The Add a Program dialog box appears; click the program or feature you want to allow or block, and then click Add. The program or feature you added appears in the Allowed Programs and Features list; select or deselect its check box, as outlined in steps 5 and 6, to allow or block it.

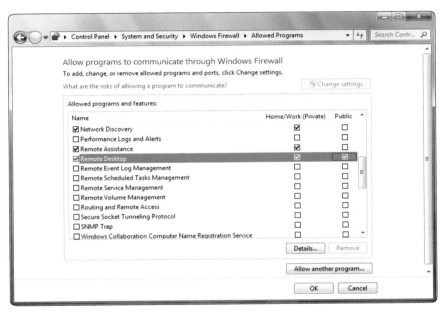

Manage Windows Firewall exceptions.

7 Press OK.

Antivirus software

Just because you use the Windows Firewall does not mean that your system does not require other forms of protection. You should use antivirus software and be careful when opening e-mail attachments or other files from any source, even a trusted one.

Also, if you download free software, such as file-sharing programs or screen savers, read the license agreement carefully to ensure that you won't receive pop-up ads from the company and that the program won't transmit data about your computing habits to the company who developed the software or to any other third parties.

Guarding against spyware with Windows Defender

Spyware is software that is installed on your computer, usually without your knowledge or consent. It can deluge your system with unwanted pop-up ads, and can also monitor and record your web-surfing activities and transmit this data to one or more third parties. Although these third parties may simply be companies in search of marketing data, they could also be more sinister forces such as hackers who want access to your personal information or use your computer for inappropriate purposes.

Even if spyware is relatively benign, its presence on your system can dramatically affect performance. To combat this, use Windows Defender to scan your system for spyware and uninstall it if detected. Windows Defender also offers a real-time protection feature—enabled by default—to alert you if a spyware program attempts to install itself on your machine or if any program attempts to change your Windows settings without your knowledge.

By default, Windows Defender is set up to run automatically on a regular basis, but you can run a scan manually.

1   Press the Start button (⬤).

2   In the Start menu's Search text field, type **Windows Defender**.

3   Windows 7 displays an entry for Windows Defender; click it.

Search for Windows Defender.

4   Windows 7 launches Windows Defender. To scan your system, press the Scan button.

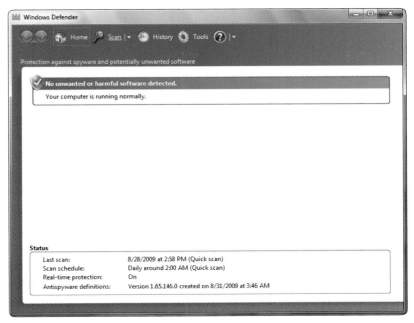

Click Scan.

5   Windows Defender scans your computer.

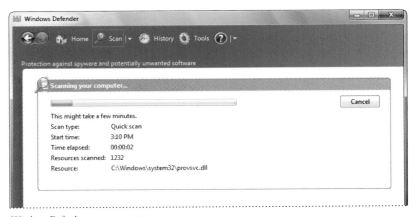

Windows Defender scans your system.

When the scan is complete, the program informs you of the results.

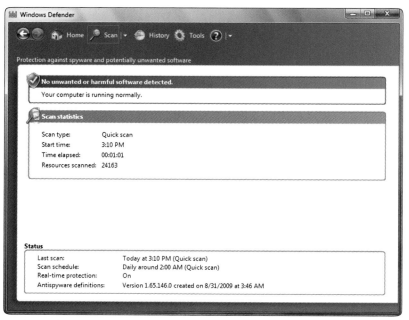

Windows Defender scans your system and informs you of the results.

To change when Windows Defender runs its automatic scan, press the Tools button in the Windows Defender window, then click the Options link. Then, in the Automatic Scanning screen, make changes as needed to the Frequency and Approximate Time drop-down lists. Finally, press Save.

Protecting kids with Content Advisor

Although the Internet can be both educational and entertaining for children, it can also expose them to inappropriate, even dangerous, content. To restrict what types of web sites and other Internet resources your children, or anyone who shares your computer, can access, you can enable the Internet Explorer 8 Content Advisor feature.

With Content Advisor, you can restrict content using four main criteria: language, nudity, sex, and violence. Content Advisor uses ratings provided voluntarily by Web sites to block or allow certain content, depending on the settings you choose. Web sites that are unrated are blocked by default when Content Advisor is enabled. You can also specify that specific Web sites be blocked or allowed. Once you enable Content Advisor, anyone who tries to access restricted material that you filter out through Content Advisor cannot do so. Moreover, no one can modify the settings or turn off Content Advisor without the supervisor password, which you can set when you activate Content Advisor.

You can also establish parental controls for your entire Windows 7 machine to limit access to certain games and programs and restrict the amount of time a user spends logged in. You can even generate reports to assess how much a particular user is using the computer. For more information about parental controls, refer to Lesson 8, "Setting Up User Accounts."

1   Open Internet Explorer 8 by clicking its icon in the Start menu or by pressing the Internet Explorer button (🌐) on the Windows taskbar.

2   In the Internet Explorer window, click Tools, then choose Internet Options from the menu that appears.

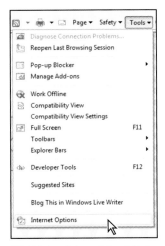

Click Tools and choose Internet Options.

4   The Internet Options dialog box opens. Click the Content tab.

5   Under Content Advisor, press Enable.

6   The Content Advisor dialog box opens with the Ratings tab displayed. Click a category in the Select a Category to View the Rating Levels list.

7   Click and drag the slider to set the desired limit

8 Repeat steps 6 and 7 for the remaining categories in the list.

Set the limit for a rating category.

9 Click the Approved Sites tab.

10 Under Allow This Website, type the URL for the site you want to allow or block.

11 Click Always or Never to allow or block the site, respectively. The site is added to the list of approved or disapproved sites.

Add sites to the list of approved or blocked sites.

12 Click the General tab.

13 To allow access to unrated sites, click the *Users Can See Sites That Have No Rating* checkbox to select it.

14 If you want to be able to override Content Advisor in order to view blocked content, click the *Supervisor Can Type a Password to Allow Users to View Restricted Content* checkbox.

Add sites to the list of approved or blocked sites.

15 Press OK to close the Content Advisor dialog box.

16 Internet Explorer launches the Create Supervisor Password dialog box. Type the password you want to use in the Password text field. Retype the password in the Confirm Password text field.

17 In the Hint text field, type a hint to help you remember your password.

Create the supervisor password.

18 Press OK to close the Create Supervisor Password dialog box.

After you set your supervisor password, be sure to write it down. If you lose your password, you will not be able to change Content Advisor settings or view blocked web sites. That said, you should not store the written password where children can find it. Also, make it a point to use a difficult password to limit the chances that a child can guess what it is. Passwords of more than six characters that combine a random mix of alphanumeric characters work the best.

19 Content Advisor confirms that it has been enabled. Press OK.

20 Press OK to close the Internet Options dialog box.

Fending off phishers and other online threats

The term *phishing* (pronounced *fishing*) refers to attempts by a malicious party to obtain private information from computer users. Often, phishing involves an e-mail message that appears to be from a legitimate source—such as a bank, credit-card company, or reputable online storefront—informing the user that his or her account information must be updated, and instructing that person to click a link in the message in order to access a web site where he or she can accomplish just that. When the user clicks the link, however, he or she is directed to a bogus site that mimics the trusted site in order to steal personal information such as passwords, credit-card numbers, social-security numbers, and/or bank-account numbers.

There are many things you can do to fend off phishers:

- If you receive an e-mail message with a suspicious link, do not click it—especially if the e-mail message is from a stranger.
- Never provide personal information, such as PIN numbers, passwords, credit-card numbers, or Social Security numbers, in an e-mail message, instant message, or pop-up window. These types of communications are notoriously insecure.
- Make it a habit to regularly review your financial statements to determine whether you have been a victim of fraud. If you discover that you have, file a report with the local police, change the passwords or PINs on all your online accounts, contact your bank and credit-card issuers, and place a fraud alert on your credit reports, your bank or financial advisor can tell you how to do this. Finally, if you are aware of any accounts that were opened fraudulently, close them.
- Only use web sites that clearly state how they use your personal information and/or include a privacy statement.

In addition to taking these common-sense steps, you can take advantage of various Windows 7 tools designed to protect you from phishers and other online threats. For example, if you use a Windows Live or Hotmail account to send and receive e-mail—your e-mail address ends in @hotmail.com or @live.com—Windows Live Mail automatically checks the sender ID of all incoming messages to determine whether that person is in your Windows Live Mail address book, and whether he or she is a legitimate sender. It then does the following:

- Windows Live Mail classifies senders who pass the sender ID check but do not appear in your contact list as *unknown*, and alerts you of this in the message's header. If the sender is someone you know, you can add him or her to your Safe Senders list (a list of e-mail addresses and domains that you trust) by clicking Allow Sender. To delete the message and block any further e-mails from the same sender, click Delete and Block.

- Windows Live Mail classifies senders who fail the sender ID check as "suspicious," and alerts you of this in the message's header. To delete the message, click Delete and Block; Windows Live Mail deletes the message and adds the sender to your Blocked Senders list. If you know the sender to be safe, add him or her to your Safe Senders list by clicking Allow Sender.

 You'll learn more about adding senders to your Windows Live Mail Safe Senders list—as well as blocking senders—in the next section of this lesson.

- If Windows Live Mail determines that the message may be an attempt at phishing, it locks the message's images, links, and content to prevent you from clicking it, and displays a *Suspected Phishing Message* alert in the message header. To delete the message, click the alert's Delete option; to unblock it, assuming you know it to be safe, click Unblock Message.

Another step you can take to protect yourself from phishers and other online threats is to use the Domain Highlighting feature in Internet Explorer 8. This feature highlights the name of the displayed Web site's domain in black in the browser window's address bar, leaving the rest of the URL gray. This helps to draw attention to misleading Web addresses, commonly used with phishing sites.

Yet another approach is to use the Internet Explorer 8 SmartScreen filter, which is enabled by default. This filter helps detect fraudulent Web sites by determining whether the URL of a Web site you visit appears on a list of known legitimate sites or on a list of known fraudulent sites. If the page you are visiting is known to be fraudulent, SmartScreen displays a warning page; there, you can indicate whether or not you want to continue on to the site. If you attempt to visit a site that doesn't appear on either list, SmartScreen analyzes it to determine whether it features characteristics of a phishing site; if so, the filter deems the site "suspicious" and notifies you of this in your browser's address bar. In addition, SmartScreen warns you if you attempt a download that has been reported as unsafe.

If you visit a site that you believe to be fraudulent but SmartScreen fails to detect the problem, then you can report the site to Microsoft for further investigation.

1   With the site you want to report open in Internet Explorer 8, click Safety, then select SmartScreen Filter, and choose Report Unsafe Website from the menu that appears.

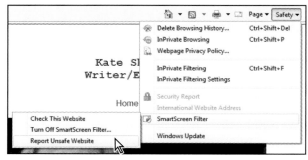

Click Safety, choose SmartScreen Filter, and select Report Unsafe Website.

4   A Microsoft web page opens. If you believe the site you are reporting is a phishing site, click the *I Think This Is a Phishing Website* checkbox to select it.

5   If you believe the site you are reporting contains malicious software, such as viruses, worms, or what have you, click the *I Think This Website Contains Malicious Software* checkbox to select it.

6   Select the language used from the Language Used on This Website drop-down menu

7 In the Characters text field, type the characters you see in the Pictures field.

Specify whether you believe the site is a phishing site, harbors malware, or both.

8 Press Submit.

If you encounter a web site that tells you to ignore warnings issued about the site by the SmartScreen filter, there's a good chance the site is indeed fraudulent. If it is not, the owner of the site should contact Microsoft to clear up the problem rather than posting such a message to site visitors.

Filtering spam and scams

The term *spam* refers to unwanted e-mail—namely, unsolicited e-mail messages sent to multiple recipients who did not request to receive it. Chances are, you sift through dozens of spam e-mails in your inbox to locate your "real" messages.

The best way to minimize spam is to avoid giving out your e-mail address except to reputable sites. Never reply to junk messages, even to *unsubscribe*. You can use Windows Live Mail's junk e-mail filter to divert spam from your inbox into a special Junk E-Mail folder. You can also block messages from specific people or domains or specify that certain people or domains be allowed.

The Windows Live Mail junk e-mail filter is enabled by default, but only moves the most obvious junk e-mail messages into your Junk E-mail folder.

1   In Windows Live Mail, click the Menus button (📄 ·).

2   Choose Safety Options.

3   The Safety Options dialog box opens with the Options tab displayed; choose the desired level of protection. If you don't want to block any junk e-mail messages, click No Automatic Filtering. Windows Live Mail will continue to block the entries in your Blocked Senders list. Click Low to block only the most obvious spam. To block yet more suspected spam, click High. For maximum blockage, click Safe List Only; Windows Live Mail will block all messages except those from people or domains on your Safe Senders list.

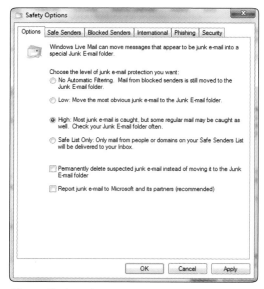

Choose a filtering option.

4   Press OK.

Blocking an e-mail sender

If you frequently receive spam or other unwanted mail from a particular sender, you can block that sender. When you do, messages from that sender are automatically diverted to your Junk E-mail folder.

1   In the Windows Live Mail inbox, right-click a message from the sender you want to block.

2   Choose Junk E-mail.

3 Select Add Sender to Blocked Senders list. Alternatively, to block all messages from the sender's domain, select Add Sender's Domain to Blocked Senders List.

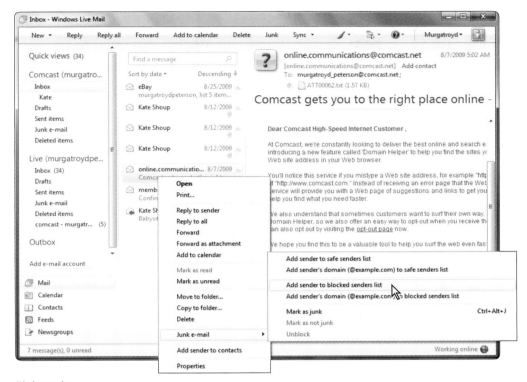

Block a sender.

4 Windows Live Mail informs you that the sender has been added to your Blocked Senders list and the message has been moved to your Junk E-mail folder. Click OK.

Adding a sender to the Safe Senders list

You should occasionally peruse the messages in your Junk E-mail folder to make sure no legitimate messages wound up there by accident. If one does, right-click it, choose Junk E-Mail, and click Mark As Not Junk to move the message to your inbox. Alternatively, you can add the sender of the message to your Safe Senders list. That way, the next time the sender e-mails you, Windows Live Mail will know to allow his or her message into your inbox.

1 In the Windows Live Mail Junk E-mail folder, right-click a message from the sender you want to add to the Safe Senders list.

2 Choose Junk E-mail.

3   Select Add Sender to Safe Senders list. Alternatively, to allow all messages from the sender's domain, select Add Sender's Domain to Safe Senders List.

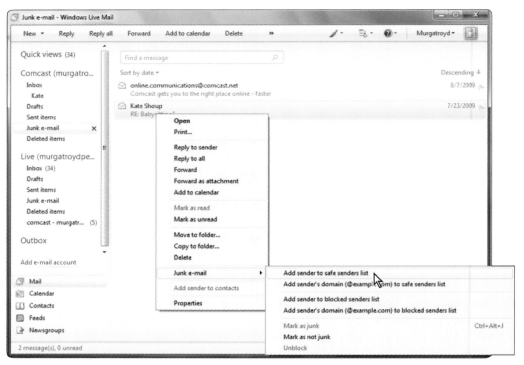

Add a sender to the Safe Senders list.

4   Windows Live Mail informs you that the sender has been added to your Safe Senders list. Press OK. Note that the message is not moved to your inbox; you need to move it yourself, either by marking it as Not Junk as described previously, or simply dragging it to the Inbox folder in the folder list.

Remove a sender from Safe Sender or Blocked Sender list

If you decide you want to remove a sender from either the Safe Senders list or your Blocked Senders list, you can easily do so using the Windows Live Mail Safety Options dialog box. As mentioned, you open this dialog box by clicking the Menus button (📑 ▾) in Windows Live Mail and choosing Safety Options. Then click either the Safe Senders or Blocked Senders tab for tools to remove or add senders to the list, as well as to set other list-related options.

 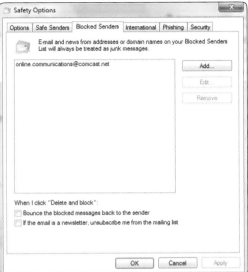

The Safe Senders and Blocked Senders tabs of the Safety Options dialog box.

Self study

1   Set a password for your Windows 7 user account.

2   Set up BitLocker to encrypt your system's primary drive. Be sure to save the recovery key in a safe place!

Review

Questions

1   What constitutes a strong password?

2   What is the difference between EFS and BitLocker?

3   What is spyware and why is it dangerous?

4   What is phishing?

5.   What is spam?

Answers

1   A strong password is one that is at least eight characters long; does not contain your username, your real name, or your company's name; does not contain a complete word; differs from passwords you have used in the past; and contains a mixture of uppercase letters, lowercase letters, numbers, symbols, and spaces.

2   You can use Windows 7's Encrypting File System, or EFS, to encrypt any files or folders that you store on your drive. With BitLocker, *all* files stored in the system drive on a computer's hard disk—including those used for startup and logon—are encrypted.

3   *Spyware* is software that is installed on your computer, usually without your knowledge or consent, that not only can deluge your system with unwanted pop-up ads, but can also monitor and record your web-surfing activities and transmit this data to one or more third parties. Although these third parties may simply be companies in search of marketing data, they could also be more sinister forces such as hackers who want access to your personal information or who want to sabotage your computer.

4   The term *phishing* (pronounced *fishing*) refers to attempts by a malicious party to obtain private information from computer users.

5   The term *spam* refers to unwanted e-mail—namely, unsolicited e-mail messages sent to multiple recipients who did not request to receive it.

What you'll learn in this lesson:

- Windows Live People
- Importing and managing contacts in Windows Live People
- Using Windows Live Calendar
- Using StickyNotes

Getting Organized with Windows 7

Boost your productivity using Windows Live People and Windows Live Calendar to manage your contacts and appointments. Windows 7's digital StickyNotes feature makes it easy to place visual reminders of important to-do items right on your desktop.

Starting up

Before you start, be sure to download all the files for this lesson from the accompanying DVD to your hard drive.

See Lesson 11 in action!

Use the accompanying video to gain a better understanding of how to use some of the features shown in this lesson. The video tutorial for this lesson can be found on the included DVD.

Windows Live People

Windows Live People is a free service offered from Microsoft's Windows Live. You can use Windows Live People to store information about people and organizations. This information can include phone numbers, fax numbers, e-mail addresses, postal addresses, Windows Live IDs, web site addresses, even a contacts birthday and notes about the contact. Windows Live People also functions as the address book for Windows Live Mail and Hotmail. You'll learn how to use your Windows Live People contacts with Windows Live Mail in Lesson 12, "Communicating via E-mail and IM." You'll see that Live People can be useful even if you don't use Windows Live Hotmail.

If you don't want to set up your address book now, you can jump ahead to Lesson 12, "Communicating via E-mail and IM."

To use Windows Live People, you must first set up a Windows Live account; once you have an account, direct your web browser to the Windows Live web site and log in. Refer to Lesson 5, "Surfing the Web with Internet Explorer 8" for more details. Finally, click the People link along the top of the page to display the Windows Live People screen.

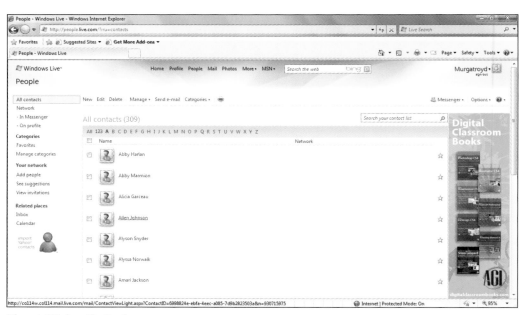

The main Windows Live People screen.

Importing contacts into Windows Live People

Windows Live People stores information you enter about people and organizations. If you've already entered information about contacts in another contact-management program, you can import the information into Windows Live People. Windows Live People can import contacts from Microsoft Outlook, Outlook Express, Windows Contacts, Windows Live Hotmail, Yahoo! Mail, and Gmail.

Before you can import contact information, you must first export it from your current program. The precise steps for this differ depending on the type of program you use. In this example, Microsoft Outlook 2007 is used.

1   In Outlook 2007, from the File menu, choose Import and Export.

2   Outlook launches the Import and Export Wizard. Choose Export to a File and press Next.

3   Choose Comma Separated Values (Windows) and press Next.

4   Select the Contacts folder and press Next.

5   Press the Browse button.

6   Choose the folder where you want to save your exported contacts.

7   Type a name for your contacts file, then press OK and press Next in the Export to File dialog box.

8   Press Finish. Outlook exports your contacts to the folder you chose.

9   Next, import your exported contacts into Windows Live People. With the Windows Live People screen displayed, click the Manage link and choose Import from the menu that appears.

Begin the import operation.

10 The Import Contacts screen appears. Click the option button next to your old contacts-management program.

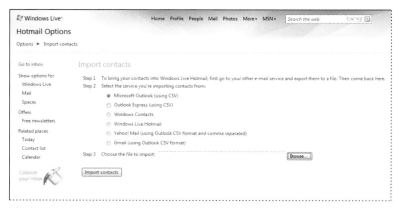

The Import Contacts screen.

11 Press the Browse button. The Choose File to Upload dialog box opens. Locate and select the file containing the contacts you want to import.

12 Press Open. The file you chose appears in the Choose the File to Import field in the Import Contacts screen. Press the Import Contacts button.

13 Windows Live People imports your contacts. To view your contacts, click the Return to Contacts link.

Your contacts are imported.

Managing contacts in Windows Live People

Windows Live People allows you to delete unwanted entries, organize your contacts by category, and quickly find the contact you need.

Adding a contact

1   In the Windows Live People screen, click the New link, located next to the All contacts link at the top of the screen.

2   Under Edit Contact Details, type the contact's first name, last name, and nickname.

Enter the requested information under Edit Contact Details.

3   Under Personal Information, type the contact's personal e-mail address, Windows Live ID, home phone number, mobile phone number, and home address.

4   Under Business Information, type the contact's company, work e-mail address, work phone number, pager number, fax number, and work address.

5   Under Other Information, type the contact's other e-mail address, other phone number, and web site address. Additionally, indicate which e-mail address is the preferred one, and enter the contact's birthday. Press Save.

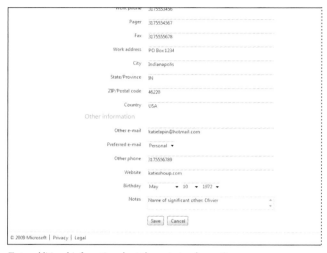

Enter additional information about the contact and press Save.

6   Windows Live People saves your contact. To view all the contact's information, click the Show full details link. To return to the Windows Live People main screen, click the Go to contact list link in the upper left corner of the screen.

Windows Live People creates a new contact entry containing the information you entered.

Finding and opening a contact

Contacts in Windows Live People are organized alphabetically by first name. To locate a contact, click a letter along the top of the All Contacts screen to reveal all contacts whose first name start with that letter; then scroll down to locate the contact you want. To open the contact, click it in the list.

If you prefer to view your contacts by last name, click the Options link in the upper-right corner of the Windows Live People screen, choose More Options from the menu that appears, and then click the Display Contacts As link under Customize Your Contacts. Click the Last, First option button to select it, then press Save.

A fast way to locate a contact in Windows Live People is to use the search function.

1   Type the contact's name in part or in full in the Search text field found in the upper right corner of the main Windows Live People screen.

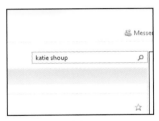

Type the name of the contact you want to find.

2   Windows Live People displays a list of contact entries that match what you typed. Click the contact you want to view.

Click the desired contact in the list to view its entry.

3   Windows Live People opens the contact entry. To view more information about the contact, click the Show full details link.

Click Show Full Details to view more information about the contact.

Editing a contact

If you need to edit a contact entry—for example, if a contact gets married and changes his or her name, or if a contact moves or changes jobs, you can do so rather easily within Windows Live People.

1   Open the contact entry you want to edit.

2   Click the Edit link.

3   Windows Live People displays the same screen you saw when you created a new contact, with this contact's information filled in. Click in a text field and type over the current contents to update them.

   An even faster way to access the Windows Live People Edit screen is to click the checkbox next to the contact you want to edit in the main Windows Live People window, then click the Edit link.

4   Press Save. Windows Live People saves your changes in the contact entry.

Categorizing contacts

You can organize your contacts into categories. For example, you might put all your contacts from a certain company into the same category. This allows you to quickly view all the contacts together.

1   In the main Windows Live People screen, click the Categories link and choose New category from the menu that appears.

Click the Categories link and choose New category.

2   Windows Live People's New Category screen appears. In the Name text field, type a name for the new category.

3   In the Members text field, type the name of a contact you want to include in the group. As you do, Windows Live People displays contact entries containing the letters you've typed; click a name in the list to select it.

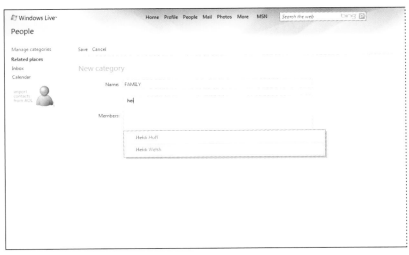

Add a contact in the Members field.

4 Repeat step 3 as needed to add more contacts to the category. Press Save when you are done adding contacts to the group.

Add more contacts to the category; then click Save.

5 Windows Live People displays the Manage categories screen, with the new category listed. Click the All contacts link in the upper left corner of the screen to return to the main Windows Live People screen.

The Manage Categories screen.

Adding another contact to a category

1 Open the entry for the contact you want to categorize.

2 Click the Categories link and choose the desired category from the menu that appears. Windows Live People categorizes the contact accordingly.

A fast way to categorize a contact is to click the check box next to the contact you want to categorize in the main Windows Live People window, click the Categories link, and then choose the desired category from the list that appears.

Setting favorites

You can give contacts *favorite* status by assigning them to a special category named *Favorites*. Favorites are denoted in your contact list with a yellow star icon ( ), making them easy to spot. To make a contact a favorite, open the entry for the contact, click the Categories link, and choose Favorites from the list that appears. Alternatively, click the checkbox next to the contact you want to make a favorite in the main Windows Live People screen, click the Categories link, and choose Favorites.

Viewing contacts

You view the contacts in a category by clicking the category name on the left side of the Windows Live People screen, under Categories.

View the contacts in a category.

Removing a contact from a category

If you need to remove a contact from a category—for example, if you've created a category for a particular company, and the contact no longer works for that company—you can easily do so. Note that removing a contact from a category does not delete the contact from your main Windows Live People list; it removes the category information from the contact entry.

1   Click the category name on the left side of the Windows Live People screen, under Categories.

2   Click the checkbox next to the contact you want to remove.

3 Click the Delete link.

*Choose the contact you want to delete from
a contact and click the Delete link.*

4 Windows Live People prompts you to confirm the deletion; press Yes. Windows Live
People deletes the contact from the category.

Deleting a category

Deleting a category does not delete the contacts in that category from your main Windows Live
People list; it removes the category information.

1 Click the Manage categories link on the left side of the main Windows Live People
screen, under Categories.

2 The Manage categories screen appears. Click the checkbox next to the category you
want to delete to select it.

3 Click the Delete link.

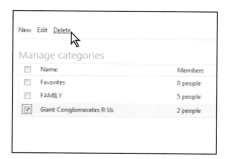

Delete a category.

4 Windows Live People prompts you to confirm the deletion. Press Yes. The category
is deleted.

Deleting a contact

1   In the main Windows Live People screen, click the checkbox next to the contact you want to delete.

2   Click the Delete link.

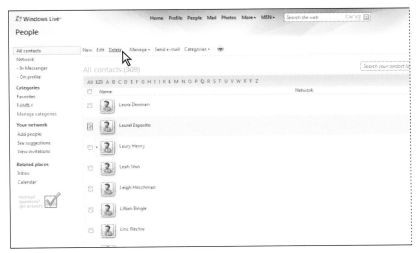

Delete a contact.

3   Windows Live People prompts you to confirm the deletion; press Yes. Windows Live People deletes the contact.

Windows Live Calendar

Windows Live Calendar is a great way to keep track of your schedule. Using this service, you can schedule one-time events, such as a lunch date, or recurring events, such as a standing meeting. You can also use Windows Live Calendar to schedule social events, such as a party. There are tools to invite others to the event, and track responses using a special event page. You can use Windows Live Calendar to keep a running list of tasks you need to complete. You can have Windows Live Calendar send you reminders about any events or to-do item. You can also create multiple calendars. For example, you might create one calendar for work and one for personal use, and you can share your calendars with others.

To use Windows Live Calendar, you must first set up a Windows Live account; once you have an account, direct your web browser to the Windows Live web site and log in. If you need to setup a Windows Live account refer to Lesson 5, "Surfing the Web with Internet Explorer 8" for more details.

Click the More link along the top of the Windows Live page and choose Calendar from the menu that appears to display the Windows Live Calendar screen, in Month view. Note that the first time you launch Windows Live Calendar, you'll be prompted to select your time zone from a drop-down menu.

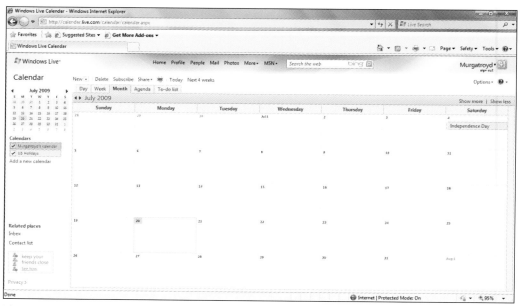

The main Windows Live Calendar screen, in Month view.

Navigating Windows Live Calendar

You can quickly switch to Day view, Week view, and Agenda view. To switch views, click the Week, Day, Agenda, or Month tab.

 Another way to switch to Day view is to click the desired day's entry in Week or Month view.

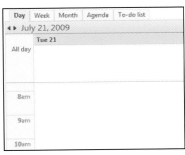

Windows Live Calendar in Month (top left), Week (top right), Day (bottom left), and Agenda (bottom right) view.

Windows Live Calendar features a thumbnail-sized calendar in the upper-left corner of the screen. You use this to display a different day, week, or month in the main calendar view. To choose a different day, make sure you're in Day view, then click the desired day in the thumbnail calendar; to change to a different week, make sure you're in Week view, then click a day that falls within the desired week in the thumbnail calendar; to change to a different month, click the left or right arrow on either side of the current month displayed in the thumbnail.

Use the thumbnail calendar in the upper left corner of the Windows Live Calendar window to display a different day, week, or month in the main calendar view.

Entering and managing events in Windows Live Calendar

You can use Windows Live Calendar to schedule events. You'll see how to view, edit, and delete these events.

Adding an event

Using the Windows Live Calendar service, you can plan your daily activities by entering appointments, which Windows Live Calendar calls events. You can also send e-mail invitations to others. By default, Windows Live Calendar sends you a reminder about an event 15 minutes before it starts, although you can send this reminder minutes, hours, or days in advance.

1   In the main Windows Live Calendar screen, click the arrow to the right of the New link and choose Event from the menu that appears.

Click the New link and choose Event.

2   The Add an Event screen appears. Type a description of the event in the What text field.

A fast way to open the Add an Event screen is click in the calendar on the date and time on which the event is to occur and to click the Add link that appears. Notice that the event's date and time are already filled in when the Add an Event screen appears.

3   Type the location for the event in the Where text field.

4   If the event will last all day, click the *All Day* checkbox to select it.

5   If the event is not an all-day appointment, click in the left-most Start text field to display a calendar; then click the date for the event.

6   Click in the right-most Start text field to display a list of times; then click the time for the event.

7   If the event will end on a different day, repeat steps 5 and 6 in the End text fields.

8   If this is a recurring event or an event for which you want to set a reminder, or an event to which you want to add more people, click Add More Details.

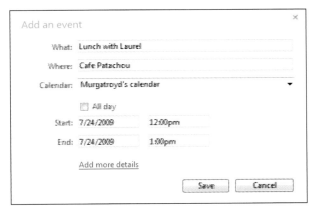

Click Add More Details.

9   The Windows Live Calendar Event Details screen appears. If the event is recurring, press Set Recurrence.

10   The Recurrence section of the page expands. From the Occurs drop-down menu, choose Daily, Weekly, Monthly, or Yearly.

11   Note that what you choose in step 10 affects the remaining options in the Recurrence section.

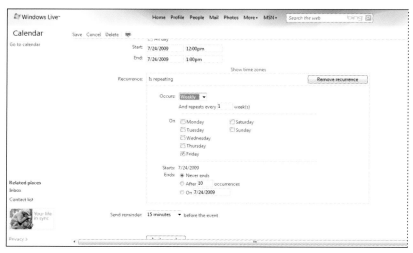

Specify when and how often the recurring event should occur.

12   To change when Windows Live Calendar sends you the event reminder, from the Send reminder drop-down menu, choose the number of minutes, hours, or days before the event the reminder should be sent.

13   To invite others to the event, press Invite People.

14   In the To text field that appears, type the name of the person you want to invite. Assuming that person's information has been entered into Windows Live People, his or her name will be displayed in a list; click the name to add it to the To text field. If the person's information has not been added to Windows Live Calendar, you must enter the person's e-mail address rather than his or her name.

15 Press Save. Windows Live Calendar adds the event to your calendar.

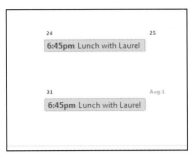

The event is added to your calendar.

 If you've invited others to this event, Windows Live Calendar will ask you whether you want to send an invitation to the event to those people; if so, press Send.

Creating and sharing calendars in Windows Live Calendar

Suppose you coach a soccer team, and need to send the upcoming season's game schedule to the other members of the team. You can create a new calendar, add events to it as needed, and share that calendar with others, while keeping your personal calendar private.

Creating a new calendar

1 In the main Windows Live Calendar screen, click the arrow to the right of the New link at the top of the screen and choose Calendar.

2 The Add a New Calendar screen appears. Type a name for the calendar in the Name text field.

 A fast way to open the Add a New Calendar screen is to click the Add a New Calendar link on the left side of the Windows Live Calendar main screen, under the list of current calendars.

3 Click a color tile. Events you create for this calendar will be displayed in this color.

4   If you want to receive a daily e-mail message containing your schedule for the day, click the *Receive a daily e-mail schedule for this calendar* checkbox to select it.

Click Save to create the new calendar.

5   Press Save. Windows Live Calendar creates the calendar, listing it with your other calendars on the left side of the screen.

Press Save to create the new calendar.

Hiding events in the calendar

By default, Windows Live Calendar displays events for all your different calendars at once, color-coding them so you can tell them apart. To hide events from view, click the calendar's checkbox on the left side of the screen to deselect it. Events from the calendar no longer appear in the main Windows Live Calendar screen. To display the events, click the calendar's checkbox again to select it.

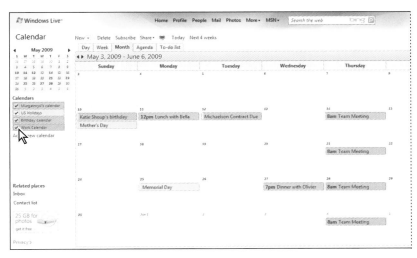

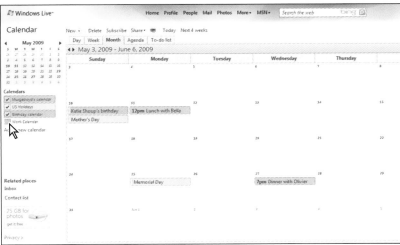

To hide events from a calendar from view, deselect the calendar's checkbox.

Sharing a calendar

You can share your calendars with others. Using three options:

- **Share Your Calendar with Friends and Family.** You specify who among your Windows Live People contacts can view, edit, and add events to the calendar. Be aware that if you choose this option, anyone you give permission to view, edit, and add events must have his or her own Windows Live ID.

- **Send Friends a View-Only Link to Your Calendar.** When you choose this options, anyone you choose will be able to view your calendar, but not to add or edit events. (No Windows Live ID is required to view your calendar in this case.)

- **Make Your Calendar Public.** Choose this option to make your calendar publicly available to anyone on the Internet.

To share your calendar with those friends and family members who have Windows Live IDs, optionally granting them permission to view, edit, and add events to the calendar, follow these steps. Note that after you share your calendar, Windows Live will e-mail the people you've selected to invite them to use your calendar.

1   In the main Windows Live Calendar screen, click the Share link and choose the calendar you want to share from the menu that appears.

Click Share and choose the calendar you want to share.

2   The Sharing Settings screen appears. Select the *Share this calendar* option.

3   A list of sharing options appears. Click the *Share your calendar with friends and family* checkbox.

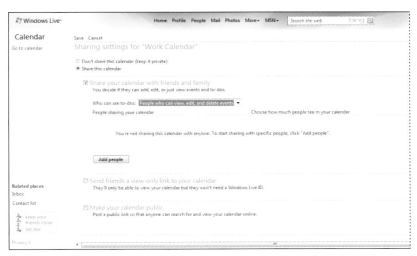

Select the Share your calendar with friends and family checkbox to reveal additional settings.

4   From the Who can see to-dos drop-down menu, specify who should be able to view your to-do items. You'll learn about to-do items shortly.

5   Press Add People. The Add People to share with dialog box opens. Type a name in the field along the top; Windows Live Calendar displays a list of contacts whose information matches what you've typed. Select a contact from the list. Alternatively, if the person you want to invite is not currently in your contact list, type his or her e-mail address; the e-mail address will be added to your contacts.

Specify the people with whom you want to share your calendar.

6 Press Add. In the Sharing Settings screen, from the drop-down menu adjacent to each contact's name and choose one of the selections from the list that appears to specify what permissions that user has. Press Save.

Save your changes.

7 Windows Live Calendar informs you that an e-mail invitation will be sent to the contacts you selected, urging them to view your calendar. Press OK.

Sending friends a view-only link to your calendar

You can also send view-only link to your calendar to your friends:

1 In the main Windows Live Calendar screen, click the Share link and choose the calendar you want to share from the menu that appears.

2 The Sharing Settings screen appears. Select the *Share this calendar* option.

3 Click the *Send friends a view-only link to your calendar* checkbox to select it.

4   Click the Get your calendar links option.

After clicking this link, a Sharing confirmation warning dialog box appears stating that you're about to publish your calendar on the Web at a private URL. Press OK.

Select the Share your calendar with friends and family *checkbox to reveal additional settings.*

5   Windows Live Calendar displays a series of links—one set for use if you want people to see all the details of your calendar, and another for use if you only want people to see when you are free and when you are busy. Click a link.

6   Windows Live Calendar displays special dialog box containing the link. Use your mouse to select the link, press Ctrl+C to copy the link, and then press Ctrl+P to paste the link into an e-mail message addressed to the people with whom you want to share your calendar.

Refer to Lesson 12, " Communicating via E-mail and IM," for help with e-mailing.

7 Press OK.

Copy the link to an e-mail message.

8 Press Save in the Sharing settings screen.

9 Send your e-mail containing the link to the calendar to those people with whom you wish to share the calendar.

Making your calendar public.

You can make your calendar public to share with anyone and everyone on the Internet:

1 In the main Windows Live Calendar screen, click the Share link and choose the calendar you want to share from the menu that appears.

2 The Sharing settings screen appears. Click the *Share this calendar* option.

3 Click the *Make your calendar public* checkbox.

4 From the Permissions drop-down menu, choose View details or View free/busy times.

5 From the Time zone drop-down menu, select the appropriate time zone—either your own or that of the people with whom you are sharing the calendar.

6 Click the Get your cal.. ..dar links option.

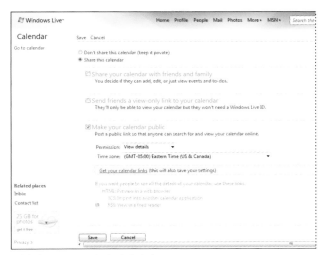

Click the Get your calendar links link.

7 Windows Live Calendar displays a series of links—one set for use if you want people to see all the details of your calendar, and another for use if you only want people to see when you are free and when you are busy. Click a link.

Click a link.

8 Windows Live Calendar displays special dialog box containing the link. Use your mouse to select the link, press Ctrl+C to copy the link, then press Ctrl+P to paste the link into an e-mail message addressed to the people with whom you want to share your calendar.

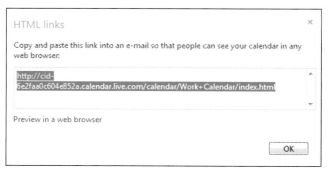

HTML links   ×

Copy and paste this link into an e-mail so that people can see your calendar in any
web browser:

http://cid-
6e2faa0c604e852a.calendar.live.com/calendar/Work+Calendar/index.html

Preview in a web browser

OK

Copy the link and paste into an e-mail message.

9 Press OK, then press Save in the Sharing settings screen.

10 Send your e-mail containing the link to the calendar of those people with whom you wish to share the calendar.

Keeping your calendar private

1 In the main Windows Live Calendar screen, click the Share link and choose the calendar you no longer want to share from the menu that appears.

2 The Sharing Settings screen appears. Choose the *Don't share this calendar* option and press Save.

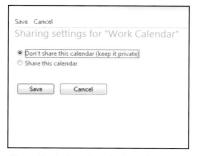

Save Cancel

Sharing settings for "Work Calendar"

● Don't share this calendar (keep it private)
○ Share this calendar

Save   Cancel

Choose Don't share this calendar and press Save.

3 Windows Live Calendar asks you to confirm that you no longer wish to share this calendar. Press Save.

Subscribing to a calendar

You can subscribe to public calendars, called iCals. For example, if an iCal exists for your favorite sports team, you can subscribe to it; when you do, entries for each game being played by that team will appear in Windows Live Calendar.

1   In the main Windows Live Calendar screen, click the Subscribe link. (This link is located to the left of the Share link.)

2   The Import or subscribe to a calendar screen appears. Click the *Subscribe to a public calendar* option.

3   Type the URL for the iCal to which you want to subscribe in the Calendar URL text field.

4   Type a name for the iCal in the Calendar Name text field.

5   Click a color tile. Events associated with this calendar will be displayed in this color.

6   Click the Subscribe to calendar button.

Subscribe to a calendar.

7   Windows Live Calendar informs you that your subscription was successful. Press Done, and entries contained in the iCal are added to your calendar.

*Windows Live Calendar adds
the iCal to your calendar.*

8   Another way to add an iCal to Windows Live Calendar is to initiate the subscription process from a calendar portal—that is, a web site offering access to multiple iCals. One such portal is MarkThisDate.com, *www.markthisdate.com*. On MarkThisDate.com, locate the iCal you want to download. Calendars are organized into categories; click a category to locate a calendar. Alternatively, use MarkThisDate.com's search text field to search for a calendar.

9   Click Add to Calendar.

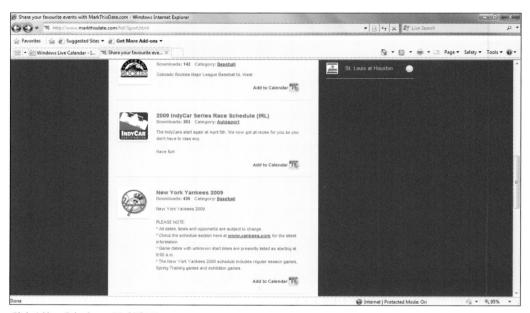

Click Add to Calendar on MarkThisDate.com.

10   Click Hotmail/Windows Live.

Choose Hotmail/Windows Live.

11 MarkThisDate launches Windows Live Calendar, with the Import or subscribe to a calendar screen displayed, the iCal's URL in the Calendar URL text field, and the calendar's name in the Calendar Name text field. Click a color tile. Repeat steps 6 and 7 to finish the subscription process.

Tracking to-do items in Windows Live Calendar

If you make lists to keep track of tasks you need to complete, you'll appreciate Windows Live Calendar's To-Do list. When you enter an item into your To-Do list, you can specify a start time, a deadline, and a priority ranking for the to-do item, as well as set a reminder. You can also enter notes about the to-do item, for example, you might list other people who are involved in completing the item or other details about it. When you complete a to-do item, mark it as complete.

1 In the main Windows Live Calendar screen, click the arrow to the right of the New link and choose To-do from the menu that appears.

Click the New link and choose To-do.

2 The Add a to-do screen appears. Type a description of the to-do item in the What text field.

To add the to-do item to a calendar other than the one currently displayed, click the Calendar down arrow and select the desired calendar.

3 If the to-do item must be completed by a certain date, click in the left-most Due date text field to display a calendar; then click the date on which the to-do item is due.

4 If the to-do item must be completed by a certain time on the selected due date, click in the right-most Due date text field to display a list of times; then click the time at which the to-do item is due.

5 Optionally, the Priority drop-down menu, choose Low priority, Normal priority, or High priority to prioritize the task.

6 If this is a to-do item for which you want to set a reminder, indicate the status, or add a description, click Add more details. Otherwise, press Save to add the to-do item to your calendar.

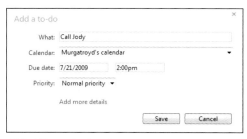

Click Add more details or Save.

7 The Add a To-Do screen expands. To indicate the status of the to-do item, from the Status drop-down menu, choose Not Started, In progress, or Done.

8 To add a reminder for the to-do item, choose the number of minutes, hours, or days before the to-do item is due that the reminder should be sent from the Send reminder drop-down menu.

9 Type any notes about the to-do item in the Description text field.

Add more details about the to-do item.

10 Press Save. Windows Live Calendar adds the to-do item to your calendar.

Viewing to-do items in Windows Live Calendar

To view your to-do items, click the To-do list tab near the top of the screen. To mark an item as complete, click the down arrow next to the item's current status and choose Done from the list that appears; Windows Live Calendar moves the to-do item to the Done section of the to-do list. To delete a to-do item, click its Delete this to-do button (×).

View your to-do items.

Using StickyNotes

Another way to keep track of tasks you need to complete is to use Windows 7's Sticky Notes. These digital notes act like their paper-based brethren; you *stick* the note to your computer screen and use your keyboard to jot down whatever it is you need to remember.

1   Press the Start button (⬤), click All Programs, click Accessories, and click StickyNotes.

2   A StickyNote appears on the desktop. Click in the StickyNote and type your reminder.

Type your reminder.

3   Change the color of the StickyNote by right-clicking it and choosing a new color from the menu that appears. The color of the StickyNote changes.

Change the color of the StickyNote.

4   To add more StickyNotes, press the New Note button (·) in an existing StickyNote. Windows 7 sticks a new StickyNote on the desktop.

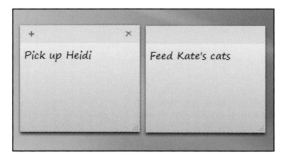

Add more StickyNotes.

5   To move a StickyNote, click the bar along the top, hold down your mouse button, and drag the StickyNote to the desired spot on your desktop. When it is situated where you want it, release the mouse button.

6   When you no longer need your reminder, you can delete your StickyNote by pressing the note's Delete Note button (×).

7   The Delete Note dialog box appears asking you to confirm the deletion. Press Yes; Windows 7 deletes the note.

Self study

1   Create a category for a group of contacts that you e-mail on a regular basis, such as the members of your immediate family, a group of close friends, or co-workers on your team.

2   Use a calendar portal such as MarkThisDate.com to find and subscribe to an iCal.

Review

Questions

1   What are three types of information you can store about a contact in Windows Live People?

2   What two mail programs use Windows Live People as their address book?

3   What are the four available views in Windows Live Calendar?

4   What are two ways to keep track of items on your to-do list?

Answers

1   You can use Windows Live People to store such information as phone numbers, fax numbers, e-mail addresses, postal addresses, Windows Live IDs, Web site addresses, birthdays, and more.

2   Windows Live People also functions as the address book for Windows Live Mail and Hotmail.

3   Windows Live Calendar offers Month view, Week view, Day view, and Agenda view.

4   One way to keep track of items on your to-do list is to use Windows Live Calendar to create to-do items. Another is to use Windows 7's StickyNotes feature to *stick* reminders about tasks you need to complete on you Windows 7 desktop.

What you'll learn in this lesson:

- Setting up Windows Live Mail

- Composing and sending an e-mail message

- Managing RSS feeds

- Windows Live Hotmail

- Windows Live Messenger

Communicating via E-mail and IM

For many, the primary purpose of a computer is to keep in touch with friends, family members, or business associates. In this lesson, you'll discover how to use both e-mail and instant messaging to stay connected.

Starting up

Before you start, be sure to download all the files for this lesson from the accompanying DVD to your hard drive. Also make sure that your computer is connected to the Internet.

See Lesson 12 in action!

Use the accompanying video to gain a better understanding of how to use some of the features shown in this lesson. The video tutorial for this lesson can be found on the included DVD.

Windows Live Mail

Windows Live Mail is an e-mail program that you can download free of charge from the Microsoft Windows Live web site. Using Windows Live Mail, you can send and receive e-mail messages, organize your messages, and subscribe to RSS feeds and newsgroups. In order to follow this exercise, you will need Windows Live Mail, which you downloaded in Lesson 5, "Surfing the Web with Internet Explorer 8," from the Windows live web site. You start Windows Live Mail just as you do any other program in Windows: by clicking the program's icon in the Start menu.

The main Windows Live Mail screen. **A**. *Folder list.* **B**. *File list.* **C**. *Preview pane.*

Setting up Windows Live Mail

To use Windows Live Mail, you must have signed up with an Internet service provider (ISP), and have an e-mail address either with that provider or with some other source, such as Hotmail. Windows Live Mail helps you organize e-mail regardless of what service you use to send or receive mail. You need your user name and password from your e-mail provider, and you may also need the URLs of the incoming and outgoing e-mail servers. You obtain this information from your e-mail provider, whether it's your ISP or some other source.

1   Open Windows Live Mail and logon.

2   Select Mail in the bottom-left corner of the window.

A Windows Live Hotmail account was set up automatically for you when you created your Windows Live account.

3 Click the Add e-mail account link from the Outbox section on the left side of the window.

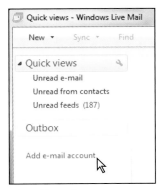

Click Add e-mail account.

4 Windows Live Mail launches the Add an e-mail account dialog box. Type the E-mail address and Password given to you by your e-mail provider in the appropriate text fields. If you don't wish to enter your e-mail account's password each time you send or receive e-mails, click the *Remember password* checkbox to select it.

5 In the Display Name text field, type the name that you want to appear in your recipient's inbox when you send an e-mail message.

6 If you are required to enter the URL of the incoming and outgoing mail servers manually, click the *Manually configure server settings for e-mail account* checkbox to select it and proceed to the next step. If not, press Next, and skip to step 20.

The first screen of the Add an E-mail Account Wizard.

7 Press Next.

8 If your e-mail provider uses an IMAP or HTTP server rather than a POP server for incoming e-mail (ask your provider if you're not sure), choose IMAP or HTTP from the My incoming mail server is a { } server drop-down menu.

9 Type the URL of your e-mail provider's incoming mail server in the Incoming server text field.

10 Type the Incoming mail server's port number in the Port text field.

11 If your e-mail provider's incoming server requires a secure connection, click the *This server requires a secure connection (SSL)* checkbox to select it.

12 If the incoming server requires some form of authentication, choose the type of authentication needed, Clear text authentication, Authenticated POP (APOP), or Secure password authentication, from the Log On Using drop-down menu.

13 If the e-mail account's Login ID, or user name, is different from the e-mail address, type it in the Login ID text field.

14 Type the URL of your e-mail provider's outgoing mail server in the Outgoing Server text field.

15 Type the outgoing mail server's port number in the Port text field.

16 If your e-mail provider's outgoing server requires a secure connection, click the *This server requires a secure connection (SSL)* checkbox to select it.

17 If your e-mail provider's outgoing server requires authentication, click the *My outgoing server requires authentication* checkbox to select it. Press Next.

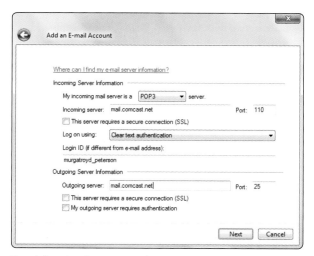

Enter information about your e-mail servers.

18 Windows Live Mail informs you that the account has been added. Press Finish.

Setting up another e-mail account

Windows Live Mail can handle more than one e-mail account. For example, if you have a personal e-mail account as well as a work account, you can configure Windows Live Mail to download messages from both, and to send messages using either account. Just complete the steps in this task for each additional e-mail account you would like to add. When you add a new account, you'll see an entry for that account in the left pane of the Windows Live Mail screen; select the account's name in that pane to view any messages associated with that account.

Deleting an e-mail account

If you no longer use an e-mail account—for example, if you've changed jobs and your old work account is no longer valid—you can delete it from Windows Live Mail.

1   In the left pane of the Windows Live Mail window, right-click the account you want to delete.

2   Select Remove account from the menu that appears.

Enter information about your e-mail servers.

3   Windows Live Mail asks you to confirm the deletion; click Yes.

Syncing Windows Live Mail with other Windows Live services

In Lesson 11, "Getting Organized with Windows 7," you learned how to manage contact information using Windows Live People, an online service offered on Microsoft's Windows Live web site. You also learned how to use Windows Live Calendar to schedule events and tasks.

You can set up Windows Live Mail to pull information from Windows Live People and Windows Live Calendar, displaying it in the Windows Live Mail window. That way, you can view your calendar and contact entries from within Windows Live Mail. When you set up Windows Live Mail to coordinate with the Windows Live Web site, you also set up Windows Live Mail to display any messages you receive using your Windows Live Hotmail account, which was set up automatically when you created your Windows Live account.

1   Press the Sign In button in the upper right corner of the Windows Live Mail window.

Press the Sign In button.

2   A Windows Live ID dialog box appears. Type your Windows Live ID in the top text field.

3   Type your Windows Live password in the bottom text field.

4   If you want Windows Live Mail to remember your Windows Live login information so you don't have to re-enter it, click the *Remember my password* checkbox to select it.

5   Press the Sign in button.

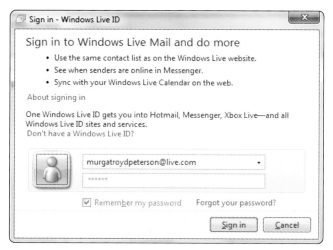

Click the Sign in button.

6   If this is the first time you have signed in to Windows Live from Windows Live Mail, you'll be prompted to download your information from Windows Live. Press Download.

Download your Windows Live information.

7   Windows Live Mail downloads your calendar entries, your contact entries, and your Hotmail e-mail account information. To access your Windows Live Calendar and Windows Live People entries, click Calendar and Contacts, respectively, below the folder list.

Composing and sending an e-mail message

Once you've set up your e-mail accounts and synced Windows Live Mail with other Windows Live services, you're ready to begin composing and sending e-mail messages.

Composing your message

The Windows Live Mail New Message window behaves much like a word processor, enabling you to enter, add, delete, move, copy, and format text.

A word on e-mail etiquette

E-mail messages can range in style from formal to flippant. Whatever your tone, you'll want to keep a few points in mind to ensure that nobody gets rubbed the wrong way. First, be aware that the recipient might misinterpret what you believe is witty sarcasm as an actual put-down. To convey that you're just kidding around, consider using an emoticon—that is, a smiley face or wink. Second, if you're angry with the recipient, give yourself time to cool down before sending a message. Third, keep things short. Your subject line and the body of your message should be clear, concise, and to the point. Finally, avoid spelling and grammatical errors—especially if your e-mail is bound for a colleague or, worse, your boss.

1   In Windows Live Mail, select the account you want to use to send your e-mail message.

2   Press the New button. A New Message window opens.

3   Click in the To text field and type your recipient's name. As you type, Windows Live Mail displays a list of contact entries that match what you typed; click an entry in the list to add that contact to the To field. If the person's contact information has not been entered into Windows Live People, you'll need to type that person's e-mail address instead of his or her name.

4 Repeat step 3 as needed to add more recipients to the To text field.

5 Click in the Subject text field and type a subject for your message.

6 Click in the main message area and type your message.

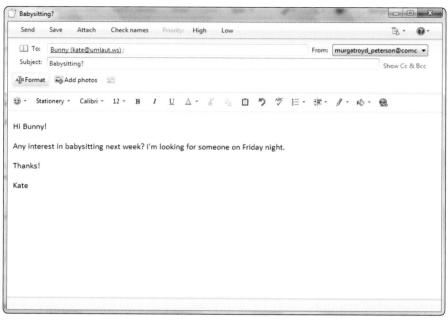

Compose your message.

Changing the look of your message

To change the look of your message, you can adjust the text's style, font, size, and color. You can also format text in a numbered list or bulleted list and change the background color. You might do this to personalize a message, or to emphasize certain points in the message.

1 Use your mouse to select the text whose font you want to change.

2   To change the font, click the current font in the formatting toolbar and choose a new font from the menu that appears.

Apply a new font.

3   To change the font size, select the text you want to change, click the current font size to the right of the font drop-down menu in the message window's formatting toolbar and choose a new size from the menu that appears.

4   To apply bold, italics, or underlining, with the text you want to change selected, press the Bold (**B**), Italics (*I*), or Underline (U) button in the message window's formatting toolbar.

Add bold, italics, or underlining.

5   To change the font color, with the text you want to change selected, press the Font Color button (△) in the message window's formatting toolbar and choose the desired color from the palette that appears.

6   To format text as a numbered or bulleted list, with the text you want to change selected, press the Format as List button (▤ ▾) in the message window's formatting toolbar and choose Numbered List or Bulleted List.

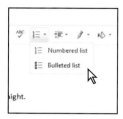

Format the selected text as a bulleted list.

7   To change the color of the message's background, press the Background Color button (◈ ▾) in the message window's formatting toolbar and choose a color from the palette that appears.

Change the background color.

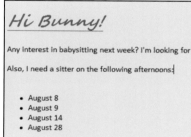

Using stationery

Another way to spruce up your message is to use Windows Live Mail stationery. This digital stationery is just like its real-world counterpart—a blank sheet of paper with some sort of design in the background. There are lots of stationery options to choose from, from paw prints to mosaics to tiles and more. To apply one of Windows Live Mail's stationery options to your message, press the Stationery button and choose More Stationery from the list that appears. Windows Live Mail launches the Select Stationery dialog box; click an option in the list to preview it. When you find one you like, press OK.

Spell-checking your message

You should take care to avoid sending messages that contain spelling errors—especially if your e-mail is bound for someone you're trying to impress. To aid you in this, Windows Live Mail supports a spell-check feature.

1   Press the Spell Check button (ᵃᵇᶜ) in the message window's formatting toolbar.

2   Windows Live Mail launches the Spelling dialog box. Notice that the first spelling error detected in your document is highlighted, with suggested fixes in the Spelling dialog box. Select one of the suggested spellings, then press Change. Alternatively, press Ignore.

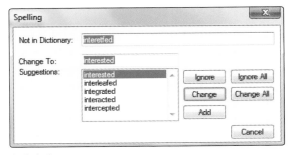

Spell-check your message.

3   The Windows Live Mail Spelling dialog box suggests fixes for any additional errors in your message. Change or ignore the errors as needed.

4   When no more errors are detected, Windows Live Mail informs you that the spell-check is complete. Press OK.

Adding a photo

Often, the purpose of an e-mail message is to share a photo with the recipient. Windows Live Mail enables you to quickly and easily insert a photo into the body of your message.

1 Click the spot in your message where you want the photo to appear.

2 Press the Add Photos button (⬚).

3 Windows Live Mail launches the Add Photos dialog box. Locate and select the photo you want to add.

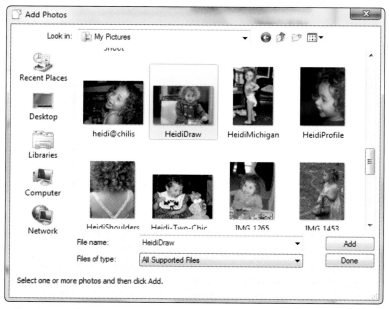

Add a photo.

4 Press the Add button.

5 If you like, follow steps 3 and 4 to add more photos.

6 When you're finished adding photos, press the Done button.

7   The photo is inserted in the body of your message. Several photo-related options appear along the top of the message, including options for framing the image, correcting the image, increasing or reducing the size and quality of the image. In this example, the medium size is selected so that the image is not too large for e-mailing.

Apply framing effects or edit the photo.

8   Press the Layout button (⊞) to reveal various layout options. These are especially helpful if you have inserted multiple images into the text.

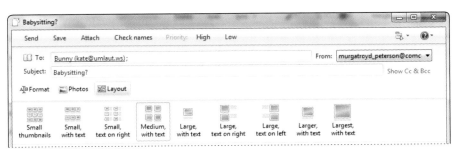

Press the Layout button to reveal layout options.

9   Press the Format button (ᴀ⌐ʙ) to display the Windows Live Mail formatting toolbar. Keep the e-mail open as you will continue to work with it in the next exercise.

Attaching a file

You may need to send attachments or files you've saved on your computer's hard drive in your e-mail messages. For example, you might want to e-mail a document containing your resume in order to apply for a job, or you might want to share a file with a friend. When your message is received, the recipient can open the attached file on his or her computer.

1   Press the Attach button, located along the top of the message window.

2   Windows Live Mail launches an Open dialog box. Locate and select the file you want to attach.

3   Press Open. An icon for the attached file appears under the message's Subject line.

Add a file attachment.

Setting a message's priority

If your message is particularly important, you may want to assign it a high priority. High-priority messages appear in the recipient's inbox with a special high-priority icon (⬆) to alert the recipient that the message is important. Likewise, you can classify messages that aren't important as low-priority. These messages are marked with a special low-priority icon (⬇).

To assign a message a high priority, press the High button, located along the top of the message window. To assign a message a low priority, press the Low button.

Prioritize a message.

Saving your message

If you don't have time to finish your message during this session, press the Save button along the top of the New Message window, then press the message window's Close button (▭). Windows Live Mail saves the message in the Drafts folder. When you are ready to work on the message again, select the Drafts folder, then double-click the message in the file list to open it.

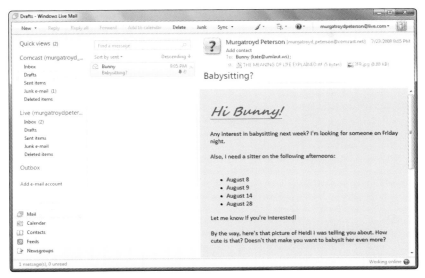

Save your message as a draft.

Sending an e-mail message

When you are ready to send your message, press the Send button. Windows Live Mail sends the message to the contact or contacts listed in the To text field, and moves a copy of your message to the Sent Items folder.

If you are not connected to the Internet when you press Send, Windows Live Mail will save your message in the Outbox folder. The next time you are connected, you can send the saved message by pressing the Sync button.

Receiving, reading, and managing e-mail messages

As easy as it is to send e-mail messages using Windows Live Mail, it's even easier to receive them. Windows Live Mail checks for new messages anytime you start the program and at 30-minute intervals while the program is running. If you don't want to wait for Windows Live Mail to run its automatic check for new messages, you can check for mail manually.

1   Click the drop-down menu to the right of the Sync button along the top of the New Message window.

2   Choose which accounts you want to check. Choose Everything to also download any changes you've made to Windows Live Calendar and Windows Live People since your last Windows Live Mail session. Windows Live Mail downloads your messages.

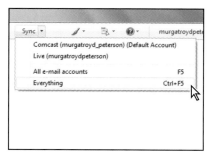

Download e-mail messages manually.

In addition to downloading your e-mail messages, Windows Live Mail also sends any messages in the Outbox folder when you click Sync.

Changing the automatic-check interval

Windows Live Mail checks for new messages any time you start the program and at 30-minute intervals while the program is running. To change this interval, press the Menus button (⊞ ▾) in the Windows Live Mail toolbar and choose Options. The Options dialog box opens; in the General tab, make sure the *Check for New Messages Every x Minute(s)* checkbox is selected, and enter a number between 1 and 480 in the spin box. Then press OK.

Previewing and opening messages

Once you've received an e-mail message, it appears in the Inbox folder. You can preview the message's contents in the Preview pane, or open it in its own message window. You can then reply to the message or forward it on to someone else. If you don't need to keep a message after it's been read, you can delete it. You can also create a folder system for storing messages you want to keep. You can even set up Windows Live Mail to filter junk mail.

Windows Live Mail displays messages you receive in the file list, with unread messages appearing in bold.

1   In the folder list, select the Inbox folder for the account to which the message was sent. Windows Live Mail displays the Inbox folder's file list. Note that new messages appear in bold.

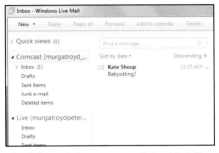

The file list, with the new message displayed in bold.

2   In the file list, click the message to view its contents in the Preview pane.

3   To open a message in its own window, double-click it in the file list.

 If you receive an e-mail from someone who is not in your Windows Live Mail contacts, click the Add Contact link that appears to the right of the sender's e-mail address. Windows Live Mail displays an Edit Contact dialog box for the contact with as much information available for the contact, filled in; add more info as needed.

Opening and saving attachments

Sometimes, you may receive messages that contain an attachment or a file appended to the message, identified by a paperclip icon.

 Be aware that attachments are known carriers of viruses. Open attachments only if they've been sent by a trusted source, and be sure you are using antivirus software.

Opening attachments

1   Open the message containing the attachment you want to open or preview the message in the Windows Live Mail Preview pane.

2   Right-click the attachment, located immediately below the message's Subject line in the message window. Choose Open from the menu that appears.

Open an attachment.

3   Windows Live Mail confirms that you want to open the file. Press Yes. The file is opened in the appropriate program, if that program is installed on your computer.

Saving attachments

1   Open the message containing the attachment you want to save or preview the message in the Windows Live Mail Preview pane.

2   Right-click the attachment.

3   Choose Save As from the menu that appears.

4   Windows Live Mail launches the Save Attachment As dialog box. Locate and select the folder in which you want to save the attachment.

5   Press Save. Windows Live Mail saves the attachment in the folder you selected.

Replying to a message

You can easily reply to a message you receive. If the message to which you are replying was sent to multiple people, you can reply to the sender as well as to everyone in the message's To list or you can reply to the sender only.

1   Open the message to which you want to reply, or preview the message in the Windows Live Mail Preview pane.

2   To reply to the sender only, Press the Reply button along the top of the New Message window. To reply to the sender and to all other recipients of the original message, Press Reply All.

3   A new message window opens with the original message text displayed. Note that the e-mail address of the sender appears in the To field. The e-mail addresses of other recipients are also displayed, if you pressed Reply All. Type your reply in the message section of the window.

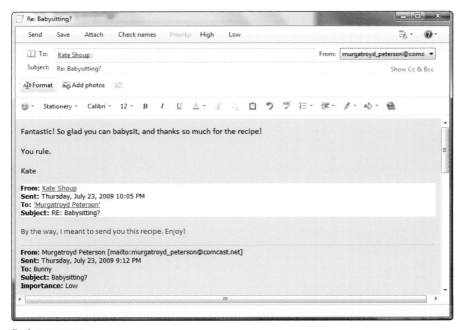

Reply to a message.

4   Press Send. Windows Live Mail sends your reply.

Forwarding a message

If you receive an e-mail message that you'd like to share with someone else, for example, a message from your boss that needs to be shared with other members of your team, you can forward the message, adding your own text to the message if desired.

1   Open the message to which you want to reply or preview the message in the Windows Live Mail Preview pane. Press the Forward button.

2   A new message window opens with the original message text displayed. Type your recipient's name in the To field. As you type, Windows Live Mail displays a list of contact entries that match what you typed; click an entry in the list to add that contact to the To field. If the person's contact information has not been entered into Windows Live People, you'll need to type that person's e-mail address instead of his or her name, repeat as needed to add more recipients to the To text field..

3   Type any text you want to add to the forwarded message.

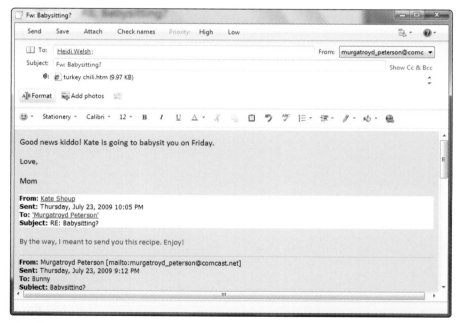

Forward a message.

4   Press Send. Windows Live Mail forwards the message to the recipient in the To field.

Deleting a message

If you determine that you do not need to keep a message, you can delete it. Deleting unwanted messages is a good way to keep your inbox organized. When you delete a message, it is moved to the Deleted Items folder; if you determine that you have deleted a message in error, you can restore it to its original location. To permanently delete the message, you must empty the Deleted Items folder.

1   Select the message to which you want to delete.

2   Press the Delete button. The message is moved to the Deleted Items folder.

To delete multiple messages at once, hold down the Ctrl key on your keyboard as you click the messages you want to delete in the file list. Then right-click any of the selected items and choose Delete from the menu that appears.

3   If you determine that you have deleted the message in error, drag it from the Deleted Items file list to the desired folder in the folder list.

4   To permanently delete the message, select the Deleted Items folder. Press the Empty This Folder button (×).

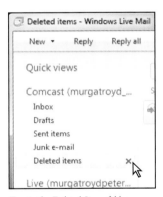

Empty the Deleted Items folder.

5   Windows Live Mail prompts you to confirm the deletion. Press Yes. The message is deleted from Windows Live Mail.

Saving a message in a folder

If you frequently receive e-mail messages from the same person, or you receive lots of messages regarding a project you're working on, you can create a folder for those messages. After you create the folder, you can move e-mail messages into that folder, much the way you file papers in file folders to keep them organized. Folders you create are added to the folder list.

1   In the main Windows Live Mail window, press New at the top of the window.

2   Choose Folder from the menu that appears.

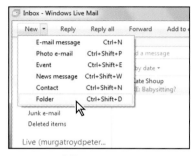

Create a new folder.

3   Windows Live Mail displays the Create Folder dialog box. Type a name for the folder in the Folder Name text field.

4   Select the e-mail folder in which the new folder should reside.

5   Press OK. Windows Live Mail creates the new folder, placing it in the folder list.

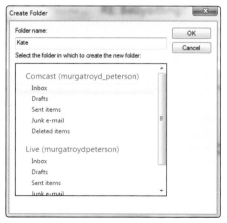
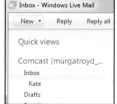

Windows Live Mail adds the folder to the folder list.

Moving an e-mail message to a folder

1 Right–click the message you want to file.

2 Select Move to Folder in the menu that appears.

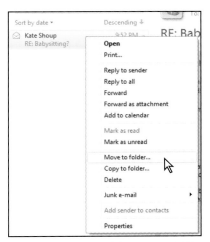

Right-click the message and choose Move to Folder.

3 Windows Live Mail launches the Move dialog box. Click the folder to which you want to move the message.

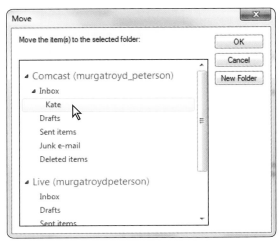

Move the message to the selected folder.

4 Press OK. Windows Live Mail moves the message to the folder you chose.

An even faster way to file an e-mail message is to drag it from the file list to the folder list, over the folder to which you want to move it. To copy, rather than move, a message to a folder, hold down the Ctrl key on your keyboard as you drag the file to the desired folder.

Finding a message

If you've misplaced an e-mail message, you can use Windows Live Mail's search tool to find it. To do so, type the name of the sender, specific keywords, an e-mail address, or anything you remember about the message, in the Find a Message field, located above the file list. As you type, Windows Live Mail displays messages that match your criteria. When you see the message you want, click to preview it in the Preview pane or double-click to open it in its own window.

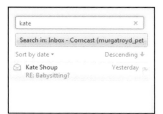

Find a message.

If Windows Live Mail fails to locate the message you need, try expanding your search to comb through more folders. To do so, click the Try Searching Again in the All E-mail link at the bottom of the file list that contains your search results.

Filtering junk mail

You'll quickly find that using e-mail opens you up to a deluge of junk e-mail messages, called spam. Indeed, you may well find yourself sifting through dozens of spam e-mails to locate your *real* messages every day, which can be a real time-waster. Fortunately, Windows Live Mail features a junk e-mail filter, which diverts spam from your inbox into a special Junk E-Mail folder.

If the junk e-mail filter, which is active by default, fails to divert a junk message to the Junk E-mail folder, you can easily move it there yourself and, in doing so, instruct Windows Live Mail to handle any subsequent messages from the sender accordingly.

1   Right-click the message you want to move to the Junk E-mail folder.

2   Choose Junk E-mail from the menu that appears.

3 Choose Add Sender to Blocked Senders list from the submenu that appears.

If you want to block all senders from the sender's domain, choose Add Senders Domain to Blocked Senders List. This diverts all messages you receive from the sender's domain or messages with the same text after the @ symbol in the sender's e-mail address to the Junk E-mail folder.

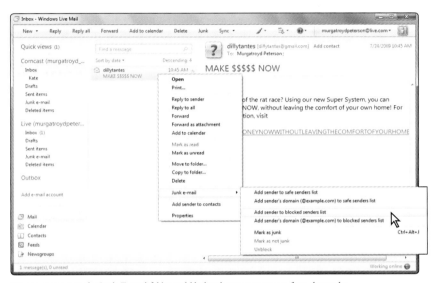

Move a message to the Junk E-mail folder and block subsequent messages from the sender.

4 Windows informs you that the sender has been added to your Blocked Senders list and that the message has been moved to the Junk E-mail folder. Press OK.

Mark as not Junk

Sometimes, Windows Live Mail's junk e-mail filter works a little too well, diverting messages that *aren't* spam into the Junk E-mail folder. For this reason, it's a good idea to check the Junk E-mail folder every few days to ensure that messages that are *not* spam have not been placed there by mistake. To view the contents of the folder, click it in the folder list. If a message has been moved there in error, follow these steps to mark the message as not junk and move it to your inbox:

1 Right-click the message in the Junk E-mail folder that you want to move to your inbox.

2 Choose Junk E-mail from the menu that appears.

3 Choose Mark as Not Junk from the submenu that appears. Windows Live Mail moves the message to your inbox.

Mark as a safe sender

1 Right-click the message in the inbox.

2 Choose Junk E-mail from the menu that appears.

3 Choose Add Sender to Safe Senders list from the submenu that appears. Windows Live Mail adds the sender to your Safe Senders list, meaning that the junk e-mail filter will not divert messages from that sender to the Junk E-mail folder.

If you want to add all senders from the sender's domain to the Safe Senders list, choose Add Senders Domain to Safe Senders List.

Changing the junk e-mail filtering level

If you find that Windows Live Mail consistently fails to divert spam messages to your Junk E-mail folder, or consistently diverts mail that is *not* junk to this folder, you can change the filtering level.

1 Press the Menus button (⊟ ·) in the Windows Live Mail toolbar.

2 Choose Safety Options from the menu that appears.

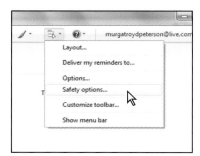

Press the Menus button and choose Safety Options.

3 The Safety Options dialog box opens, with the Options tab displayed. Choose the desired level of protection.

- **No Automatic Filtering**. Select this option to divert only those messages from senders you have blocked to the Junk E-mail folder.

- **Low**. When you choose this option, the junk e-mail filter will divert only the most obvious junk e-mail to the Junk E-mail folder. As a result, some messages that are junk mail may not be diverted.

- **High**. When you choose this option, the junk e-mail filter diverts messages with a medium or high likelihood of being junk e-mail to the Junk E-mail folder. As a result, some messages that aren't junk e-mail may be diverted.

• **Safe List Only**. Choosing this option diverts all messages from people who are not on your Safe Senders list to the Junk E-mail folder.

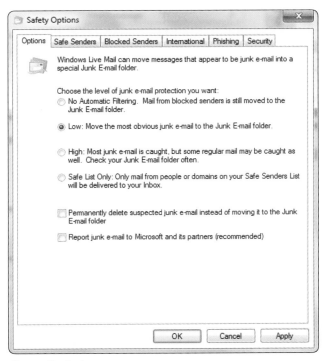

Choose a filter level.

4   Press OK.

Managing RSS feeds

Really Simple Syndication (RSS) enables web content, such as blogs, podcasts, and news to be *syndicated* or converted to a web feed, also called an RSS feed, to which you can subscribe. In Lesson 5, "Surfing the Web with Internet Explorer 8," you learned how to subscribe to RSS feeds using Internet Explorer 8. What you didn't learn was that when you do so, that feed is also added to Windows Live Mail—meaning that like Internet Explorer 8, Windows Live Mail automatically checks for and downloads feed updates. You can view these updates right from the Windows Live Mail window.

1   Click Feeds in the bottom-left corner of the Windows Live Mail window, under the folder list.

2   Feeds to which you are subscribed appear in the folder list. Click a feed to view it.

3   Posts for that feed appear in the file list. Select a post to view it in the Preview pane.

If the post you want to view is not displayed in full in the Preview pane, click the View Online link at the top of pane. This launches the post in its own web page.

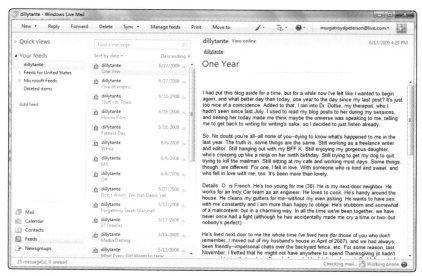

View a feed.

Reading and participating in newsgroups

In addition to functioning as an e-mail program, Windows Live Mail can also act as a newsreader, enabling you to download, read, and post newsgroup messages. A *newsgroup* is an online discussion forum for users from all over the world with common interests. Newsgroups live on special servers called *news servers*, which typically house thousands of newsgroups and offer access to countless more by communicating with other news servers. To access them, you usually must establish a newsgroup account with your Internet service provider or some other source. Contact your Internet Service Provider for more information. In addition, you must create a newsgroup account within Windows Live Mail. To get started, click Newsgroups in the bottom-left corner of the Windows Live Mail window, click the Add Newsgroup Account link in the folder list, and follow the onscreen prompts.

Windows Live Hotmail

You can also use Windows Live Hotmail with your Windows Live Mail application. Windows Live Hotmail is a free, web-based e-mail service that you can access from any computer with an Internet connection using a web browser such as Internet Explorer 8. Assuming you created a Windows Live account, as discussed in Lesson 5, " Surfing the Web with Internet Explorer 8," you already have a Windows Live Hotmail account. To access your Windows Live Hotmail account, direct your web browser to the Windows Live web site and log in. Then click the Mail link along the top of the page to display the Windows Live Hotmail screen.

A quick glance at the main Hotmail screen reveals that it is similar to the main Windows Live Mail screen. For example, there's a folder list; it contains an Inbox folder, a Junk folder, a Drafts folder, a Sent folder, and a Deleted folder. There's also a file list, which displays the messages in the selected folder, as well as a Preview pane, which displays the contents of the message selected in the file list. If the Preview pane is not visible, press the Options button in the upper-right corner of the Windows Live window and choose Right or Bottom to display it.

The main Windows Live Hotmail screen.

You can reply to and forward messages you receive, as well as create new messages. Like Windows Live Mail, Hotmail uses contact information stored in Windows Live People. Many of the same formatting tools are also available, for example, you can change the font, font size, and font color, apply bold, italics, or underlining, or format text as a bulleted or numbered list. You can also add attachments, spell-check your message, save your message as a draft, and prioritize your message. Finally, you can filter unwanted messages using Hotmail's junk e-mail filter, and create folders to manage your messages, just as you can in Windows Live Mail.

Hotmail offers many of the same messaging tools as Windows Live Mail.

Windows Live Messenger

When you send an e-mail, there may be a delay between the time you send the message and the time it appears in your recipient's inbox. Even if the e-mail message arrives quickly, if your recipient is offline, there is no telling when he or she will actually see your message.

In contrast, instant messaging (IM) allows for instantaneous communication, enabling two or more people to communicate in real time using typed text. An IM program enables you to determine whether any of your contacts are currently online and running a compatible IM program. If a contact is online, you can use the program to send and receive messages with none of the delays that can occur in e-mail communications.

Windows Live Messenger is an IM program that you can download free of charge from Microsoft's Windows Live web site. You learned how to download this program in Lesson 5, "Surfing the Web with Internet Explorer 8." In order to use Windows Live Messenger, you must have an account, and if you created a Windows Live account, you are ready to start using IM. Start Windows Live Messenger just as you do any other program in Windows: by clicking the program's icon in the Start menu.

Adding contacts to Windows Live Messenger

Before you can communicate with someone using Windows Live Messenger, you must add that person as a Windows Live Messenger contact, and invite him or her to chat online with you.

1   Press the Windows Live Messenger button (⬚) in the Windows 7 taskbar. If this button is not visible, launch Windows Live Messenger by selecting its program icon in the Start menu.

2   The Windows Live Messenger window opens. Press the Add a Contact or Group button (⬚).

3. Choose Add Contact.

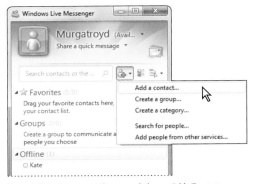

Press Add a Contact or Group and choose Add Contact.

4 A Windows Live Messenger dialog box appears. Type the person's IM address in the Instant Messaging Address text field and press Next.

Type your contact's IM address.

5 In the next screen, type a message to the person you want to invite to chat. Press Send Invitation.

Type your contact's IM address.

6 Windows Live Messenger informs you that you've added the person to you contacts, and that as soon as he or she accepts your invitation, you will be able to chat. Press Close.

Receiving and responding to an IM

When someone sends you an IM, Windows 7 displays it near the taskbar's notifications area located in the bottom right of your screen if Windows Live Messenger is running on your computer.

When someone sends you an IM, you'll see it near the taskbar's notification area.

To respond, click the message. A Windows Live Messenger window opens; type your reply and press Enter.

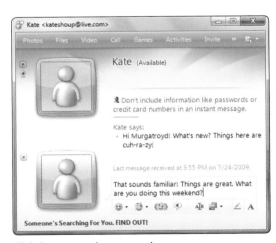

Click the message and type your reply.

Starting a new IM thread

1 Press the Windows Live Messenger button (🦋) in the Windows 7 taskbar. If this button is not visible, launch Windows Live Messenger by selecting its program icon in the Start menu.

2 The Windows Live Messenger window opens, listing who among your contacts is available. Right-click the entry for the person you want to IM.

3 Choose Send an Instant Message from the menu that appears.

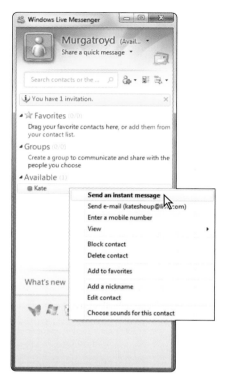

Choose your contact.

4 A Windows Live Messenger window opens; type your message and press Enter.

In addition to typing text in an IM, you can also add emoticons to your messages. An emoticon is a special graphic meant to convey a facial expression or an emotion. Using emoticons can help prevent others from misinterpreting your messages. Also available are winks, which are animated greetings you can send to your contacts, and nudges, which cause the conversation window to vibrate.

Self study

1   Set up Windows Live Mail to handle any additional e-mail accounts you use on a regular basis.

2   Set up Windows Live Mail to operate as a newsreader. If your ISP does not host a news server, search the Internet to locate any number of companies that do.

Review

Questions

1   What are three ways to change the look of an e-mail message you're composing?

2   How often does Windows Live Mail check for new messages?

3   Why are e-mail attachments sometimes considered dangerous?

4   What is the difference between Windows Live Mail and Windows Live Hotmail?

5   How is IM different from e-mail?

Answers

1   You can change the look of your message by adjusting the text's style, font, size, and color. You can also format text in a numbered list or bulleted list and change the background color. You can also apply one of Windows Live Mail's stationery options.

2   By default, Windows Live Mail checks for new messages every 30 minutes.

3   E-mail attachments are known carriers of viruses. You should open e-mail attachments only if they've been sent by a trusted source.

4   Windows Live Mail is an e-mail program, or client, that is installed on your computer. Windows Live Hotmail is a free, Web-based e-mail service that you can access from any computer with an Internet connection using a Web browser such as Internet Explorer 8.

5   When you send an e-mail, depending on how your e-mail program, and that of your recipient, are set up, there may be a delay between the time you send the message and the time it appears in your recipient's inbox. In contrast, instant messaging (IM) allows for instantaneous communication, enabling two or more people to communicate in real time using typed text.

What you'll learn in this lesson:

- Managing images in Windows Live Photo Gallery
- Viewing and editing images in Windows Live Photo Gallery
- Obtaining photo prints
- Sharing your pictures with others

Working with images

Windows 7 has many tools that help you store, organize, edit and print your photos right from your computer.

Starting up

Before you start, be sure to download all the files for this lesson from the accompanying DVD to your hard drive.

See Lesson 13 in action!

Use the accompanying video to gain a better understanding of how to use some of the features shown in this lesson. The video tutorial for this lesson can be found on the included DVD.

Windows 7 imaging software

Windows 7 includes multiple tools for working with images, some with more features than others. Here's a brief run-down:

- **The Pictures folder.** The Pictures folder acts as a central repository for digital image files that are imported from a digital camera or scanner. The window displaying the contents of the Picture folder contains special toolbar buttons for viewing your pictures in a slide show, printing your pictures, sharing them with others, and burning them to a CD or DVD. The Pictures folder enables you to see all your pictures in one place and to sort them by name, date, tag, rating, and other file properties. For more information about tagging, rating, and sorting files, refer to Lesson 3, "Working with Files and Folders."

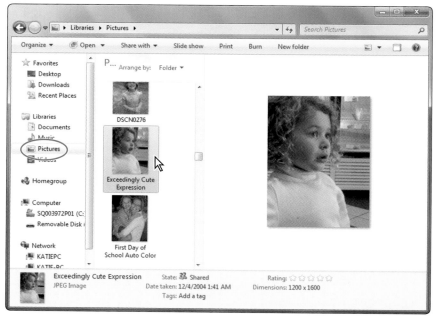

The Pictures folder.

- **Windows Photo Viewer.** You can use Windows Photo Viewer to open photos you locate in the Windows Pictures folder. Windows Photo Viewer enables you to view, rotate, and zoom in on your pictures, as well as view them as a slide show, print them, and e-mail them to others.

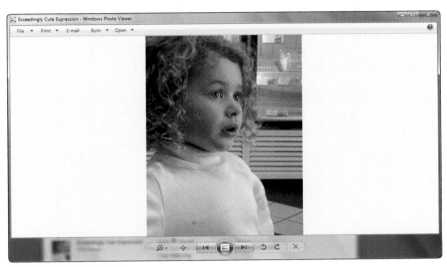

Windows Photo Viewer.

- **Windows Paint.** You can use the drawing tools located in the Windows Paint Ribbon to create doodles on a blank canvas. You can also open digital photos in Paint and rotate, crop, or resize them, or use the drawing tools to draw on them.

Windows Paint.

- **Windows Live Photo Gallery.** Windows Live Photo Gallery can be downloaded free of charge from the Microsoft Windows Live web site. You learned how to create a Windows Live account and download this program in Lesson 5, "Surfing the Web with Internet Explorer 8." Using Windows Live Photo Gallery, you can view, organize, and edit your digital pictures. For example, you can change an image's colors, improve its brightness and contrast, straighten the image, crop it, remove red eye, and more. Windows Live Photo Gallery also makes sharing your photos a snap, with tools to expedite printing your photos, ordering prints online, e-mailing them, or, assuming you are signed in to your Windows Live account, posting them online on the Windows Live web site.

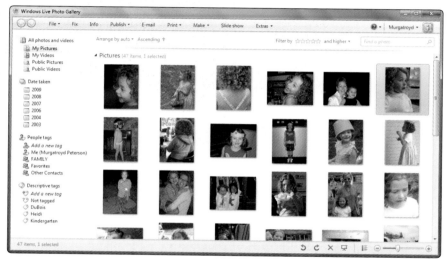

Windows Live Photo Gallery.

Windows Live Photo Gallery is the most robust tool for managing and editing your images. For this reason, the remainder of this chapter focuses on Windows Live Photo Gallery, even though some of the tasks discussed can be completed in other Windows 7 programs. You start Windows Live Photo Gallery just as you do any other program: by clicking its icon in the Start menu.

Importing images to your computer

To view and edit a digital photo on your computer, you must first import it from the digital camera you used to take the photograph. Most digital cameras store the images they capture on a memory card, or a small, removable storage device. Memory cards come in a variety of formats: SD card, Smart Media, CompactFlash, or Sony Memory Stick.

One way to import the images stored on your camera's memory card is to use a universal serial bus (USB) cable to connect the camera directly to your computer. Another method is to remove the memory card from the camera, insert it into a memory-card reader, and then plug the memory-card reader into your computer's USB port. Some computers include a built-in memory-card reader. If your computer has a built-in reader, insert the memory card into it.

Regardless of which method you choose, Windows 7 launches the AutoPlay dialog box.

The AutoPlay dialog box.

If Windows 7 fails to launch the AutoPlay dialog box, open the Computer folder, right-click the icon for the digital camera or memory card, and choose Open AutoPlay from the menu that appears.

1   Click Import Pictures and Videos Using Windows.

2   The Import Pictures and Videos dialog box opens. If all the photos you're importing share some characteristic in common—for example, they all depict the same person or they were all taken during your vacation—you can enter a relevant tag in the Tag These Pictures field; the tag you type will be applied to all the pictures you import. If you don't wish to apply the same tag to all the pictures you're importing, you can tag them individually either from the Pictures folder, as discussed in Lesson 3, "Working with Files and Folders," or within the Windows Live Photo Gallery window, as discussed later in this lesson.

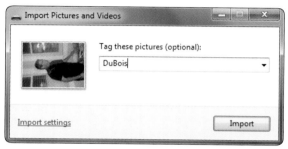

The Import Pictures and Videos dialog box.

3   Press the Import button. Windows creates a subfolder for the pictures in the Pictures folder and imports the pictures into the folder.

Windows 7 imports the pictures.

Scanning images

If you have photos taken with a traditional film-based camera—holdovers from before you went digital. You can use a scanner to convert these photo prints to digital images. To do so, connect your scanner to your computer and place a photo print in the scanner as outlined in the scanner's manual. Then, in Windows Live Photo Gallery, select File, and choose Import from a Camera or Scanner, select the scanner in the list of devices that appears, press Import.

Managing images using Windows Live Photo Gallery

Digital photos can be stored, located, and viewed on your computer with the press of a button.

Photos in your Pictures folder appear in Photo Gallery by default. You can click All pictures and video in Windows Live Photo Gallery's Navigation pane and sift through all the images in these folders, but doing so can be time-consuming, especially if you store many digital photos on your computer. To make it easier to find the photos you're looking for, you can tag and rate your image files. You can also rename image files in batches, replacing the filenames your camera creates with more meaningful names for several image files at once. You can sort or search files based on their tag, rating, or name. You can also locate your image files by file type or by date taken.

 If you don't have your own images in your Pictures folder, copy the Sample Images folder from the DVD supplied with this book into the Pictures folder on your computer.

Tagging photos in Windows Live Photo Gallery

Tagging photo files in Windows Live Photo Gallery is similar to tagging files in Windows 7's Documents, Pictures, and Music folders.

1   In the Windows Live Photo Gallery window, select the picture or pictures you want to tag.

2   If necessary, press the Info button along the top of the window to display the Info pane.

3   Click the Add descriptive tags link under the Descriptive tags header on the right side of the window.

4   Type the tags you want to apply, separating them with a comma, and press Enter. Windows Live Photo Gallery applies the tag.

Tag your photos in Windows Live Photo Gallery.

Add a people tag

In addition to enabling you to apply descriptive tags, you can also apply people tags—that is, tags that indicate who appears in the photo.

1   In the Windows Live Photo Gallery window, select the picture or pictures you want to tag.

2   If necessary, click the Info button along the top of the window to display the Info pane.

3   Click the Add people tags link below the People tags header on the right side of the window.

Click the Add people tags link.

4   If the tag you want to apply appears in the list, click it to apply it to the selected image, otherwise, type the tag in the text field and press Enter. Windows Live Photo Gallery applies the tag.

Tag the people in your photos.

Rating photos in Windows Live Photo Gallery

As with tagging photos, you can rate photos within Windows Live Photo Gallery using the Info pane. Windows Live Photo Gallery uses Windows 7's star rating system, with five stars being the highest rating.

1   In the Windows Live Photo Gallery window, select the picture you want to rate.

2   If necessary, press the Info button along the top of the window to display the Info pane.

3   In the Info pane, next to the Rating entry, click the star that represents the rating you want to apply. For example, to give the file a two-star rating, click the second star; to apply a five-star rating, click the fifth star. Windows Live Photo Gallery applies your rating.

Click a star in the Info pane.

Batch-naming photos in Windows Live Photo Gallery

Batch-name image files in batches replaces the filenames your camera creates, for example, DC000591.jpg, with more meaningful names such as, ParisTrip2009.jpg, for several image files at one time.

1   In the Windows Live Photo Gallery window, select the pictures you want to batch-rename by holding down the shift key and clicking two images you would like to include or clicking in the checkbox that appears in the upper left hand corner when you hover over the image.

2   Right-click a selected picture and choose Rename in the menu that appears.

3   The Info pane opens with the contents of the Filename field selected. Type a name for the files and press Enter. Windows Live Photo Gallery applies the name to each selected picture along with a sequential number to differentiate the files.

Batch-rename your photos.

Locating photos in Windows Live Photo Gallery

One of the great things about Windows Live Photo Gallery is that it makes finding the image you want to view or edit a snap. You can sort files by name, date, rating, file type, or tag. You can also direct the program to display only those photos shot on a certain date, or containing a certain tag.

1   In the Windows Live Photo Gallery Navigation pane, click the folder containing the photos you want to sort. Choose All Photos and Videos if you're not sure which ones to select.

2   Click the Arrange By down arrow near the top of the screen. Arrange by auto is selected by default.

3 Choose how you want to sort your images. Windows Live Photo Gallery sorts your pictures accordingly.

Sort photos by name.

Locating files by date

1 In the Navigation pane, click the folder containing the photo you want to find. Choose All Photos and Videos if you're not sure where the image is loaded.

2 Still in the Navigation pane, click Date Taken.

3 Click the year that the photo you're searching for was taken. Windows Live Photo Gallery displays all photos taken during the year you clicked.

4 Click the month in which the photo was taken. Windows Live Photo Gallery displays all photos taken during the month you clicked.

5 Click the day on which the photo was taken. Windows Live Photo Gallery displays all photos taken on the day you clicked.

View photos taken on a certain day.

Locating all photos containing a certain people tag or descriptive tag

1   In the Windows Live Photo Gallery Navigation pane, click the folder containing the photo you want to find.

2   In the Navigation pane, click People Tags or Descriptive Tags. A list of tags you've applied to your photos appears.

3   Click a tag to see all pictures that contain that tag. Photos containing the selected tag are displayed.

View photos containing a specific tag.

If you're not sure of the location of a file, select All Photos and Videos when searching.

Locating all photos with the same rating

1   In the Windows Live Photo Gallery Navigation pane, click the folder containing the photo you want to find.

2   Next to Filter By, near the top of the screen, click a rating. Photos with the rating you selected are displayed.

View photos given the same rating.

Searching for a file

1   In the Windows Live Photo Gallery Navigation pane, click the folder containing the photo you want to find.

2   Type some part of the file's name, a tag, a caption, or a file extension in the Search text field and press Enter. Windows Live Photo Gallery displays photos matching the criteria you entered.

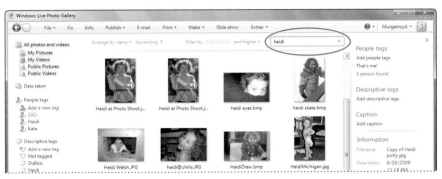

Search for a photo.

Viewing images in Windows Live Photo Gallery

You can view your images in Windows Live Photo Gallery in a few different ways: displaying a preview of the image, opening the image in its own screen, and by setting up a slideshow.

Previewing an Image in Windows Live Photo Gallery

Windows Live Photo Gallery displays photos as thumbnail-sized images by default. To see a preview of an image, hover your mouse pointer over the thumbnail.

Preview an image.

Opening an Image in Windows Live Photo Gallery

To open an image in Windows Live Photo Gallery in its own screen, double-click the image. Windows Live Photo Gallery opens the image in its own window.

Open an image.

 After you open an image, you can return to the main Windows Live Photo Gallery window by clicking the Back to Gallery button in the upper-left corner of the window.

Viewing photos as a slideshow

You can use Windows Live Photo Gallery to view your pictures in a full-screen slide show. You can specify which images appear in the show, and indicate the speed at which the show should play. While the slideshow runs automatically by default, moving from one picture to the next, you can control the show whenever you like using the slideshow buttons that appear when you move the mouse.

1　In the Windows Live Photo Gallery window, select the pictures you want to include in your slideshow.

2　Press the Slide Show button (⬜) at the bottom of the Windows Live Photo Gallery Window. The slideshow starts.

3   To access the slideshow controls, right-click on the screen. A context menu appears with various menu options, including Play, Pause, Next, Back, Shuffle to shuffle the order of the photos displayed, and Loop to run the slideshow continuously. Also available are settings for controlling the speed of the slideshow.

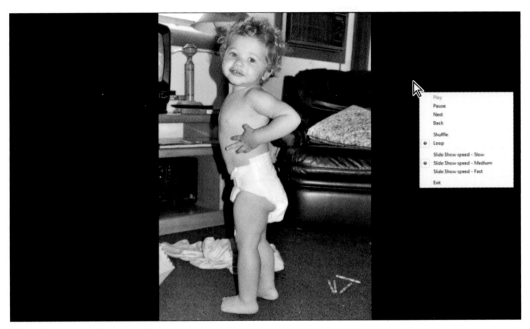

Right-click to access slideshow controls.

4   Click Exit in the context menu to exit the slideshow.

Editing images in Windows Live Photo Gallery

Suppose you discover that one of your images is rotated 90 degrees, lacks in contrast, seems slightly off color-wise, or is a bit blurry. Or you might discover that your subject has red eyes, requiring correction. Maybe you think the image would look better if it were cropped or straightened, or that it needs to be a different size. You can use the Windows Live Photo Gallery editing tools to fix all these problems and more.

Before you edit an image, you should always make a copy of it and preserve the original. That way, if you are unhappy with the edits, the photo isn't permanently damaged. To make a copy of a photo, double-click it, click File, click Make a Copy, and click Save. If you don't like the results of an adjustment, you can click the Undo button at the bottom of the Fix pane to undo it. To undo all changes made to the image, click the arrow next to the Undo button and click Revert to Original.

To access the Windows Live Photo Gallery editing tools, you click the picture you want to edit, then press the Fix button along the top of the screen. The available tools appear in the Fix pane. One approach is to use Windows Live Photo Gallery's Auto Adjust tool to automatically apply the Adjust Exposure, Adjust Color, and Straight Photo fixes at once; alternatively, you can apply these fixes individually. In addition, you can use the Crop Photo tool to crop your photo, the Adjust Detail tool to sharpen the image, the Fix Red Eye tool to eliminate red eye, and the Black and White Effects tool to convert your image from color to black and white. You can also use the Rotate buttons along the bottom of the screen to rotate your image.

Rotating an Image in Windows Live Photo Gallery

If your image appears sideways in Windows Live Photo Gallery, you can rotate it.

1 Open the image you want to rotate in Windows Live Photo Gallery.

2 Click either the Rotate Counterclockwise (ↄ) or Rotate Clockwise button (ↄ), located along the bottom of the Windows Live Photo Gallery screen. Windows rotates the image.

Rotate an image.

Auto-adjusting a photo

If you discover that your image lacks in contrast, seems slightly off color-wise, or is a bit skewed, you can use Windows Live Photo Gallery's Auto Adjust tool to fix these problems automatically.

1 Open the image you want to auto-adjust in Windows Live Photo Gallery.

2 Press the Fix button along the top of the screen. The Fix pane opens.

3 Click Auto Adjust in the Fix pane. Windows Live Photo Gallery assesses your image and applies the necessary exposure and color settings and straightens the image as needed.

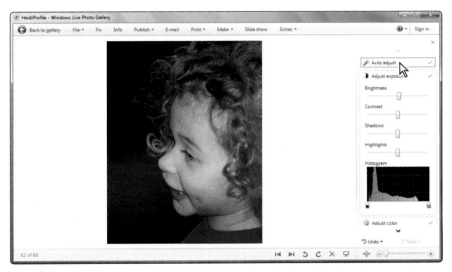

Auto-adjust an image.

If clicking Auto Adjust doesn't yield the desired results, click Adjust Exposure and drag the Brightness, Contrast, Shadows, and Highlights sliders to adjust these levels manually. Then click Adjust Color and dragging the Color Temperature, Tint, and Saturation sliders. Finally, click Straighten Photo and drag the slider as needed to straighten the photo.

Cropping a photo

A key aspect of image composition is ensuring that only what should appear in the image does appear in the image. If you discover that your image contains some unwanted elements—for example, a telephone pole that appears to be growing out of your subject's head, or someone you want to remove from the image, you can crop those elements to remove them.

1   Open the image you want to crop in Windows Live Photo Gallery.

2   Press the Fix button along the top of the screen. The Fix pane opens.

3   Click Crop Photo. Cropping-related options appear.

4   To change the picture's size, click the down arrow and choose a standard print proportion. Alternatively, select Custom to set a custom size, as shown in this example.

5   To rotate the crop frame vertically or horizontally, click Rotate Frame.

6   Drag the crop frame to the desired spot on the photograph.

7   To resize the crop frame, click one of the sizing handles. Then drag inward to make the frame smaller or outward to make it larger.

Crop a photo.

8   Press Apply. Windows Live Photo Gallery crops the photo.

Adjusting a photo's detail

If an image appears a bit blurry, you can use Windows Live Photo Gallery to sharpen it. Windows Live Photo Gallery can also reduce noise in an image—that is, the specks that sometimes occur when the wrong exposure has been used. Here's how:

1   Open the image you want to crop in Windows Live Photo Gallery.

2   Press the Fix button along the top of the screen. The Fix pane opens.

3   Click Adjust Detail.

4   To sharpen the picture, drag the Sharpen slider to the right.

5   To reduce specks on a digital photo, called noise, click the Analyze button under Reduce Noise. Windows Live Photo Gallery analyzes the image's noise level and adjusts the Reduce Noise slider accordingly. You can also adjust this manually by using the slider below the Analyze button.

Sharpen a photo and reduce noise.

Removing red eye

If the subject of your photograph has red eyes, you can use the Fix Red Eye tool to rectify the problem.

1   Open the image you want to crop in Windows Live Photo Gallery.

2   Press the Fix button along the top of the screen. The Fix pane opens.

3   Click Fix Red Eye.

4   Click the upper left corner of an eye that needs correcting.

5   Drag the cursor to the lower right corner of the eye to select the eye.

Drag a square around the red eye.

6   Windows Live Photo Gallery removes the red eye. Repeat steps 4 and 5 to remove red eye from any remaining eyes in the photo.

Windows Live Photo Gallery removes the red eye.

Converting a color image to black and white

For many, black-and-white images have a timeless quality. You can use Windows Live Photo Gallery to convert a color image to black and white. Here's how:

1   Open the image you want to crop in Windows Live Photo Gallery.

2   Press the Fix button along the top of the screen. The Fix pane opens.

3   Click Black and white effects. Several black-and-white effect options appear.

4 Click a black-and-white effect option to apply it to your image.

Convert your color photo to black and white.

Creating a panoramic image

Some settings are best captured in panorama, but not everyone has a camera that can snap such wide-angle photos. Fortunately, Windows Live Photo Gallery can "stitch" together photos to create a panoramic image.

1 In the Windows Live Photo Gallery window, select the pictures you want to include in your panoramic image.

2 Press the Make button.

3 Choose Create Panoramic Photo.

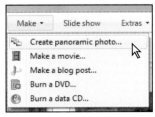

Click Make and choose Create Panoramic Photo.

4   Windows Live Photo Gallery stitches the selected photos together. When the stitching operation is complete, the Save Panoramic Stitch dialog box appears. Locate and select the folder in which you want to save the panoramic photo.

5   Type a name for the panoramic photo in the File Name text field.

6   Press Save. Windows Live Gallery saves the panoramic photo.

The panoramic photo.

Obtaining photo prints

As great as it is to store and view photos on your computer, sometimes there's no substitute for a photo print. Assuming you have a printer capable of printing photos, you can make prints of your digital pictures from within Windows Live Photo Gallery. Alternatively, you can order prints online.

Using your printer to print photos

You can use your printer to print your photos. The quality of your prints depends on the overall quality and resolution of the digital picture, the type of paper you use, the type of ink you use, and your printer settings.

1   Open the image you want to print in Windows Live Photo Gallery. Alternatively, select multiple images to print in the main Windows Live Photo Gallery window.

2   From the Print drop-down menu, choose Print.

3   The Print Pictures dialog box opens. Choose the printer you want to use from the Printer drop-down menu.

4   Choose the paper size from the Paper Size drop-down menu.

5   Choose the image quality from the Quality drop-down menu.

6   Choose the paper type from the Paper Type drop-down menu.

7   Specify how many photos should appear on each page.

8   Use the Copies of Each Picture spin box to indicate how many prints you want.

9   Click the *Fit Picture to Frame* checkbox to select it if you don't want your print to contain a border.

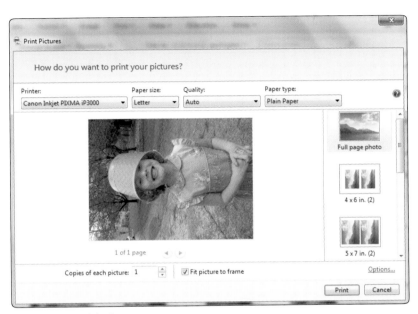

The Print Pictures dialog box.

For additional print-related options—such as Sharpen for Printing—as well as for access to color-management and printer-properties settings, click the Options link.

10   Press Print. Windows Live Photo Gallery prints the picture.

Ordering Prints Online

You can also use Windows Live Photo Gallery for ordering prints via an online printing company. You can order a variety of products bearing your images, for example, greeting cards, calendars, T-shirts, mugs, or mouse pads.

To order prints online, you launch the Order Prints Wizard and select the printing company you want to use:

1   In the Windows Live Photo Gallery window, select the pictures you want to order.

2   From the Print drop-down menu, choose Order Prints.

3   Windows Live Photo Gallery launches the Order Prints Wizard, which displays a list of available printing providers (note that the providers in this list may vary depending on your location). Click the printing provider you want to use—in this case, Kodak. Press Send Pictures.

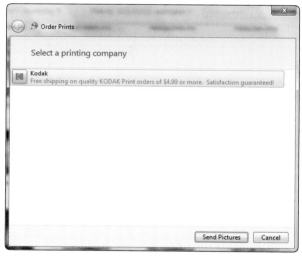

Choose a printing provider.

At this point, the precise steps you take may vary depending on which printing provider you chose in step 3. Follow the Order Prints Wizard's instructions to indicate how many prints you want of each photo and what size each print should be. Logon to your account with the provider or create a new one, enter your billing and shipping information, and place your order.

Sharing your pictures with others

Of course, you can always share your pictures with others by giving prints away, but if the people with whom you want to share live far away, you may quickly find yourself overwhelmed by the hassle and expense. A better way is to share your images via e-mail or by posting them on a picture-sharing web site.

E-mailing a picture

Assuming you have an e-mail program installed on your computer and that your computer is connected to the Internet, you can send your photos to others via e-mail. One way to do so is to launch your e-mail program and follow the steps in the section "Adding a photo" in Lesson 5, "Surfing the Web with Internet Explorer 8." Another is to initiate the send operation from within Windows Live Photo Gallery.

1   In the Windows Live Photo Gallery window, select the picture or pictures you want to share via e-mail.

2   Press the E-mail button along the top of the screen.

3   Windows Live Photo Gallery launches the Attach Files dialog box. Click the Photo Size down arrow and choose a size from the list that appears. Smaller photo sizes yield smaller file sizes, which will enable your recipient to download your image more quickly.

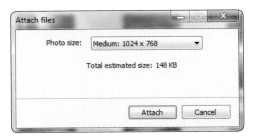

Choose a photo size.

4   Press the Attach button. Windows 7 launches a New Message window, inserting the photo or photos in the body of the message. Enter your recipients or recipients in the To text field.

5 Type a subject for the message.

6 Type your message text.

Edit your e-mail.

7 Press Send.

Creating and publishing an online photo album

You can also publish your photos in an online album using Windows Live. After you post the album, you can share it with others by e-mailing them a link to the album. When you share photos in this way, others can view and even comment on your photos. You must be online and signed in to Windows Live to publish an album. An easy way to sign in is to click the Sign In button in the upper-right corner of the Windows Live Photo Gallery window, type your Windows Live ID and password in the dialog box that appears, and click Sign In.

1 In the Windows Live Photo Gallery window, select the pictures you want to include in the album.

2 From the Publish drop-down menu along the top of the screen, choose Online Album.

3 The Publish Photos on Windows Live dialog box opens. To add the photos to an album you've already created, click it. Otherwise, create a new album by typing a name for the album in the empty field.

4   Choose who should be permitted to view the album from the drop-down menu below
    the album's title.

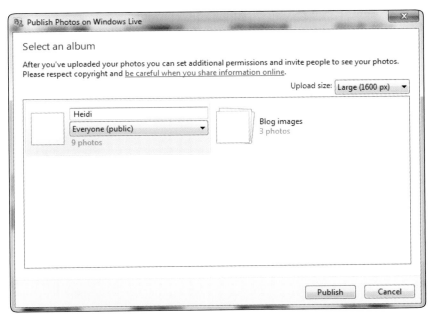

Create a new album.

5   Press Publish. Windows Live Photo Gallery uploads the selected images to the Windows
    Live web site, notifying you when the upload operation is complete. Press View Album to
    view the album online; alternatively, press Close.

Windows Live Photo Gallery uploads your photos.

6 Windows Live opens in your web browser, with the page containing your album on display. Select an image to view it in its own window.

View your album online.

Backing up your photos online

When you import new photos into Windows Live Photo Gallery, you should get in the habit of publishing them online at your earliest opportunity. Not only does publishing an online album enable you to share your photos, it also protects you in the event your hard drive were to fail by giving you access to copies of all your precious photos. Another option is to use Windows Live Photo Gallery to burn your photos onto a recordable CD or DVD. To do so, select the photos you want copy and from the Make drop-down menu, choose Burn a DVD or Burn a Data CD, and follow the onscreen prompts.

Viewing your album online

You can view your album online immediately after publishing it. But what if you want to view it at a later time?

1   Direct your web browser to the Windows Live web site (www.windowslive.com) and sign in to your account. For help signing in, refer to the section "Signing in to Windows Live" in Lesson 5, "Surfing the Web with Internet Explorer 8."

2   Click the Photos link along the top of the Windows Live main page.

3   If the album you want to view is listed under Recent Photo Albums, click it. Otherwise, click the All Albums link on the left side of the screen.

4   A list of your albums appears. Click the album you want to view; Windows Live opens the album. Click an image in the album to view it in its own window.

View your album online.

Sharing an online album with others

As mentioned, you can e-mail others a link to the album after you post it online. One way to do so is to select the album's URL in your browser's address bar, press Ctrl+C to copy it, launch your e-mail program, create a new e-mail message, and press Ctrl+V to paste the link into the body of the message. A faster way is to initiate the operation from within Windows Live, using your Live or Hotmail e-mail account.

1   Open the album you want to share.

2   Click the More link located just above the images in your album.

3   Choose Send a Link.

4 Windows Live launches the Send a Link screen. Enter your recipient or recipients in the To field. Alternatively, select the check box next to a category name to send your message to all people in that category.

5 Optionally, include a message by typing it in the Include Your Own Message text field.

6 If you've included recipients who do not have Windows Live accounts, click the *Don't Require Recipients to Sign In with Windows Live ID* checkbox to select it.

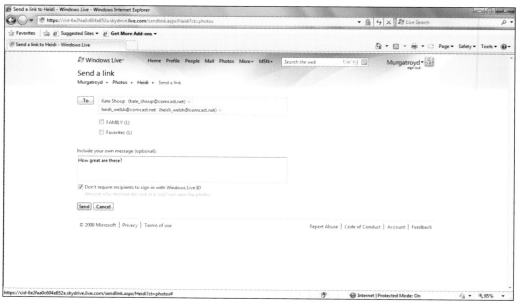

E-mail a link to your album.

7 Press Send.

Changing an online album's permissions

Suppose, after publishing an album, you decide you want only certain people to be able to view it. If so, you can edit the album's permissions to limit who has access to the album. You can also edit permissions to grant access to everyone on the Internet.

1 Open the album whose permissions you want to change.

2 Click the More link located just above the images in your album.

3 Choose Edit Permissions.

4 The Edit Permissions screen appears. To grant permission to everyone on the Internet, click the *Everyone (Public)* checkbox to select it.

5 To grant permission only to those in your network, deselect all other checkboxes, then click the *My Network* checkbox to select it.

6 To grant permission only to those people in a particular category, deselect all other checkboxes, then click the category's checkbox to select it.

7 To grant permission only to certain individuals, deselect all check boxes, then click the checkbox next to each individual you want to include to select them.

8 To grant an individual rights to add, edit details, and delete photos in the album, choose Can Add, Edit Details, and Delete Photos from the drop-down menu to the right of the individual's name and checkbox.

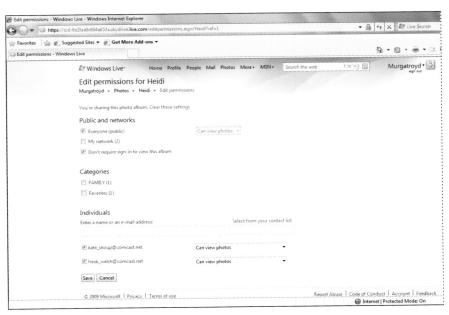

Edit album permissions.

9 Press Save.

To rename or delete an album, choose Rename or Delete respectively from the More drop-down menu located just above the images in your album and follow the onscreen prompts.

Self study

1 Experiment with using the Auto Adjust tool to correct an image automatically versus using the Adjust Exposure, Adjust Color, and Straight Photo sliders to correct an image manually.

2 Create and publish an online album, and then share it with others.

Review

Questions

1 What are three ways to view your images in Windows 7?

2 What is a memory card?

3 What is noise?

4 What are two factors on which the quality of a photo print depends.

5 Why should you back up your photos?

Answers

1 You can view your images in the Pictures folder, Windows Photo Viewer, Windows Paint, Windows Media Player, and Windows Media Center, all of which come bundled with Windows 7. In addition, you can use Windows Live Photo Gallery.

2 A memory card is a small, removable storage device, often used in cameras to store digital images. Memory cards come in a variety of formats: SD card, Smart Media, CompactFlash, or Sony Memory Stick.

3 In photography, the term noise refers to the specks that sometimes occur when the wrong exposure has been used to capture an image.

4 How good your print will look depends on several factors, among them the overall quality and resolution of the digital picture, the type of paper you use, the type of ink you use, and your printer settings.

5 Backing up your photos—either by publishing them online or burning them onto a recordable CD or DVD—protects you in the event your hard drive were to fail by giving you access to copies of all your photos.

What you'll learn in this lesson:

- Displaying mobility settings
- Prolonging battery life
- Connecting to the Internet via a wireless connection
- Configuring presentation settings

Using Windows 7 on a Laptop or Netbook Computer

Certain Windows 7 settings and features that apply only to laptops and netbooks, helping you to get the most out of your mobile device.

Starting up

Before you start, be sure to copy all the files for this lesson from the accompanying DVD to your hard drive.

See Lesson 14 in action!

Use the accompanying video to gain a better understanding of how to use some of the features shown in this lesson. The video tutorial for this lesson can be found on the included DVD.

Displaying mobility settings

Windows Mobility Center serves as a starting point for adjusting laptop-specific Windows 7 settings. Many of these settings relate to conserving power—especially critical when using a battery to power your laptop. Others pertain to connecting to the Internet via wireless access points, synchronizing your laptop with another computer, and giving presentations.

1 Press Start (⬤) and choose All Programs. The All Programs menu appears.

2 Click the Accessories folder. A list of Windows 7 accessories appears.

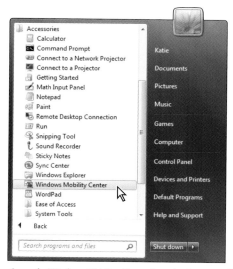

Access the Windows Mobility Center from the Accessories folder in the Start menu.

3 Click Windows Mobility Center. The Windows Mobility Center window opens.

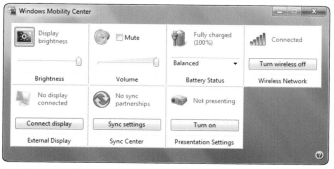

The Windows Mobility Center enables you to change various mobility settings.

A fast way to open the Windows Mobility Center window is to right-click the battery icon (▣) in the taskbar's notification area and choose Windows Mobility Center.

Adjusting display settings

Your laptop's display likely consumes more power than any other part of your computer. One way laptops conserve power is by dimming the display after a period of inactivity. You can also set your laptop to conserve power by adjusting the brightness of the display.

1 Open the Windows Mobility Center window from the Accessibility folder in the Start menu.

2 Drag the Brightness slider to the left to dim the screen, or to the right to brighten it.

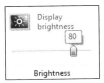

Adjust the Display brightness.

3 To see additional brightness settings, press the Change Display Brightness button (🖼). The Control Panel's Edit Plan Settings window appears.

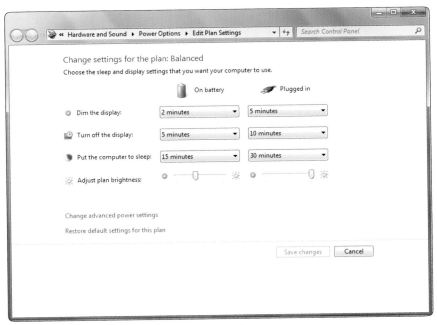

Use the Edit Plan Settings window to change various screen-display options.

4   Depending on which power plan you are using, Windows 7 dims the screen display automatically after the system has been idle for a specified period of time. For example, using the Balanced power plan, which is the default, Windows 7 dims the display after two minutes when the laptop is running on battery power, or five minutes if the laptop is plugged in. To change these settings, choose the desired duration click the Dim the Display drop-down menu under On Battery, then choose the desired duration under Plugged In.

You'll learn about power plans for mobile computers in the upcoming section, "Prolonging Battery Life."

5   Windows 7 turns off the display after the system has been idle for five minutes. If the laptop is plugged in, the display is turned off after ten minutes of idle time. To change these settings, choose the desired duration from the Turn Off the Display drop-down menu under On Battery, then choose the desired duration under Plugged In.

6   Windows 7 puts the computer to sleep after the system has been idle for 15 minutes. If the laptop is plugged in, the computer is put to sleep after 30 minutes of idle time. To change these settings, choose the desired duration from the Put the Computer to Sleep drop-down menu under On Battery, then choose the desired duration under Plugged In.

7   If your computer is running on a battery using either the Balanced or Power Saver power plan, its screen will be dimmer by default to conserve power. To adjust this default setting, drag the Adjust Plan Brightness slider under On Battery. If you prefer a dimmer screen when the laptop is plugged in, drag the Adjust Plan Brightness slider to the left under Plugged In.

8   Press the Save Changes button to close the Edit Plan Settings window.

9   Press the Close button (▄▄) to close the Windows Mobility Center window.

Adjusting volume settings

Windows 7 makes it easy to adjust audio settings from the Windows Mobility Center window.

1   Open the Windows Mobility Center window.

2   Drag the Volume slider to the left to decrease the volume, or to the right to increase it.

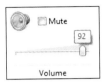

Adjust the volume.

3   To mute the system, click the *Mute* checkbox to select it.

4   To access additional audio settings, press the Change Audio Settings button (⊚). The Sound dialog box opens. For more information about the options in this dialog box, refer to the section, "Changing the Sound Scheme," in Lesson 4, "Customizing Windows 7."

Use the Sound dialog box to change various system sound settings.

5   For now, press the Cancel button to close the Sound dialog box.

6   Press the Close button (▭) to close the Windows Mobility Center window.

 A fast way to adjust your system's volume is to click the volume icon in the taskbar's notification area. Windows 7 displays a volume slider; drag the slider up to increase the volume or down to decrease it. To mute or unmute your speakers, click the Mute button under the slider.

Prolonging battery life

If you are using a battery to power your laptop, rather than plugging it in, you should take care to monitor the battery level. You can do this by observing the power icon in the taskbar's notification area. To see how much power remains, simply click the icon (⟁). The window that appears also enables you to select a different power plan, adjust screen brightness to conserve power, and access additional power options.

Monitor the battery level by clicking the power icon in taskbar's notification area.

Choosing a power plan

One way to prolong battery life is to change power plans. Windows 7 offers three power plans for laptop computers: Power Saver, High Performance, and Balanced. The plan you choose depends on whether your laptop is plugged in or running on battery power.

- The Power Saver plan is designed for use when the laptop is running on battery power. It increases battery life by shutting down various components, such as the display and the hard drive, after the system has been idle for a short period of time—meaning you must wait for these components to restart before you can recommence using your laptop.

- The High Performance plan is designed for use when the laptop is plugged in. It improves performance by waiting longer to shut down components when the system is idle, decreasing the likelihood you will need to wait for them to restart.

- The Balanced plan offers a happy medium between the Power Saver and High Performance plans. It is best if you don't want to bother changing plans each time you unplug your computer or plug it back in.

1   Open the Windows Mobility Center window.

2   Click the Battery Status drop-down arrow.

3   Choose a different power plan.

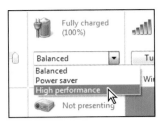

Select a different power plan in the
Windows Mobility Center window.

4   Press the Close button (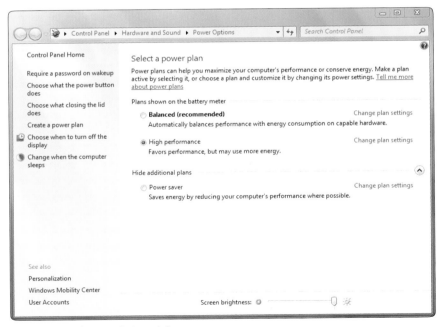) to close the Windows Mobility Center window.

Creating a custom power plan

If none of the three available plans quite fit your needs, you can create a custom plan. Custom plans are also great if, for example, you frequently take long airplane flights; you can create a plan that conserves maximum energy and use that plan whenever you're on the plane. Here's how to create a custom power plan:

1   Open the Windows Mobility Center window.

2   Press the Change Power Settings button (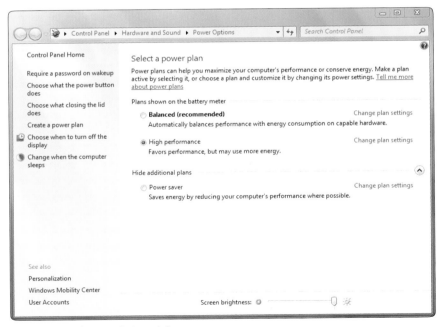). The Control Panel's Power Options window appears.

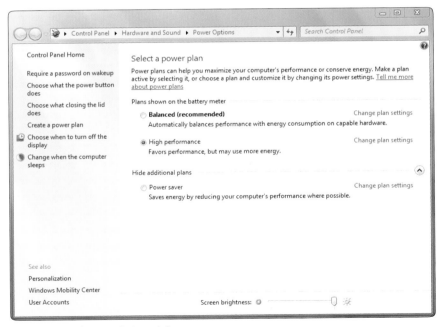

The Control Panel's Power Options window.

A fast way to open the Control Panel's Power Options window is to right-click the power icon in the taskbar's notification area and choose Power Options from the menu that appears.

3 Click the Create a Power Plan link in the left panel of the Power Options window. The Control Panel's Create a Power Plan window opens.

4 Click to select the plan that most closely resembles the one you want to create.

5 In the Plan Name text field, type a name for your power plan.

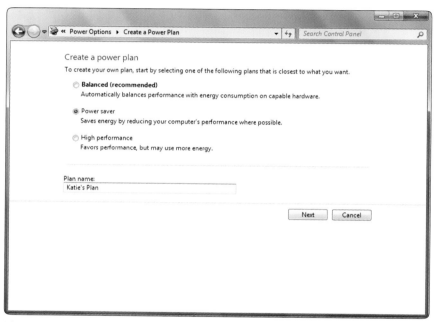

The Control Panel's Create a Power Plan window.

6   Press Next. The Control Panel's Edit Plan Settings window appears.

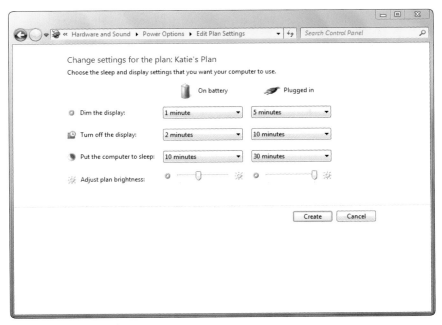

Set up your custom power plan.

7   Make any desired changes to the Dim the Display, Turn Off the Display, Put the Computer to Sleep, and Adjust Plan Brightness settings.

8   Press Create. Windows 7 creates a new power plan that uses the settings you chose.

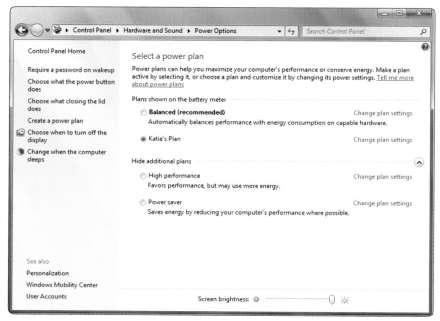

Windows 7 creates a new power plan, based on the settings you chose.

9   Press the Close button () to close the Power Options window.

10   Press the Close button () to close the Windows Mobility Center window.

To delete a custom power plan, first select another plan for use. Then, in the Power Options window, click Change Plan Settings for the custom plan you want to delete. The Edit Plan Settings window opens; press Delete This Plan. Windows 7 prompts you to confirm the deletion; press Yes.

Modifying a power plan

1   Open the Windows Mobility Center window.

2   Click the Change Power Settings button (). The Control Panel's Power Options window appears.

A faster way to open the Control Panel's Power Options window is to right-click the power icon in the taskbar's notification area and choose Power Options from the menu that appears.

3   Click the Change Plan Settings link for the power plan you want to change. The Edit Plan Settings page appears.

4   Make any desired changes to the Dim the Display, Turn Off the Display, Put the Computer to Sleep, and Adjust Plan Brightness settings.

5   Click the Change Advanced Power Settings link. The Power Options dialog box opens. Here, you can change many additional power settings. To change a setting, press the plus button (·) to the left of the feature you want to change. In this case, the plus button next to the plan name is selected.

6   Here, a Require a Password on Wakeup sub-entry appears. Press the plus button (·) next to this sub-entry.

7   To require a battery on wakeup when the system is running on a battery, click On Battery to reveal a drop-down menu. Choose Yes from the drop-down menu.

To undo changes you've made in the Power Options dialog box, click the Restore Plan Defaults button. To undo other changes to power settings, click the Restore Default Settings for This Plan link in the Edit Plan Settings dialog box.

Make additional changes to a power plan in the Power Options dialog box.

8   Press OK to close the Power Options dialog box.

9   Press Save Changes to close the Edit Plan Settings window.

10 Press the Close button (═) to close the Power Options window.

11 Press the Close button (═) to close the Windows Mobility Center window.

Setting battery alarms

You can set up Windows 7 to alert you when your laptop's battery levels are low. This enables you to save your work before your laptop runs out of power and shuts down. You can also specify the battery level at which you are notified.

1   Open the Windows Mobility Center window.

2   Click the Change Power Settings button (🔋). The Control Panel's Power Options window appears.

3   Click the Change Plan Settings link for the desired power plan. The Edit Plan Settings page appears.

4   Click the Change Advanced Power Settings link. The Power Options dialog box opens.

5   Press the plus button (·) to the left of the Battery entry.

6   Press the plus button (·) to the left of the Low Battery Level sub-entry.

7   Click On Battery to reveal a drop-down menu. Click the up or down arrow that appears, to specify the battery level your system should reach before Windows 7 notifies you of a low battery.

8   Press the plus button (·) to the left of the Low Battery Notification subentry.

9   Click On Battery to reveal a drop-down menu. Choose On from the drop-down menu.

Set a battery alarm in the Power Options dialog box.

You can specify what the laptop should do when it runs out of power. By default, Hibernate is selected; other options are Shut Down and Sleep. To change this setting, press the plus button (⊕) next to Critical Battery Action, click On Battery, choose the desired option from the drop-down menu that appears.

10 Press OK to close the Power Options dialog box.

11 Press Save Changes to close the Edit Plan Settings window.

12 Press the Close button (▭) to close the Power Options window.

13 Press the Close button (▭) to close the Windows Mobility Center window.

Configuring power buttons

By default, pressing the power button on your laptop or closing its lid puts the machine in Sleep mode. If you prefer, you can set up your Windows laptop to switch to Hibernate mode when you press the power button or close the lid. A third option is to configure your Windows laptop to shut down when you press the power button or close the lid. In this case, Windows 7 closes any programs, folders, or files open on your desktop before shutting down completely; when you restart the computer, you experience a completely fresh start. Finally, you can configure Windows 7 to do nothing when you press your laptop's power button or shut the lid.

Sleep is essentially a stand-by mode. Power is withheld from non-essential components and operations in order to conserve energy. When a sleeping system is awakened, it resumes operation quickly. In contrast, Hibernate mode, saves your data to your hard disk and powers down your computer. When you are ready to use the computer again, the system restarts, reverting to the state it was in before it entered hibernation—with all the same programs, folders, and files displayed on the desktop.

1 Open the Windows Mobility Center window.

2 Press the Change Power Settings button (▥). The Control Panel's Power Options window appears.

A fast way to open the Control Panel's Power Options window is to right-click the power icon in the taskbar's notification area and choose Power Options from the menu that appears.

3   In the left panel, click the Choose What the Power Button Does link. The System
     Settings window appears.

The System Settings window.

4   Choose Do Nothing, Sleep, Hibernate, or Shut Down from the When I Press the Power
     Button drop-down menu under On Battery, then choose one of these options under
     Plugged In.

5   Choose Do Nothing, Sleep, Hibernate, or Shut Down from the When I Close the Lid
     drop-down menu under On Battery, then choose one of these options under Plugged In.

*If you like, you can instruct Windows 7 to require your account password when your laptop wakes
from sleep. To do so, click the Require a Password radio button in the System Settings window.
If necessary, click the Change Settings That Are Currently Unavailable link in order to activate
this radio button.) To find out how to set a password for your user account, refer to the section,
"Password-Protecting Your Computer," in Lesson 10, "Securing Your Computer."*

6   Press Save Changes to close the System Settings window.

7   Press the Close button (●●) to close the Power Options window.

8   Press the Close button (●●) to close the Windows Mobility Center window.

Connecting to the Internet via a wireless connection

If you are using your laptop somewhere that offers wireless Internet access—for example, at a library or café you can easily connect.

1   Open the Windows Mobility Center window.

2   If necessary, press the Turn Wireless On button. Notice that it toggles to a Turn Wireless Off button after you click it.

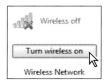 

Press the Turn Wireless On button.

3   Press the Change Wireless Network Settings button (⣿). A list of wireless access points in your area appears.

Pressing the Change Wireless Network Settings button displays a list of wireless connections in your area.

A fast way to display the list of wireless access points in your area is to click the wireless networks icon in the taskbar's notification area.

4   Click the wireless access point you want to use to connect. Its entry in the list expands to include a *Connect Automatically* checkbox and a Connect button.

5   If you want your laptop to connect to the selected network automatically whenever it is detected, click the *Connect Automatically* checkbox to select it. Press the Connect button.

Press the Connect button.

6   Windows 7 connects to the wireless access point.

Windows 7 connects to the wireless access point.

7   If prompted for a password or network security key, enter it, and press OK. Windows 7 connects you to the wireless access point.

If prompted, enter the password or network security key.

8   If this is the first time you have connected to this wireless access point, Windows 7 prompts you to specify what type of access point it is: home, work, or public. This is so that Windows 7 can determine what security settings to apply. Click your wireless access point type, in this example, Public Network.

Specify whether you are connecting to a home, work, or public wireless access point.

9   Windows 7 confirms your selection. Press Close.

Public networks may not be secure. E-mail messages you send and information you enter into web sites, including passwords, could be intercepted, so you should be careful about what information you enter when using a public network.

Windows 7 confirms your selection.

10 The Windows Mobility Center window indicates your connection status. Press the Close button (━━) to close the Windows Mobility Center window.

Windows Mobility Center indicates that you are connected to the wireless access point.

11 If you are connecting to a public wireless access point, you may need to create an account and log on with the wireless access point provider. To find out, launch your web browser. If you are automatically directed to a login web page, then you need to create an account and log in to use the wireless access point.

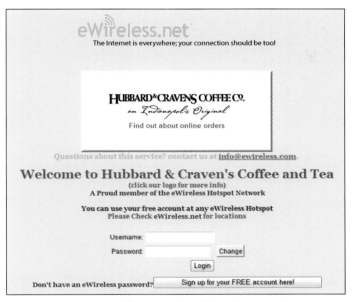

You must create an account and log in to use this public wireless access point.

Remote App and Desktop Connections

RemoteApp and Desktop Connections is a Windows 7 feature that enables you to access a computer remotely and work on it as though it is local. For instance, you might use RemoteApp and Desktop Connections on your mobile computer to connect via the Internet to your desktop machine at work, to gain access to programs, files, and network resources on your work computer. In order to use this feature, your workplace's network Administrator must first "publish" these programs, files, and network resources to make them available to you. He or she must then tell you how to access them—either by accessing a special file called a setup file or by launching a specific URL. For more information, see your system Administrator or the Windows 7 Help and Support information.

Disconnecting from the wireless access point

1   Open the Windows Mobility Center window.

2   Click the Change Wireless Network Settings button (￼). A list of wireless access points in your area appears.

Display the list of wireless access points in your area.

An even faster way to display the list of wireless access points in your area is to click the wireless networks button in the taskbar's notification area.

3   Click the entry for the wireless access point to which you are currently connected. A Disconnect button appears.

A Disconnect button appears.

4 Press the Disconnect button. Windows 7 disconnects from the wireless access point.

5 Press the Close button (▭) to close the Windows Mobility Center window.

Configuring presentation settings

One common use for mobile computers is to give presentations—but when you do so, certain settings in the typical configuration can prove problematic. For example, while you might normally want your computer to display a screen saver after a period of inactivity, you would not want it to do so while you were giving a presentation. Fortunately, you can configure Windows 7 to prevent such occurrences, as well as prevent your laptop from entering Sleep mode, changing your desktop background image, and adjusting your laptop's speaker volume.

1 Open the Windows Mobility Center window.

2 Click the Change Presentation Settings button (⊜).

Click the Change Presentation Settings button.

3 The Presentation Settings dialog box opens. Click the *Turn Off the Screen Saver* checkbox to select it.

4 Click the *Set the Volume To* checkbox to select it.

5 Drag the Set the Volume To slider to the left to reduce the volume, or to the right to increase it.

6 Click the *Show This Background* checkbox to select it.

7 Choose the background you want to be displayed by default when you give a presentation. An image file containing your company's logo might be a good choice.

If the image you want to display does not appear in the list, click the Browse button. Windows 7 displays a Browse dialog box; locate and select the desired image and click Open.

8 Choose Center, Tile, or Fit to Screen from the Position drop-down menu to specify how the image should be positioned.

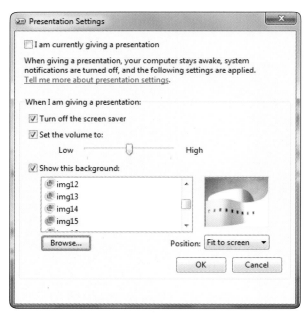

Establish your presentation settings.

9 Press OK to close the Presentation Settings dialog box.

10 Press the Close button (▭) to close the Windows Mobility Center window.

Once you've configured your presentation settings, you can turn them on whenever you are preparing to give a presentation. To do so, simply press the Turn On button in the Presentation Settings section. The Turn On button changes to a Turn Off button; click it when you are finished with your presentation to revert to your mobile computer's regular setup.

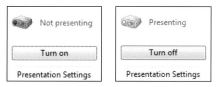

Press Turn On to switch to the presentation settings.

Self study

1 Create a custom power plan—for example, one for use on long airplane flights.

2 Set a battery alarm to alert you when your mobile computer's battery levels are low.

Review

Questions

1 What is the name of the Windows 7 feature that serves as a starting point for adjusting laptop-specific Windows 7 settings?

2 What three power plans does Windows 7 support?

3 What is the difference between Sleep mode and Hibernate mode?

4 What are two ways to view available wireless access points in your area?

5 What is RemoteApp and Desktop Connections?

Answers

1 Windows Mobility Center serves as a starting point for adjusting laptop-specific Windows 7 settings.

2 Windows 7 supports three plans: the Power Saver plan, designed for use when the laptop is running on battery power; the High Performance plan, designed for use when the laptop is plugged in; and the Balanced plan, which offers a happy medium between the Power Saver and High Performance plans and is best if you don't want to bother changing plans each time you unplug your computer or plug it back in.

3 Sleep is essentially a stand-by mode. Power is withheld from non-essential components and operations in order to conserve energy. In contrast, in Hibernate mode, Windows 7 saves your data to your hard disk and powers down your computer.

4 One way to view available wireless access points in your area is to open the Windows Mobility Center window, click the Turn Wireless On button, and click the Change Wireless Network Settings button. Alternatively, you can click the wireless networks icon in the taskbar's notification area.

5 RemoteApp and Desktop Connections is a Windows 7 feature that enables you to access a computer remotely and work on it as though it is local.

Appendix

Which version of Windows 7 do you have?

In all, there are six versions of the Windows 7 operating system, each with more features than the last:

- Windows 7 Home Premium Edition
- Windows 7 Professional Edition
- Windows 7 Ultimate Edition

The following table shows which features are supported by each version of the Windows 7 operating system. You'll learn about many of the features mentioned in this table throughout this book.

WINDOWS 7	WINDOWS 7 HOME	WINDOWS 7 PROFESSIONAL	WINDOWS 7 ULTIMATE
Home Group	Yes	Yes	Yes
Improved Taskbar and jump lists	Yes	Yes	Yes
Live thumbnail previews and enhanced visual experience	Yes	Yes	Yes
Ad-hoc wireless networks and Internet connection sharing	Yes	Yes	Yes
Windows Mobility Center	Yes	Yes	Yes
Aero Glass and advanced windows navigation	Yes	Yes	Yes
Easy networking and sharing across all computers and devices	Yes	Yes	Yes
Windows Media Center	Yes	Yes	Yes

WINDOWS 7	WINDOWS 7 HOME	WINDOWS 7 PROFESSIONAL	WINDOWS 7 ULTIMATE
Improved media format support and enhancements to Windows Media Center and media streaming, including Play To	Yes	Yes	Yes
Multi-touch and improved handwriting recognition	Yes	Yes	Yes
Domain Join	No	Yes	Yes
Encrypting File System	No	Yes	Yes
Location Aware Printing	No	Yes	Yes
Remote Desktop Host	No	Yes	Yes
BitLocker	No	No	Yes
BitLocker To Go	No	No	Yes
DirectAccess	No	No	Yes
BranchCache	No	No	Yes
AppLocker	No	No	Yes
MUI multiple languages support	No	No	Yes
Boot from VHD disk image	No	No	Yes
Maximum running applications	Unlimited	Unlimited	Unlimited

Windows 7 keyboard shortcuts

General shortcuts

SHORTCUT	ACTION
F1	Display Help
Ctrl+C (or Ctrl+Insert)	Copy the selected item
Ctrl+X	Cut the selected item
Ctrl+V (or Shift+Insert)	Paste the selected item
Ctrl+Z	Undo an action
Ctrl+Y	Redo an action
Delete (or Ctrl+D)	Delete the selected item and move it to the Recycle Bin
Shift+Delete	Delete the selected item without moving it to the Recycle Bin first
F2	Rename the selected item
Ctrl+Right Arrow	Move the cursor to the beginning of the next word
Ctrl+Left Arrow	Move the cursor to the beginning of the previous word
Ctrl+Down Arrow	Move the cursor to the beginning of the next paragraph
Ctrl+Up Arrow	Move the cursor to the beginning of the previous paragraph
Ctrl+Shift with an arrow key	Select a block of text
Ctrl with any arrow key+Spacebar	Select multiple individual items in a window or on the desktop
Ctrl+A	Select all items in a document or window
F3	Search for a file or folder
Alt+Enter	Display properties for the selected item
Alt+F4	Close the active item, or exit the active program
Alt+Spacebar	Open the shortcut menu for the active window
Ctrl+F4	Close the active document (in programs that allow you to have multiple documents open simultaneously)
Alt+Tab	Switch between open items
Ctrl+Alt+Tab	Use the arrow keys to switch between open items
Ctrl+Mouse scroll wheel	Change the size of icons on the desktop

SHORTCUT	ACTION
Windows logo key (⊞) +Tab	Cycle through programs on the taskbar by using Aero Flip 3-D
Ctrl+Windows logo key (⊞) +Tab	Use the arrow keys to cycle through programs on the taskbar by using Aero Flip 3-D
Alt+Esc	Cycle through items in the order in which they were opened
F6	Cycle through screen elements in a window or on the desktop
F4	Display the address bar list in Windows Explorer
Shift+F10	Display the shortcut menu for the selected item
Ctrl+Esc	Open the Start menu
Alt+underlined letter	Display the corresponding menu
Alt+underlined letter	Perform the menu command (or other underlined command)
F10	Activate the menu bar in the active program
Right Arrow	Open the next menu to the right, or open a submenu
Left Arrow	Open the next menu to the left, or close a submenu
F5 (or Ctrl+R)	Refresh the active window
Alt+Up Arrow	View the folder one level up in Windows Explorer
Esc	Cancel the current task
Ctrl+Shift+Esc	Open Task Manager
Shift when you insert a CD	Prevent the CD from automatically playing
Left Alt+Shift	Switch the input language when multiple input languages are enabled
Ctrl+Shift	Switch the keyboard layout when multiple keyboard layouts are enabled
Right or Left Ctrl+Shift	Change the reading direction of text in right-to-left reading languages

Dialog box shortcuts

SHORTCUT	ACTION
Ctrl+Tab	Move forward through tabs
Ctrl+Shift+Tab	Move back through tabs
Tab	Move forward through options
Shift+Tab	Move back through options
Alt+underlined letter	Perform the command (or select the option) that goes with that letter

SHORTCUT	ACTION
Enter	Replaces clicking the mouse for many selected commands
Arrow keys	Select a button if the active option is a group of option buttons
F1	Display Help
F4	Display the items in the active list
Backspace	Open a folder one level up if a folder is selected in the Save As or Open dialog box

Windows logo shortcuts

SHORTCUT	ACTION
Windows logo key (⊞)	Open or close the Start menu.
Windows logo key (⊞) +Pause	Display the System Properties dialog box.
Windows logo key (⊞) +D	Display the desktop.
Windows logo key (⊞) +M	Minimize all windows.
Windows logo key (⊞) +Shift+M	Restore minimized windows to the desktop.
Windows logo key (⊞) +E	Open Computer.
Windows logo key (⊞) +F	Search for a file or folder.
Ctrl+Windows logo key (⊞) +F	Search for computers (if you're on a network).
Windows logo key (⊞) +L	Lock your computer or switch users.
Windows logo key (⊞) +R	Open the Run dialog box.
Windows logo key (⊞) +T	Cycle through programs on the taskbar.
Windows logo key (⊞) +*number*	Start the program pinned to the taskbar in the position indicated by the number. If the program is already running, switch to that program.
Shift+Windows logo key (⊞) +*number*	Start a new instance of the program pinned to the taskbar in the position indicated by the number.

SHORTCUT	ACTION
Ctrl+Windows logo key (⊞) +number	Switch to the last active window of the program pinned to the taskbar in the position indicated by the number.
Alt+Windows logo key (⊞) +number	Open the Jump List for the program pinned to the taskbar in the position indicated by the number.
Windows logo key (⊞) +Tab	Cycle through programs on the taskbar by using Aero Flip 3-D.
Ctrl+Windows logo key (⊞) +Tab	Use the arrow keys to cycle through programs on the taskbar by using Aero Flip 3-D.
Ctrl+Windows logo key (⊞) +B	Switch to the program that displayed a message in the notification area.
Windows logo key (⊞) +Spacebar	Preview the desktop.
Windows logo key (⊞) +Up Arrow	Maximize the window.
Windows logo key (⊞) +Left Arrow	Maximize the window to the left side of the screen.
Windows logo key (⊞) +Right Arrow	Maximize the window to the right side of the screen.
Windows logo key (⊞) +Down Arrow	Minimize the window.
Windows logo key (⊞) +Home	Minimize all but the active window.
Windows logo key (⊞) +Shift+Up Arrow	Stretch the window to the top and bottom of the screen.
Windows logo key (⊞) +Shift+Left Arrow or Right Arrow	Move a window from one monitor to another.
Windows logo key (⊞) +P	Choose a presentation display mode.
Windows logo key (⊞) +G	Cycle through gadgets.
Windows logo key (⊞) +U	Display the address bar list in Windows Explorer
Windows logo key (⊞) +X	Open Windows Mobility Center.

Windows Explorer shortcuts

SHORTCUT	ACTION
Ctrl+N	Open a new window
Ctrl+W	Close the current window
Ctrl+Shift+N	Create a new folder
End	Display the bottom of the active window
Home	Display the top of the active window
F11	Maximize or minimize the active window
Ctrl+Period (.)	Rotate a picture clockwise
Ctrl+Comma (,)	Rotate a picture counter-clockwise
Num Lock+Asterisk (*) on numeric keypad	Display the contents of the selected folder
Num Lock+Plus Sign (+) on numeric keypad	Open the Run dialog box.
Num Lock+Minus Sign (-) on numeric keypad	Collapse the selected folder
Left Arrow	Collapse the current selection (if it's expanded), or select the parent folder
Alt+Enter	Open the Properties dialog box for the selected item
Alt+P	Display the preview pane
Alt+Left Arrow	View the previous folder
Backspace	View the previous folder
Right Arrow	Display the current selection (if it's collapsed), or select the first subfolder
Alt+Right Arrow	View the next folder
Alt+Up Arrow	View the parent folder
Ctrl+Shift+E	Display all folders above the selected folder
Ctrl+Mouse scroll wheel	Change the size and appearance of file and folder icons
Alt+D	Select the address bar
Ctrl+E	Select the search box
Ctrl+F	Select the search box

Taskbar shortcuts

SHORTCUT	ACTION
Shift+Click on a taskbar button	Open a program or quickly open another instance of a program
Ctrl+Shift+Click on a taskbar button	Open a program as an administrator
Shift+Right-click on a taskbar button	Show the window menu for the program
Shift+Right-click on a grouped taskbar button	Show the window menu for the group
Ctrl+Click on a grouped taskbar button	Cycle through the windows of the group

Ease of Access shortcuts

SHORTCUT	ACTION
Right Shift for eight seconds	Turn Filter Keys on and off
Left Alt+Left Shift+PrtScn (or PrtScn)	Turn High Contrast on or off
Left Alt+Left Shift+Num Lock	Turn Mouse Keys on or off
Shift five times	Turn Sticky Keys on or off
Num Lock for five seconds	Turn Toggle Keys on or off
Windows logo key (⊞) +U	Open the Ease of Access Center

Magnifier shortcuts

SHORTCUT	ACTION
Windows logo key (⊞) + Plus Sign (+) or Minus Sign (-)	Zoom in or out
Ctrl+Alt+Spacebar	Preview the desktop in full-screen mode
Ctrl+Alt+F	Switch to full-screen mode
Ctrl+Alt+L	Switch to lens mode
Ctrl+Alt+D	Switch to docked mode
Ctrl+Alt+I	Invert colors
Ctrl+Alt+arrow keys	Pan in the direction of the arrow keys
Ctrl+Alt+R	Resize the lens
Windows logo key (⊞) + Esc	Exit Magnifier

Windows Help viewer shortcuts

SHORTCUT	ACTION
Alt+C	Display the Table of Contents
Alt+N	Display the Connection Settings menu
F10	Display the Options menu
Alt+Left Arrow	Move back to the previously viewed topic
Alt+Right Arrow	Move forward to the next (previously viewed) topic
Alt+A	Display the customer support page
Alt+Home	Display the Help and Support home page
Home	Move to the beginning of a topic
End	Move to the end of a topic
Ctrl+F	Search the current topic
Ctrl+P	Print a topic
F3	Move the cursor to the search box

Index

Wiley Publishing, Inc.
End-User License Agreement

READ THIS. You should carefully read these terms and conditions before opening the software packet(s) included with this book "Book". This is a license agreement "Agreement" between you and Wiley Publishing, Inc. "WPI". By opening the accompanying software packet(s), you acknowledge that you have read and accept the following terms and conditions. If you do not agree and do not want to be bound by such terms and conditions, promptly return the Book and the unopened software packet(s) to the place you obtained them for a full refund.

1. **License Grant.** WPI grants to you (either an individual or entity) a nonexclusive license to use one copy of the enclosed software program(s) (collectively, the "Software") solely for your own personal or business purposes on a single computer (whether a standard computer or a workstation component of a multi-user network). The Software is in use on a computer when it is loaded into temporary memory (RAM) or installed into permanent memory (hard disk, CD-ROM, or other storage device). WPI reserves all rights not expressly granted herein.

2. **Ownership.** WPI is the owner of all right, title, and interest, including copyright, in and to the compilation of the Software recorded on the physical packet included with this Book "Software Media". Copyright to the individual programs recorded on the Software Media is owned by the author or other authorized copyright owner of each program. Ownership of the Software and all proprietary rights relating thereto remain with WPI and its licensers.

3. **Restrictions on Use and Transfer.**

   (a) You may only (i) make one copy of the Software for backup or archival purposes, or (ii) transfer the Software to a single hard disk, provided that you keep the original for backup or archival purposes. You may not (i) rent or lease the Software, (ii) copy or reproduce the Software through a LAN or other network system or through any computer subscriber system or bulletin-board system, or (iii) modify, adapt, or create derivative works based on the Software.

   (b) You may not reverse engineer, decompile, or disassemble the Software. You may transfer the Software and user documentation on a permanent basis, provided that the transferee agrees to accept the terms and conditions of this Agreement and you retain no copies. If the Software is an update or has been updated, any transfer must include the most recent update and all prior versions.

4. **Restrictions on Use of Individual Programs.** You must follow the individual requirements and restrictions detailed for each individual program in the "About the CD" appendix of this Book or on the Software Media. These limitations are also contained in the individual license agreements recorded on the Software Media. These limitations may include a requirement that after using the program for a specified period of time, the user must pay a registration fee or discontinue use. By opening the Software packet(s), you agree to abide by the licenses and restrictions for these individual programs that are detailed in the "About the CD" appendix and/or on the Software Media. None of the material on this Software Media or listed in this Book may ever be redistributed, in original or modified form, for commercial purposes.

5. **Limited Warranty.**

   (a) WPI warrants that the Software and Software Media are free from defects in materials and workmanship under normal use for a period of sixty (60) days from the date of purchase of this Book. If WPI receives notification within the warranty period of defects in materials or workmanship, WPI will replace the defective Software Media.

(b) WPI AND THE AUTHOR(S) OF THE BOOK DISCLAIM ALL OTHER WARRANTIES, EXPRESS OR IMPLIED, INCLUDING WITHOUT LIMITATION IMPLIED WARRANTIES OF MERCHANTABILITY AND FITNESS FOR A PARTICULAR PURPOSE, WITH RESPECT TO THE SOFTWARE, THE PROGRAMS, THE SOURCE CODE CONTAINED THEREIN, AND/OR THE TECHNIQUES DESCRIBED IN THIS BOOK. WPI DOES NOT WARRANT THAT THE FUNCTIONS CONTAINED IN THE SOFTWARE WILL MEET YOUR REQUIREMENTS OR THAT THE OPERATION OF THE SOFTWARE WILL BE ERROR FREE.

(c) This limited warranty gives you specific legal rights, and you may have other rights that vary from jurisdiction to jurisdiction.

6. Remedies.

(a) WPI's entire liability and your exclusive remedy for defects in materials and workmanship shall be limited to replacement of the Software Media, which may be returned to WPI with a copy of your receipt at the following address: Software Media Fulfillment Department, Attn.: *Windows 7 Digital Classroom*, Wiley Publishing, Inc., 10475 Crosspoint Blvd., Indianapolis, IN 46256, or call 1-800-762-2974. Please allow four to six weeks for delivery. This Limited Warranty is void if failure of the Software Media has resulted from accident, abuse, or misapplication. Any replacement Software Media will be warranted for the remainder of the original warranty period or thirty (30) days, whichever is longer.

(b) In no event shall WPI or the author be liable for any damages whatsoever (including without limitation damages for loss of business profits, business interruption, loss of business information, or any other pecuniary loss) arising from the use of or inability to use the Book or the Software, even if WPI has been advised of the possibility of such damages.

(c) Because some jurisdictions do not allow the exclusion or limitation of liability for consequential or incidental damages, the above limitation or exclusion may not apply to you.

7. U.S. Government Restricted Rights. Use, duplication, or disclosure of the Software for or on behalf of the United States of America, its agencies and/or instrumentalities "U.S. Government" is subject to restrictions as stated in paragraph (c)(1)(ii) of the Rights in Technical Data and Computer Software clause of DFARS 252.227-7013, or subparagraphs (c) (1) and (2) of the Commercial Computer Software - Restricted Rights clause at FAR 52.227-19, and in similar clauses in the NASA FAR supplement, as applicable.

8. General. This Agreement constitutes the entire understanding of the parties and revokes and supersedes all prior agreements, oral or written, between them and may not be modified or amended except in a writing signed by both parties hereto that specifically refers to this Agreement. This Agreement shall take precedence over any other documents that may be in conflict herewith. If any one or more provisions contained in this Agreement are held by any court or tribunal to be invalid, illegal, or otherwise unenforceable, each and every other provision shall remain in full force and effect.

The on-line companion to your Digital Classroom book.

DigitalClassroomBooks.com

Visit DigitalClassroomBooks.com for...

 Updated lesson files

 Errata

 Contacting the authors

 Video Tutorial samples

 Book Samples

DIGITAL CLASSROOM

For information about the Digital Classroom series
visit www.DigitalClassroomBooks.com

You have a personal tutor in the Digital Classroom.

978-0-470-41093-6

978-0-470-41091-2

978-0-470-41092-9

978-0-470-41090-5

978-0-470-41094-3

978-0-470-43635-6